FRANCIS DODD SKETCH OF A. E. HOUSMAN

A. E. Housman:
Man Behind A Mask

by MAUDE M. HAWKINS

From Far, from eve and morning
And yon twelve-winded sky,
The stuff of life to knit me
Blew hither: here am I.

A Shropshire Lad

HENRY REGNERY COMPANY
CHICAGO · 1958

PR
4809
H15
H33

Contents

Preface

THE REMARKABLY COMPLETE A. E. Housman collection of original rough drafts of poems at the Library of Congress was given to the Library in 1940 by Mrs. M. J. Whittall, of Washington, D. C., and was exhibited to the public in small representative selections from time to time, but was not bound in its completed form, or really open to inspection, until 1947. It contains the rough drafts and a few fair copies of nearly the entire poetic output of A. E. Housman, with the exception of his nonsense verse. All of the serious poetry that has been preserved from his original notebooks is included, with every early draft known to be extant, and many later drafts and fair copies.

The notebooks themselves had been described previously with much detail by the poet's brother and literary executor, Laurence Housman, in his preface to *More Poems,* 1936, and more intimately in his *Memoir: My Brother A. E. Housman,* 1937. There, in his analysis of the contents of the published poems, he listed 731 pages of manuscripts in four notebooks, which he named A, B, C, and D, to indicate as nearly as possible their chronology.

The difference in the number of pages in the original notebooks and the number of notebook manuscript pages received from

Laurence Housman represents the fulfillment of the poet's request to his brother that all poems unfinished or below a certain standard should be destroyed.

Later the manuscripts were removed from the folios, cleaned of adhesive, and repaired, hinged and remounted on the original folio sheets, by which means they will better stand the wear of time. The order of the pieces as arranged when received was not disturbed.

The rough drafts show that the best of A. E. H's poetry came with the most difficulty, and the handwriting of these particular poems shows the stress under which the poet produced them. The lines of very personal poems, such as *A Shropshire Lad* XXX and XXXIII, are typical examples of drafts which in the handwriting, marginal notes, words rejected, and erasures or obliterations, testify to the "great excitement" that A. E. H. said had possessed him during the time he wrote *A Shropshire Lad,* and also furnish significant biographical material.

Since many of the poems were written in fragments—often one or two lines or a four line stanza appearing totally unrelated to the poem it became a part of ultimately—separate indices were prepared by the Library of Congress for the sections of Housman's poetry as it has appeared in published form. The entire collection was microfilmed in August, 1947. However, these fragments must not be called "unpublished lines." They were merely work-shop bits to be completed. Very few lines or quatrains are in the collection which did not appear in new form in *The Collected Poems of A. E. Housman,* Jonathan Cape, London, 1939.

I corresponded with Laurence Housman from 1949 to 1951, and during this passage of letters, a plan was formed for me to visit him in England and to gather first hand information about A. E. Housman from him and from others. My summer at "Longmeadow" with the Housmans furnished the basis of truth about his life without which it would be useless to publish anything more about a poet too long misunderstood by the public, and often by his own friends when he lived.

This book does not discuss A. E. Housman as a classical scholar; that has already been done in A. S. F. Gow's admirable book *A. E. Housman: A Sketch*. While his scholarship must enter these pages as a part of his life, it appears only in relation to his character. Likewise, no attempt has been made to present a critical analysis of Housman's poetry. There might be a place for such an analysis, but it is not here. Only the poems are mentioned at any length which disclose either his hidden life, or which clarify his social and religious attitudes.

The many agencies through which this book found form deserve thanks for cooperation and information. The book would have been impossible without the one hundred or so letters that passed between Mr. Laurence Housman and me, and the three weeks spent with Clemence and Laurence Housman in Somerset, England, when they generously gave me their permission to write this book. They gave me much direct and indirect information about the life of their brother and some valuable unpublished photographs, and in the long hours spent in "Elbow Room," Laurence Housman's study, surrounded by the books, pictures, and furniture of A. E. H., I absorbed from Laurence Housman the essence of the truth which now I present as I believe it was—a truth which recently he has confirmed.

I also have to thank the Library of Congress for unfailing courtesy and aid during the time I did the work there on the rough drafts of A. E. Housman.

To the other sources I found in England I wish to express appreciation:

To Sir R. E. Mortimer Wheeler, Institute of Archaeology, University of London, for letters and for allowing me to examine several of his cartoons of A. E. Housman.

To Mr. E. Slade, Senior Dean, St. John's College, Oxford, for the right to publish the Francis Dodd portrait of Housman.

To Trinity College Library, Cambridge University, for permission to study the Housman fair copy of *A Shropshire Lad* and to quote from *The Name and Nature of Poetry*.

To the Fitzwilliam Museum, Cambridge, for the privilege of examining the fair copy of Housman's *Last Poems*.

To Mrs. Joan Thomson Charnock, daughter of Sir J. J. Thomson, Master of Trinity, and to Mr. Andrew S. F. Gow, Tutor of Trinity College, both of them long-time friends of A. E. Housman, for conferences at Cambridge, and for valuable letters which gave me information.

To Colonel R. K. Morcum and his niece, Miss Darrent, and to Colonel C. L. Wood, of Fockbury, Worcestershire, and Bromsgrove, Worcestershire, respectively, for permission to enter and to study Housman's early homes, in which they now reside.

To the University of London for permission to quote from Housman's Introductory Lecture (1892), and to Cambridge University for permission to quote from Housman's Inaugural Lecture (1911) and to quote from Housman's *The Name and Nature of Poetry* (1933).

To The Bromsgrove School, *Memorial to A. E. Housman,* (by Katherine E. Housman Symons, A. W. Pollard, Laurence Housman, R. W. Chambers, Alan Ker, A. S. F. Gow, John Sparrow), five hundred copies of which were published (November, 1936) for permission to quote material.

I also have to thank the following publishers for their permission to quote certain poems and passages: Henry Holt and Company, from *The Collected Poems of A. E. Housman;* The Oxford Press, from Grant Richards' *Housman: 1897-1936;* Scribners, from Laurence Housman's *My Brother: A. E. Housman;* Bobbs-Merrill, from Laurence Housman, *The Unexpected Years;* Jonathan Cape, London, from Percy Withers' *A Buried Life;* and Colby College Library, Waterville, Maine, *A Shropshire Lad,* with notes by Carl J. Weber, (1946).

To the research libraries of the University of South Carolina, Duke University, The Library of Congress, and the University of Cincinnati, for the use of material, and to Mr. Laurence Housman, Miss Clemence Housman, Mr. Edmund Wilson, Mr. Ben Lucien Burman, Mr. Melville Cane, and Mr. Witter Bynner for permission to quote from published works and letters.

To my husband, whose aid was constant, both on our English summer of research and at home; to my daughter, Mrs. Lynn Kalmbach, whose devotion gave me the time to complete the book; to Mr. Charles Lee, at that time of the University of South Carolina, for unfailing interest and aid; to Miss Ruby Kitchens, who performed my secretarial labor loyally and accurately over a period of three years, and to Mrs. Catherine Furney, who completed this labor.

MAUDE M. HAWKINS
"Hawkinshurst"
Hopkins, South Carolina

ALFRED EDWARD HOUSMAN
1859-1936

1859   Born March 26

1870-1877   Attended Bromsgrove Preparatory School

1877-1881   Attended St. John's College, Oxford

1881-1882   Taught Latin at Bromsgrove Preparatory School

1882-1892   Worked in Her Majesty's Patent Office
Procured a Pass Degree from Oxford and later, an
M. A. Degree from Oxford

1892-1911   Professor of Latin, University College, London
Author of classical papers on textual criticism

1896   *A Shropshire Lad*

1911-1936   Professor of Latin, Cambridge University and
Fellow of Trinity College, Cambridge
Author of numerous classical papers and books,
notably a five volume textual criticism of *Manilius*

1922   *Last Poems*

1933   *The Name and Nature of Poetry*

1936   Died, April 30

1936   *More Poems,* published posthumously by
Laurence Housman

1938   *Additional Poems,* published posthumously by
Laurence Housman in *My Brother, A. E.
Housman*

1939   *Collected Poems* (Jonathan Cape, London)

KEY TO ABBREVIATIONS

ASL   *A Shropshire Lad*

LP   *Last Poems*

MP   *More Poems*

AP   *Additional Poems*

One

Fabric of the Mask

That is the land of lost content
I see it shining plain,
The happy highways where I went
And cannot come again.

A Shropshire Lad

1

An Ancient Lineage

FOR GENERATIONS the Housmans lived in and around Bromsgrove, Worcestershire, where several of their ancestral homes remain to this day. The town of Bromsgrove threads its way by the pattern of ancient roads through the banks and misty meadows of the northwest corner of Worcestershire. It is rich with the flavor of old days, and stretches out like a patchwork quilt laid by Time, the blocks composed of contrasting designs of new and old dwellings. Some of the ancient Tudor structures have a unique effect of propped-up solidarity; their upper stories lean precariously forward toward the street like the shoulders of old men bent with the weight of years. Viewed from a distance, they appear to be huddled crookedly together, as if the new houses to left and right had pushed them off balance in the shock of collision with modern progress.

To the southeast, some twenty miles away, Stratford glorifies the gentle Avon river and commercially immortalizes Shakespeare. The mystical blue hills of Shropshire curve the horizon to the west. Birmingham hustles and hums with business fourteen miles to the northeast, developing the manufactures for which it was noted even a century ago. Thirty-two miles almost straight east of Bromsgrove spreads the war-scarred city of Coventry, rich in literary and historical associations.

[3]

Today, the complete peace of the English countryside disguises the bitter struggles fought so recently for the survival of the English people. The yeoman with his inbred and eternal love of the land tills his soil as earnestly as if two devastating wars had not passed over his head in one generation; and Nature, with her casual indifference to the plight of man and the armies that trample on his breast, nonchalantly casts her opulence over fields and valleys, obliterating the scars of war and human sacrifice. Grass and grain cover the earth with their healing, and orchard trees lift their heads again to bloom in May.

So it is at Bromsgrove. True, the lorries roar all night through High Street, which lies along the main thoroughfare to Birmingham; but two miles north lies a realm calm with quiet living. In valleys green and suddenly still, the road where Housman walked as a boy winds among hawthorn hedges and snug little farms. Gray stone fences are sprayed with roses, and bearded barley ripples in the breeze.

Within this area of northwest Worcestershire a century ago lived several notable families: The Housmans, the Brettells, the John Adams family, and the wealthy Holden family which owned extensive property two miles north of Bromsgrove in the region known as Catshill. These families intermarried and from them descended the poet, A. E. Housman.

The Holden estate two miles outside Bromsgrove centered about The Clock House,[1] a dignified old mansion that dated back to 1640, so named because from part of the house rose an ancient clock that used to give time to the little hamlet of Fockbury. The clock was taken down when extensive repairs were made in the nineteenth century, and thereafter the house was called Fockbury House, though it is spoken of to this day as "The Clockus" by the elderly villagers.

[4]

The Clock House came into the Brettell family through Joseph Brettell, who married the heiress Ann Holden. There were several Brettells and this one should not be confused with his cousin, Joseph Brettell, to whom Herbert Spencer traced his lineage in his *Autobiography*, nor with the Joseph Brettell two generations earlier, of Finstall House, who was a Bromsgrove attorney and a Governor of the Bromsgrove School, then known as King Edward's School.

The Rev. Thomas Housman, grandfather of Alfred Housman, was the son of a distinguished scholar, the Rev. Robert Housman, of whom there is an account in the *Dictionary of National Biography*. Rev. Thomas Housman was educated at Oxford, and married Joseph Brettell's daughter Ann. He had come first from Oxford to Bromsgrove in 1836 as assistant Curate of the Parish Church. He married Ann Brettell soon after, and in 1839 he moved into The Clock House, with his wife and child, in order to live with the bereft Joseph Brettell, whose wife, Ann Holden Brettell, had recently died.

In 1838, the parochial district of Catshill, which included the hamlet of Fockbury, was formed out of the large parish of Bromsgrove, and a new church was built there. Since Rev. Thomas Housman was permanently settled in The Clock House he naturally became the first Vicar of Catshill, and thereafter "The Clockus" served as parsonage.

The Catshill church nestled in a shady lane and was surrounded by an iron fence which enclosed the old churchyard with its zig-zag tombstones. The verger looked as old as the church. Warped, bent, gray, he was the living symbol of the tombstones around him.

At Catshill, Bromsgrove seemed far away, and although its town clock struck the hour, here time stood still. This was the parish church where the Housman family worshiped for three generations; this was the walk they traversed to worship the conventional religion inherited from their forefathers, and here Grandfather Housman, less familiarly known as the Rev. Thomas Housman, in his decorous clergyman's attire gravely led the rites for the community—christenings, communions, marriages, and burials—for many years.

The church was simple, with an impressive square Norman tower, and the interior of the building had changed very little in a hundred years. The Housman pews remained sober and stiff, as they were when the governess herded the little Housmans into them. In the vicar's study to the left of the altar Grandfather Housman's stern picture was conspicuously framed on the wall, with those of two vicars that followed him placed below his portrait. The very old baptismal font in the rear of the nave marked the place where Alfred Housman was christened by his grandfather, and the time worn registry near it gave the date of his birth. The six brothers and sisters that followed him were not recorded there, but at Bromsgrove in the church on Adams' Hill, for they were all born at Perry Hall in Bromsgrove.

Outside the parish church, "God's Acre" sadly spread itself, a half-forgotten crop of lonely graves stood gone to seed. The modern cemetery for Catshill was across the road and was better kept. The old verger knew the churchyard well, and went at once to the large family lot of the Housmans. Not all those buried there were Housmans; some were Brettells and Adamses. In the center there was the monument over Grandfather and Grandmother Housman, who had been Ann Brettell; and the tombstones of the parents and the stepmother of Alfred Housman, whose lives are stories in themselves. The marbles were overgrown with volunteer grasses, and the verger explained that their unkempt appearance was due to the fact that the Bromsgrove Borough Council had not been able of late to appropriate the required funds to pay a caretaker.

"It's been this way many a-days and a-days," the verger said sadly; "and I doan' like it meself. But we do the best we can."

He was humbly delighted with a two-shilling piece, which he seemed to think amply repaid him for giving away an hour of his leisurely time.

The powerful personality of Grandfather Thomas Housman dominated Catshill parish. Handsome, intelligent, well-balanced but severe, he brought his Oxford University education into the bounds of a simple country community. He was a lover of the classics but also a lover of humanity in a rather grudging way. Although he could not make a very generous allowance for those who did not go through church doors to find their salvation, he was a man who believed in fairness and justice, and who tried to give the devil his due, so that when he died he was considered the leader and protector of the entire parish, and all the country-side was full of closed blinds.

The father of Thomas Housman had been a man much more distinguished as a scholar and clergyman than his son. Alfred Housman was evidently proud of his great-grandfather, for he mentioned Robert Housman especially in personal data he compiled for an inquiring periodical after his slowly kindling fame as a poet began to make people curious about him. That his ancestors were well grounded on the firm foundation of those "saints of the Lord" who cemented the strength of their blood and bones into the noble structure that built the Church of England was of less importance to Alfred than were their ancient lineage and superior intelligence.

When Edward Housman, the eldest son of Thomas Housman

and father of Alfred, was growing up, he knew with complacency that he belonged to a distinguished family, with considerable holdings of land around Catshill, including two charming old houses, The Valley House and The Clock House. There is reason to suppose that Edward Housman felt a comfortable and lazy security in regard to his family's financial prosperity when he looked upon the wide estates that he would inherit. He was not as much interested in politics as he was in poetry and literature, and he failed to acquaint himself with the danger signals threatening the survival of the social caste system, upon which the success of landed gentlemen depended.

The fact that Edward's father was a landed proprietor had influenced him to remain as vicar of Catshill during his lifetime, although his talents could have carried him to much higher livings in the Church of England. He was known best to his parishoners as "The Squire," an appellation they used very naturally, because of the large and pleasant acreage he owned, and because of the fact that a number of families in his parish were in his employ, either as workers of the land or household servants and gardeners. To be employed by "The Squire," especially on his own dwelling place, carried a shade more social distinction than to work for anyone else, and his house servants were supposed to be the last word in virtuous respectability. That they were not is another story. Thomas Housman's life was a varied and busy one, a combination of vicar, adviser, and administrator, not only for himself, but for the entire area. Such a combination of vicar and squire was unusual in England, and suggests that Thomas Housman was a man of versatility.

The preference for the title "Squire" instead of "Vicar" among his communicants also implies that they were cannily interested in their material relationship with their employer more than they were in his spiritual interventions. There is no way of knowing

[8]

whether Thomas Housman liked being called a squire instead of a vicar, but we do know that his honesty, dignity, and wisdom not only brought his flock to his feet on Sunday but also led them to his fields and gardens on Monday, both actions based on the fact that his parishoners seem to have prospered according to their just deserts. His son, Edward, was sometimes called "Squire" in after years, as a title inherited from his father, although the land inheritance had diminished considerably by that time.

Thomas Housman's marriage was appropriate for one of his social position and was advantageous financially. His wife was closely related to John Adams, who in the late eighteenth century had taken over the ownership of Perry Hall, located on an estate of two acres in Bromsgrove. Perry Hall was a spacious and impressive mansion that had formerly been the home of the historical Lowes of Chadwick. Thomas Lowe was probably the son of Roger Lowe of Bromsgrove, who, although a strong Royalist, was fined ten pounds for not taking a knighthood at the Coronation of Charles I. His name appears in the list of disclaimers at the visitation of 1634.

John Adams was great-uncle to Thomas Housman's children. He was in his day the local controller or custodian of stamps and kept in Perry Hall several thousand pounds' worth of government property which had to be guarded against thieves. Therefore heavy fittings of iron were provided against burglary across doors and windows. The outer doors were three inches thick, and the drawing-room shutters were locked at night by crossbars and screws. Swing bells were attached to the outer doors, and on the roof was an alarm bell in case outside help was needed to protect the property. The ritual of shutter-closing and the barring of the doors went on long after John Adams and his stamps were gone, and was one of the ceremonials the Housmans remembered most vividly from childhood, although not very much of great value was in the house at the time.[2] John Adams has his name remembered, for the fine Bromsgrove church is built upon Adams' Hill; thus his dynamic personality is perpetuated by a verbal monument. The children of Edward Housman, all but Alfred, were destined to be born in Perry Hall surrounded by the stalwart traditions of their ancestors who left them the legacy of "Blood, boots and bones," (a motto used by Sir Francis Drake, ancestor of Alfred Housman's mother), which later was to stand them in good stead when they entered a world where they had to make their own way.

Grandmother Housman was dominated, almost obliterated, by her husband and there is no account of her activities or influence outside the family circle. Her picture in late life shows a face with strong character lines and pronounced features. Her life was especially bound by conventionalities imposed both by the Victorian code and by the Church of England. As the vicar's wife she had many solemn responsibilities, but she was in love with Thomas Housman, not the vicar, and in private was able to throw her Victorian robes aside, as she disclosed in a conversation on her death bed.

She outlived her husband a few years, and at last lay dying in the house of her son Edward. One day when she was very weak, she asked one of her daughters a decidedly fleshly question: "Do you think I'll know my old man in heaven as I did on earth?" Her daughter, a maiden lady, knew her mother meant "know" in the Biblical sense, and blushingly stammered some nonsense; but her innocent young grandson, overhearing her inquiry, peeped through the golden bars of his infant paradise and cried out with great assurance, "Why Grandmother, of *course* you will!"[3]

Grandmother Housman brought twelve children into the world, but only six arrived at maturity: Edward, Thomas, Joseph, Mary, Jane, and Agnes. Edward was born at Kinver, in Staffordshire, January 25, 1831. He went to the local school there, but had finished before his father moved to Catshill. When he went to London to study law, he stayed in lodgings with relatives until he was articled and came home to practice in Bromsgrove, about 1855. Uncle Tom, as the children called Thomas, was something of an adventurer, for he made and lost three fortunes, one in gold-mining. He was a widower at forty, and was far enough along on making his fourth fortune to leave each of the seven children of Edward Housman two hundred pounds when he died. He also distinguished himself once by running away with their governess, a good-looking woman of thirty. Uncle Joe was educated at Bromsgrove School, became a parson, and was fond of shooting and fishing. He was much liked by his parishoners, as well as by his relatives. He was first the curate of Charlton Bishop in Devonshire, and later for many years its rector. He retired about 1905, and died about two years later. Aunt Mary and Aunt Jane remained spinsters; Aunt Agnes married fortunately, but died in childbirth. She was Clemence Housman's godmother and left her a legacy of one thousand pounds.

The ancestry of Alfred Housman on his mother's side was also cultured and distinguished. At the picturesque village of Woodchester, in historic Woodchester Hall on Selsley Hill near the larger town of Stroud, in Gloucestershire, lived another Housman family, the first cousins of Edward Housman. They were a talented, self-reliant group and Edward occasionally visited them. Of the three girls, Lucy was eldest—statuesque and efficient. There were two sons among the cousins, who later became university men, one of them a rector and distinguished naturalist. Lucy joked with Edward on one of his visits, telling him to be sure not to marry until he had met her bosom friend Sarah Jane Williams, the daughter of their rector at Woodchester, the Rev. John Williams, D. D. Sarah Jane was, indeed, a close friend of all the Housman sisters. The meeting was arranged at an afternoon tea party, and the result of it was fully up to Lucy's expectations. Edward and Sarah Jane fell in love at once; the flush and excitement in their faces was not due to the tingling of tea.

Sarah Jane had been born into an environment similar to Edward's, a fact which contributed to their congeniality. Her father was a highly educated rector, a graduate of Oxford University, and much more of an accomplished scholar than Thomas Housman.[4] From 1833 to his death, he presided over the gem of a Gothic church at Woodchester. He was also a tutor in the classics, and possessed some creative ability in verse, for he composed a number of hymns. He translated easily from Greek or Latin into English as long as he lived. Along with his talents he also was known for great gentleness and sweetness of disposition. Sarah Jane's portrait bears a strong resemblance to that of her father, whose picture reveals him in the gown and bands of his doctorate. He was a soulful, unworldly man, who must have been concerned with the needs of the spirit more than those of the flesh, but his daughter's personality was more intense and passionate.

Dr. Williams traced his lineage directly back to the family of Sir Francis Drake, and he had inherited some family plate bearing the Drake Crest, which appeared in the shape of a distorted dragon more like the fabulous wivern.

As long as the annual Drake family dinners lasted, Doctor Williams attended them, but after 1845 they were discontinued. The right to the Drake crest was passed down to the Housmans by the widow of their mother's brother, who together with Sarah Jane, were the only two children out of a family of thirteen who survived to maturity.

When Edward proposed marriage to Sarah Jane, he was accepted with warmer than Victorian acquiescence. Thomas Housman blessed his son for his highly suitable choice of a wife. Plans were made for an early marriage; the girls began to sew the hundreds of yards of ruffles and lace suitable for the trousseau of an attractive and well-born young lady. But the wedding was delayed by the serious illness and death of Sarah Jane's father in 1857.

Two years passed before the vows were taken, June 17, 1858, in Woodchester church. The wedding complied with the conventionality due high church ceremonies, but the faces of the bride and groom were full of unconventional happiness. Lucy and Julia Housman were the bride's attendants and they were the last to wave good-byes as Edward's carriage sped away.

After an idyllic honeymoon at the seaside, Edward took his new wife back to the quiet beauty of Catshill, and established her in the Valley House, close to The Clock House, for her first home.

The Valley House

The Valley House is the only one of the three childhood homes of A. E. H. that remains, both inside and out, almost exactly as it was then, except for the fact that when Edward and Sarah Jane lived there, it was covered with creepers which have since been removed. The romance of age is woven around that dwelling, for it was built in the seventeenth century. Today its mellow hand-made bricks and native stones fit the landscape as if, like a hill, the house had been made by nature. The valley would not be the valley it is without that old house; it shelters itself in the bosom of the hills as much a part of them as are their own banks. The lane to the Clock House winds around it, leading to the second ancestral Housman dwelling a short distance up the slope. The rose-covered stone fences conceal from the passer-by most of the flower garden and lawn at the Valley House. Beyond these stretch the kitchen gardens with apples, plums, gooseberries, and currants planted beyond the vegetables, so well cultivated that they appear more artistic than utilitarian. Ivy runs over part of the house in a restrained manner; yew trees centuries old offer shade, but the cedar tree that one hundred years ago dominated the front lawn is gone. The Valley House today is the home of Dr. Pugh, a dentist of Birmingham.

Today the yeomen pass each other in the narrow lane as the tenant farmers did one hundred years ago—their horse-drawn carts creak in the quietude; every fifteen minutes the clock at the Clock House warns humanity of the flight of time. Yet here, time has perversely stood still; the house seems impervious to its marks. The second story lattice window in the front of the structure looks out from Alfred's birth room, and marks the same yews it looked on a century ago; it throws itself open to the same breath of spring and song of the cuckoo as it did in 1859. The place drowses in the sun, gathering new strength for generations to come. The valley folk say it is truly bewitched, for they whisper that the attic has its restless ghost that can still be seen at the single attic window if one passes at midnight by the light of the moon.

The winds of late March, 1859, swept up the roads and fields from Bournheath. Within the Valley House there was a rustling hush, an expectancy. Doors opened and closed quietly; the doctor had been upstairs for hours. Lights shone in the latticed windows all night. In the morning, Sarah Jane begged for her old family doctor from Woodchester, and when he arrived in the afternoon, in the midst of gusts and rain, Alfred Edward Housman was born, March 26, 1859.

Housman's birth year was a miracle year of English literature. Darwin published *The Origin of Species*—the most important book of its time. George Meredith tried out his queer genius on *The Ordeal of Richard Feverel*. Carlyle had just issued the first volumes of *Frederick the Great*; Dickens produced a *A Tale of*

Two Cities; Thackeray finished *The Virginians*; Tennyson brought out *The Idylls of the King*. George Eliot came before the public with her great novel, *Adam Bede*. Those were all epochal publications, marking significant changes in religious and social philosophy. And Browning had declared (not without inner doubt, however) that "God's in his heaven, all's right with the world."

In Memoriam had buttressed the Faith nine years earlier, and was still the religious watchword of Queen Victoria. The wretched Crimean War was over. Although mines and factories were increasing, and Birmingham was outgrowing its boundaries, the streets of Bromsgrove and the country lanes beyond lay untouched and unhurried, outside the rush of change. The "corn" was cut with the sickle or the scythe; the art of making nails by hand still persisted in the nailer's shop, and the blacksmith had business enough to keep him at his trade. Haste and mechanization had not invaded the peace of country living.

The location of the Valley House accounts for the discrepancies in texts about the birthplace of A. E. Housman. Although some reputable authorities have blamably given Shropshire as his birthplace, others have more understandably given Bromsgrove as the exact location; A. E. H. himself in the family tree that he prepared put his birthplace accurately as Catshill, County of Worcester. Catshill was the name of the parish in which the Valley House was located, and referred not to a village, but to the area presided over by the parish church, comprising several square miles of farm land. The hamlet of Fockbury is more closely associated with the Clock House where he lived later. Bromsgrove, of course, is the town, two miles south of both, where Perry Hall is located, the home of Alfred's formative years.

Not much is known about Alfred's first year. His mother was soon carrying her second child, and she had to give Alfred over in part to a nurse, who often wheeled him up to the Clock House to call on his grandparents. He seems to have been a reasonably healthy child, not very prone to childish illness, and not hard to govern. He says that he remembers his christening; but although he had a remarkable memory, it is probable that he confused his brother Robert's christening a year later with his own.[5]

The lane on which Alfred made his first journeys with his nurse turns slightly to the right at the Valley House and leads up by trim hedges flanked with oaks and evergreens to the Clock House. The path stretches smooth, sweet with the odor of boxwood and honeysuckle, and soft with bracken ferns along the sides. Farther west the Shropshire hills break the horizon with curves of blue, veiled in mist. In the miles of valleys between Catshill parish and Shropshire the thatched or tiled homesteads huddle together in gregarious groups, nudging each other in the most friendly fashion, as if to call attention to their companionable dispositions. Orchards in springtime mass their scented clouds of pink and white over the dales, foretelling the rain of cherries and apples that help to make Shropshire rich in summer. The old verse, "Clunton and Clunbury, Clungunford and Clun, are the quietest places under the sun"[6] comes to mind as one looks down later from the heights of Clun Forest upon this hinterland of easy living.

Early in life, Alfred Housman looked to "The West" (*LP* I) and centered his dreams and broodings upon the Shropshire Hills. The direction of west dominates the viewpoint in much of his poetry.

> Westward, on the high-hilled plains. . . .
> —*ASL* LV

> Far in a western brookland
> That bred me long ago. . . .
> —*ASL* LII

[16]

The west winds out of the west land blow, ...
                    —*ASL* XXXVIII

West and away from here to heaven
Still is the land!
                    —*MP* XIV

Comrade, look not on the west—
    'Twill have the heart out of your breast. ...
                    —*LP* I

In Catshill parish and Bromsgrove the serious little boy grew up with his brothers and sisters in the outdoor world of orchard-blooming in Maytime, fruit gathering in summer, and nutting parties in the autumn. He saw the beauty of October change, death-struck by the year, and saw the smoke of comfortable firesides rising in misty plumes. In early autumn he saw the farmers "dressed to the nines" on their way to the fairs and agricultural shows; all of these activities of men and nature made lasting impressions on his sensitive mind.

He gathered in through all his senses the impressions that later were to make him a poet: the russet of fallow land ploughed in squares on hillsides; the burnished glow of beech leaves on the ground; the sheen of harvest moons on sheaves and ricks of garnered grain. On solitary walks he learned to know all the flowers, leaves, and grasses by name, and developed a life-long intolerance of people who misnamed them. If he was a dreamer, he was precise about his imaginings and began to show a remarkably orderly mind by the time he was ten years old.

The sound of parish bells was particularly delightful to him, and soon his life was unconsciously tuned by them. The striking clocks at Bromsgrove measured the quarter hours, but in his day the clock in the Clock House tower was a thing of the past, and had been taken down. The chimes of Bromsgrove church, however, shot the air with silvery songs, and the nearer parish bell at Catshill tolled solemnly across the fields. To Alfred, clocks and bells were a part of the experience of living. Later he was to intensify this impression when he personified the bells in several instances, and made them actors that either prophesy or determine men's fate. These early conceptual images were integrated years later into the tragic love story "Bredon Hill," *ASL* XXI, and much later the striking clock became the literal hangman in the stark eight lines of "Eight O'clock," *LP* XV.

About the time Alfred was born in this charmed spot, Perry Hall in Bromsgrove became vacant through the death of Edward Housman's great-uncle, Captain John Adams, at the age of ninety-one. Edward Housman had been working with him for several years as a Solicitor, and upon the Captain's death, the Hall became Edward's property. Immediately it was made the home and place of business of Edward Housman, when Alfred was a year old.

The change from the Valley House to Perry Hall was a momentous one for Sarah Jane. She now became the mistress of a mansion. Perry Hall with its great reception rooms, high frescoed ceilings, banquet rooms, smaller dining room, long ell with a cloakroom and servants' quarters challenged her greatest efforts. The planning and arrangement of her new home was a delight to her and Edward spared no expense to make it the perfect residence of a landed gentleman and his lady. Sarah Jane had no fears for the future. She did not know that Edward had mortgaged farm property to furnish Perry Hall and staff it as he desired.

Most of Alfred's early development occurred at Perry Hall. The mansion continued to be the home of the Housmans until 1873, the fourteenth year of Alfred's life. It was well suited to the needs of a growing family and to Edward's social position. Edward's optimism made him believe that more opportunity to practice his business as solicitor would open if he lived at Bromsgrove, and the large mansion offered excellent opportunity for the expansion of his own offices, as well as a wing ideally built for schoolroom, nursery quarters, and servants' rooms. Edward's provision for a large family was providential, for by 1868 six more children had been born.

The christenings and registries of each child born to Edward and Sarah Jane were sponsored by the Church of England with due ceremony. Alfred was baptized on Easter Sunday, April 24, 1859, at Catshill. If the single entry in the Catshill parish church in Grandfather Housman's hand is, for the sake of clear chronology, proscribed before the other six names in the Bromsgrove register, the list represents the roster of a family remarkable for both versatility and fair distribution of talent:

Alfred Housman (Catshill) b. March 26, 1859
    (Poet and scholar; Fellow of Trinity College, Cambridge)
Robert Holden Housman, b. August 30, 1860
    (B.S.M.I.E.E.; professor and brilliant investigator of scientific research)
Clemence A. Housman, b. Nov. 23, 1861
    (Wood engraver, exhibitor in the Tate Gallery; novelist, and short story writer)
Katherine Elizabeth Housman (Symons), b. Dec. 10, 1862
    (Author of a history of King Edward's School, Bath, and author of sketches about A. E. Housman)
Basil Williams Housman, b. January 16, 1864
    (F.R.C.S., Doctor of Medicine)
Laurence Housman, b. July 18, 1865
    (Dramatist, poet, novelist, journalist and essayist, illustrator and artist—the most versatile of all the Housmans)
George Herbert Housman, b. July 19, 1868
    (Soldier, killed in the Boer War)

Such a combination of abilities and potentialities in one family is rare, and it is no wonder that in his seventies Alfred once remarked in a laughing mood of reminiscence to Laurence:

"Was there ever such an interesting family as ours!"[7]

Not one of these seven Housmans is buried either in the Catshill parish churchyard, or at Bromsgrove, nor will they ever be.

When Alfred Housman was born, his father planted a little chestnut tree in the side garden east of Perry Hall, and another chestnut was planted as each of his children was born. Later, when they moved from Perry Hall to the Clock House, the trees were presented to Catshill church, then bare of trees, and were re-planted in the churchyard and set in the order of the children's ages along the western and northern walls. Six of these trees are living today. The one that died, strangely enough, was the smallest one that commemorated the birth of the youngest child, Herbert, who died in early manhood under tragic circumstances in the Boer War.

2

Life at Perry Hall

PERRY HALL remains externally today quite as it was when Alfred Housman lived there. The mansion centered in two acres of pleasant lawns and gardens furnished an ideal place to rear a family. The rooms were spacious with wide marble fireplaces and frescoes that bespoke elegance, and the atmosphere was restful and congenial, with green expanses and broad vistas. East of the house on Adams Hill the quaint steeple of ancient Bromsgrove church rose over a high bank of yew, laurel, birch, laburnum, and lime trees to a height of 200 feet, and dominated the landscape from almost any position. Its impressive tower was built in the fourteenth century and was completed with spire before the dawn of the fifteenth century. The church itself consists of examples of twelfth, thirteenth, fourteenth, and fifteenth century masonry, and contains the tomb of the famous Sir John Talbot. It stands a hundred yards across the road from the side gate of Perry Hall garden. How many times during childhood the Housmans were dressed in starched fine collars and linens to be herded into the family pew for the formal rites of the Church of England, it would be difficult to estimate. The Church was made an obligatory part of their existence, and continued to be so for many years.

Perry Hall is an ell-shaped structure of great solidarity, with floor-to-ceiling windows. It was erected at various times, as was the church, and some of the inner walls are of unusual thickness. During recent structural alterations the entrance to a secret passage was discovered near the side of one of the fireplaces. It is believed that this passage led to one of the many underground exits used during the persecution days of the seventeenth century. Apparently Edward Housman and his children knew nothing about this passage, and therefore the supposition is that John Adams had known nothing about it, and that it had been built by the Lowes of Chadwick, or their immediate descendants to insure safety at times of political persecution.

After Edward Housman's death, Perry Hall passed through the hands of several owners, and has at last reached the fate of many of the English estates in the last few years. Its history illustrates the decadence of a great social order that was the backbone of England and the source of the brains that produced much of her momentum. On March 11, 1950, Perry Hall was officially opened as an exclusive residential clubhouse for Birmingham professional men and executives. Important notices of this fact together with a picture of Perry Hall appeared in *The Birmingham Mail* of that date. Under the picture was the title: "The Home of the Housmans." The clubhouse is directed at present by Col. C. L. Wood.

The local prestige of Edward Housman and his family temporarily increased in 1860 by his removal to Perry Hall. Here Alfred Housman lived during the most impressionable years of his life, from babyhood to adolescence, and here he and his brother Laurence did their first exploratory work in verse-making. All the children roamed at will through the high-ceilinged drawing rooms, library, dining room, greenhouse, even the stable house and kitchen, but they all liked outdoors best: the garden, with its well-defined sections of ornamental lawns, flowers, and shrubbery, with neat rows that produced vegetables, and the "rubbish garden," which belonged to them, whereby they let it largely take care of itself.[1] Here were two splendid old apple trees that became "climbing trees" for the children and were sweet with fruit in season; here were plum trees for damson jam, and also for climbing; and rows of rampant black currant bushes to be picked for jam and "flan" (a Worcestershire fruit pudding). Here, too, the children had a clay hill all their own, where they built play fortresses and enacted imaginary battles that became very real at times, for the youngsters were all self-willed and individual, making it inevitable that they would quarrel violently. Old drain pipes became cannon under force of Alfred's imagination, and pieces of wood were transformed into guns and torpedoes by Robert. Alfred one day encouraged the children to pick out their favorite trees, but since he reserved the beech for himself, most of them had to accept second choices. Although the children were high-strung and given to rebellion among themselves, they could never remember a time when any of them quarreled with Alfred, who was their leader in planning games and later in directing the writing of verses and stories. Laurence Housman recalls that they united as one man against all intruders, developing then a family loyalty which afterwards remained one of their most outstanding characteristics.

It is natural to assume that with children as talented as were the Housmans, their parents must have had elements of greatness in them. But the seven Housmans would individually have disclaimed "greatness" as an inherited trait, and would have modestly substituted "cleverness." They would point out that cleverness is hereditary, but would affirm that greatness is a sheer fluke—it comes from you know not where; it goes you know not whither; and that many famous men had unremarkable fathers and mothers.

[23]

The Housman parents were both of them clever, but probably psychological analysis would not attribute greatness to either of them. Sarah Jane certainly had much more strength of will and quiet tenacity of purpose than her husband possessed. She was more intelligent and witty than her husband; she occasionally wrote skits in verse about the people she wanted to ridicule—a talent A. E. H. inherited with good measure. She was no prude; in fact she enjoyed a bit of Rabelaisian humor and at heart she was not much inhibited by Victorian conventionalities. A. E. H. was much like her in his sense of humor and ability to use barbed wit against people he disliked. He inherited her tenacity and will power; likewise in appearance he resembled his mother more than his father. But he was reserved and inhibited by Victorian conventionalities.

Sarah Jane had been reared as strictly as Edward, and her religion colored her inner life with earnestness. She spared no pains to teach her children reverence although she never cared for family prayers and seldom appeared until they were over. She preferred to hear her children pray in private by their beds at night, and one of Alfred's vivid memories was his mother in a long house-robe of pale fabric, bending over her brood with folded hands leading them in the Lord's Prayer.[2] She never flaunted her religion and was not sanctimonious, but one day when she found the children quarreling violently as to which ones could claim ownership to certain lovely clouds they saw in the sky, she reprimanded them for fighting over God's gifts, which she explained were sacred and universal. Similarly, each child was thoroughly instructed in the creeds and rituals of the church and attended services as regularly as the Sabbath came.

Sarah Jane's picture, taken about two years before her death, discloses a noble and meditative face, both handsome and feminine, with much purposeful determination. Her dress is delightfully

Victorian, but it almost disguises the woman herself, and makes her appear a little stout; Laurence Housman said that effect was the result of the conventional seven petticoats and various paddings the costumes of the time demanded, and that his mother was really quite slender. He remembers her as "dear and kind," and has a recollection of hearing her long skirts swish down the stairs and across the hall, and of her leaning over him in a brown muslin dress once. Her dark hair was abundant, but severely combed back down over her ears as was the fashion of the day for married women, who apparently were expected to minimize their personal charms and devote themselves to domestic duties and child rearing. The acquiline cast of her nose was inherited by Alfred, Clemence, and Kate—the three who resembled her. Her usual expression was spirited yet serious, as well it might be, with a rapidly increasing family of dynamic little individuals, all quite different, on her hands.

Regardless of Sarah Jane's Victorian disguise of the matron, she was naturally romantic and emotional. The village curate fell in love with her. He never told her so, and she would possibly have been shocked to know it; but his longing for her was so great that he faithfully maintained her memory for twenty-one years after her death, when he finally married a woman somewhat similar to her. He was a great friend of the family, and was chosen to be Laurence's god-father. Many years later, when Laurence called on the old man who was then ninety, the secret of his love was finally disclosed through lips loosened with age. He solemnly kissed the son of Sarah Jane at parting, and never saw any of the Housmans again, for he died soon afterwards, a retired vicar, quite alone.[3]

Edward Housman was the opposite of his wife in personality. He was naturally amiable and gentle—in these qualities he was like her—but he was easy-going, rather vain, and self-indulgent, with a tendency to procrastinate and to be indecisive, which grew on him with the years. He had natural talents beyond the ordinary, especially in oratory, for he had an excellent vocabulary and a beautiful voice. But his too dreamy nature was reflected in his large hazel eyes, which were the best feature of a face rather too loose and full-lipped in expression to be impressive. He seems not to have worried much about his future finances when the children were small, for he was indulgent and gave them about as much of his time and money as they asked for. As a result they worshipped him when they were young, but became more and more critical of him as they grew older.

Katherine Housman Symons remarked in her memoir of A. E. H. published at Bromsgrove School in 1936 for the Housman Memorial Fund: "Our father was a man of many hobbies—too many—shooting, fishing, music, photography, firework-making, besides his chief interest, horticulture."

Edward Housman was inordinately proud of his unusual brood, but his conceit made him take the credit of their achievements on himself when he could. He had an absurd notion that of anything they produced he was, at least, part-author. One day he found a translation from the Latin in the form of verses by Alfred written as a school exercise. The poem was originally by Horace, but he made some alterations in Alfred's rendition, which he regarded as improvements, put his own initials to it, and sent it to the local newspaper. What his eldest son thought of this incident is not recorded.

Some of Edward's own stories about himself illustrate his vanity, and one of the funniest was about an entirely different kind of prowess. He told it himself to one of his more tolerant sons years later, without knowing how humorous it was. In his early manhood he was helping one day to clean out a fish-pond, and to do

this job he turned up his trousers above the knee, disclosing a fine
pair of calves. A susceptible maiden lady gazed at them with awe-
struck delight, and declared that she had "never seen such a sight
in all her born days!"

Edward's comment, "That was the properest compliment I ever
got," was followed by this: "But what else could she expect from
a man who was able to beget such a fine large family as *I* have!"
So greatness can be credited to Edward Housman's calves, at any
rate.[4]

In a popular novel at Perry Hall there was a character who put a
rickety ladder on a table, and immediately fell off it, who was so
like Edward that his offspring went into gales of laughter whenever they read the passage, for they could call to mind many such
incidents that proved the similarity. There was the time, for instance, when their father put on two waistcoats of different colors,
and absent-mindedly buttoned them across as though they were
one. Sarah Jane had to watch over him in these matters as if he
were one of the children, and once said resignedly, "I suppose a
fortnight after my death, Edward will go ambling down High
Street in lavender gloves and a pair of pepper and salt trousers!"

"And did you?" somebody inquired later.

Edward hesitated. "I don't think so," he replied evasively.[5]

Certainly there was no greatness in Edward Housman but there
was much talent, canceled by increasing eccentricity. The poor
man managed to outlive the respect and appreciation of everybody
but himself, and died at sixty-three, the victim of indecision and
of the drink he took to drown his bereavement, failures, and final
despair. Two pictures of him remain: the family portrait when he
was a young man of twenty-four, and a candid camera snapshot
taken shortly before his death—a side view picture, which shows
a stout and flabby bearded stranger—the wide hat drawn down

over his forehead giving him a rather forlorn appearance. Not a vestige of the man he once had been remained.

Yet Edward Housman was originally a very intelligent and cultured gentleman. Trained for the law, he came at once to be the trusted local Solicitor, an opportunity which, if he had applied himself, would have brought him ample means. He was known as a fluent orator who argued his cases well. His filing cabinet, six feet high and equipped with many narrow drawers for his case papers, now stands in "Elbow Room" at "Longmeadow," the home of Laurence Housman, and is used for his manuscripts. During the early years of his father's practice, the case was well-filled with clients' papers from a number of miles around. What caused the change in him?

Sarah Jane's health waned after the birth of her fourth child. Her decline was gradual but evident, and was probably the main reason that Edward, solicitous for her welfare, began to neglect his practice. Strength failed rapidly during her sixth pregnancy, when Laurence was born, and during the time before Herbert, her seventh child, arrived, she was an invalid. At first her marriage had been rich with physical delight; Edward had known that his wife was in love with him, for she was passionate enough to suit him as well as herself. Along with the fires of her erotic ardor, she possessed feminine graciousness and intellectual vivacity that furnished an antidote for his easily discouraged temperament. Their early years of marriage had been ideally happy; now the black fear of her death blocked his energies.

Edward had always appreciated his wife's discrimination and fastidious good taste. She had brought to Perry Hall from her Woodchester home some dignified old furniture which she loved and Edward admired for the air of elegance it gave to the spacious drawing room and entrance hall. These pieces were beautifully refinished later in London. At least two of them turned out to be objects of art worthy of museum exhibition. They stand today in the second parlor of "Longmeadow," the home of Laurence Housman; one is a large inlaid chest of drawers of seventeenth century Dutch design, the other is a small and exquisite cabinet of tortoiseshell, ebony, and ivory, dating back to the days of Queen Elizabeth I, and inherited through the Drake lineage.

The old rectory at Woodchester had been torn down the year after Sarah Jane's marriage, and thereafter Grandmother Williams spent part of her time at Perry Hall, with not very happy results for the children. In a bedroom at "Longmeadow" there is a portrait of her in an oval frame, which shows her as beautifully dressed and bonneted, with ringlets framing a contemplative face and sad eyes, as well they might be, after she had lost eleven of thirteen children. None of the Housmans except Alfred had any mature recollection of either grandfather. Their remembrances of Grandmother Williams were austere, for they knew her in old age when she was crippled with rheumatism, and had to be attended by a nurse, who massaged her shrunken legs and carried sippy meals to her room at Perry Hall. She had too much Victorianism and too testy a temper to brook any nonsense on the part of her mischievous grandchildren. One Sunday afternoon, when Laurence was swinging innocently on the front lawn, she put her head out of the window and called sharply:

"Stop that, you naughty boy! You will go to the devil!"

The reply came with the defiance and exuberance of five years: "I *like* the devil!"[6]

This candid retort evidently baffled his grandmother and for once the child was given the satisfaction of having the last word.

No doubt her mother instructed Sarah Jane to stress strict adherence to the sham conventionalities that became the bugaboo of the seven Housmans during their formative years. It was a rather terrible and rigorous code of conduct, filled with the taboos of the 1880's. Not only was church attendance a requirement, but the children must attend family prayers and scripture reading every morning before breakfast. This ritual was conducted by their father in a perfunctory manner, and was only occasionally brightened by the unexpected appearance of the family cat, whose antics were delightedly observed by those indecorous members of the group who were not above peeping through their fingers. Their mother almost never came to morning prayers, but if the children failed to arrive, or slipped in late, they were punished by losing bacon for breakfast.

They were taught that it was impolite if not positively immoral to be seen approaching or leaving the toilet, and that these perfectly natural processes of their little bodies must be veiled by a horrid secrecy. They slipped in on tip-toe as best they could, and out again, shamefaced. Later their stepmother was to be even more strict regarding such false codes as these.

Once, years later, when their stepmother was visiting Alfred in London, she noticed on street corners the shocking signs, "W. C. 1," "W. C. 2," and asked Alfred what they meant. He explained to her that these signs referred to the particular sections of London they represented, West Center 1, West Center 2, and had been put there as traffic aids.

"Very unfortunate!" was her explosive reply.

If the legacy of too strict a rearing was detrimental, the other legacies were for the most part valuable and constructive, and there is no time on record when Alfred did not acquiesce with apparent willingness to a regime which seems exceptionally harsh measured by standards of conduct today. As long as Sarah Jane was able, she watched his mind develop with pride and understanding. She was a master of understatement in a humorous way, especially when pleased, and her remarks to Edward in praise of their eldest son were probably as laconic but fully as appreciative as one which she wrote about her young husband in a letter to her friend, Lucy Housman, after their honeymoon was over:

"I find him to be a very decent fellow!"

As Sarah Jane grew inactive during the last two years of her life, she made her eldest son more of a companion and confidant than he had been before. Up to this time Alfred had stammered a good deal, especially when he was excited, but now he began to overcome this habit. During long hours alone with his mother he was perfectly happy, his shyness disappeared, and she talked to him as if he were a grown person. They read together, wrote humorous skits, and he translated his Latin to her. Perhaps it was to please his mother that Alfred conformed tractably to all the artificial standards of conduct becoming to little English gentlemen. He was always quiet, reserved, and "nice" in the English sense of the word; and was developing the appearance which in later life was to cause him to be described as "looking as if he had come from a long succession of maiden aunts."[7]

The children during their mother's prolonged illness relied on Alfred a great deal to guide them; the younger ones called him "Wa-Wa," a name used by them as a term of endearment for many years. His brother Robert was his closest companion, and though according to Laurence Housman, Robert had a violent temper and was a natural bully, Alfred got along with him very well, although once when he was badgering the younger children, Alfred fell on him and trounced him soundly, to Robert's frozen amazement. Katherine Symons described her brother Robert as "a delicate little fellow, full of fun and mischief, but troubled by asthma." For three years in the early '70's Robert was sent away for health's sake to

Sydney College, Bath. Left without Robert, Alfred turned more to his mother, his school work, and his books for companionship. He became gradually an introvert.

Two years before their mother's death, Alfred, and later Robert, had won Foundation Scholarships to Bromsgrove School, an excellent preparatory institution for boys fortunately located a short walking distance from Perry Hall. Alfred was eleven years old when he won the Scholarship. Thereafter his small and solemn person was seen less at home. He devoted long, determined hours to his new studies, from seven in the morning through the noon hour and from four to six in the afternoon, making rapid progress in both Greek and Latin.

At the end of his first year he carried off the honors in these studies; and his classmates, who had been at first inclined to belittle him and call him "Mouse" because of his shy aloofness, discovered that this boy was not to be badgered, and that he could defend himself with his fists if he had to.[8] Moreover, they lived in a day when boys went to school to learn; a healthy respect for knowledge was bred in them, high rank in scholarship was a goal to be reached; and when one in their midst stood above them in his marks, he had to be treated with consideration. Regardless of a poor beginning at a dame school in Bromsgrove, and later the ordeal of a governess at home, Alfred made up his mind to take the classical prizes at Bromsgrove preparatory school, and he spared no pains to accomplish this end.

Sometimes he had amusing stories to carry home to his mother— of boys who cribbed their Greek from a Bible under their desks; or of his asking Dr. Blore, the head master, a question that stumped him. Many years later, when Dr. Blore had become head of King's School, Canterbury, and Alfred had become famous, Dr. Blore commented wryly on his old pupil:

"I remember him as the sort of boy who I was afraid would ask me some questions I could not answer."

Alfred was happier at Bromsgrove School when Dr. Blore was succeeded by Herbert Millington as head, because Millington was especially able in the classics, and Alfred got on particularly well with him for that reason.

"May all my boys be like him!" he appended to Alfred's final school report at graduation. He had achieved first place of all the members of his class in the sixth and last form, and had gained more prizes than any of the others. The prizes he enjoyed competing for most were those offered for original poetry, and to win these became a solemn obligation as well as a delightful adventure. All his life he considered his classical research to be a double portion of both sweetness and bitterness; bright with the thrill of exploration, but shadowed by the grave responsibility of absolute accuracy in the discovery and disclosure of new truths and tinctured by acid scorn for sham scholarship, and alas, darkened also by the desire for atonement.

Poetry was later to be his emotional outlet and supreme expression of personal sorrow; scholarship was to be a thing apart—reserved for the work-a-day hours of labor expended in the necessity of not only earning a living, but climbing to the height of complete authority in the classical world. Alfred never had any illusions about the monetary reward of poets, and he had little faith in fame for himself through the writing of verses. There is no doubt that many years later he took a melancholy satisfaction in reaping the fruits of his labor at Trinity College, where he sat in his cell-like study and sent out lightning thrusts of barbed wit directed against his less accurate contemporaneous critics. To this end he worked like a slave for many years. He always thrived under arduous research well enough to keep from breaking down under it, but poetry was to be his salvation when release of passion was required.

During her last year of life, Sarah Jane felt the consciousness of approaching death at her side. Her illness was particularly painful; she grappled with it, determined to outdo it as long as possible. Finally her bed was removed from her upper latticed chamber to a downstairs room just off the dining room, converted into a bed-chamber, where she could be waited on and visited by the members of her family to better advantage. She lay there restlessly, but outwardly uncomplaining. Through the long weary nights she slept intermittently troubled by her dreams, which were based on her fears, not for herself, at first, but for her family. No doubt she wondered how her aimless Edward would chart his course without her hand beside his on the wheel. How would that brilliant, sensitive eldest son react to the loss of the parent that well she knew he loved best? How would the little girls, Clemence and Kate, who still lived in the land of fairy tales and dolls, adapt themselves to the loss of their mother? How would delicate Laurence, still weak and somewhat crooked in his legs, though he was now five years old, get along without her? And Herbert, her baby, what would become of him?

She thought of all the brilliant individual capacities of her children, and intuition told her they would do well in the world after she had long left it. Her pangs of rebellion must have been strong, when she realized that she could not live to witness their successes; and she began to wonder if in the future world she would know how their paths lay on earth. She became troubled about the state of her soul: was her faith strong enough to make her sure of a life hereafter? She turned to the Roman Catholic Church in her distress; she caused a crucifix to be placed at the foot of her bed, and commanded that candles should be burned before it day and night; but remembering a promise she had made to her brother before he died that she would never be a Catholic, she resisted what to him was papal nonsense, but to her would have been a solace.

She had learned to say nothing to Edward of the things that tortured her mind because of his depression afterwards. She once mentioned to him, however, that she feared her death would cause Alfred to lose his religious faith. As a result, after she was gone, Alfred received a letter from his father telling him of his mother's anxiety about his faith; this letter he never acknowledged until he told his brother Laurence about it when he was seventy-five years old.[9]

The rapidly increasing seriousness of Sarah Jane's illness was kept from the children as long as possible, but as the end approached, Aunt Mary Housman and her sister Jane arrived at Perry Hall to take over the household. Grandfather Housman had passed away not long before 1870, and the spinster aunts, kind of heart, were free to help Edward and his family through their sorrow. Their presence gave Edward a chance to be with his wife more, and instead of fiddling with photography or hunting he spent his spare time at her bedside, brave enough not to fail her when she needed him most. Finally, when she was about to die, Alfred was sent to the Wise family, lifelong friends of his mother's at Woodchester. Here the family which was destined to become his own lifelong friends spared him the agony of parting from his mother, an ordeal neither of them could well endure.

One day Sarah Jane called her oldest daughter Clemence, nearly eleven years old, to her bedside. She had for some time rejoiced in Clemence's dependability and great intelligence, and now she made a request of her: "Take care of little Laurence for me. His legs are weak, and he will need you." Clemence solemnly promised, and her mother would have been happy if she had been able to foresee the journeys afoot these two Housmans were to take together, when twenty-five miles a day across the hills was not unusual for them.

Sarah Jane Housman died in the early morning of March 26, 1871, on Alfred's twelfth birthday. The children were dressed in mourning at once. The little girls cried themselves sick; Laurence in his exuberance of grief had thrown himself down on a favorite toy lying on the sofa, and broken it; and he remembers his sorrow to have been a mixed feeling of loss, his mother and the toy becoming united in his childish mind as a cause for mourning.[10] Alfred came home with the Wise family, pale and silent, to take his place at his mother's burial in Catshill parish churchyard. During the two-mile drive back to Perry Hall, the children said nothing, true to their trained repressions, and thereafter they seldom spoke of their mother. In a few days both Alfred and Robert were back at Bromsgrove school.

Life went on outwardly according to its established pattern, but there was really a tragic difference. Aunt Mary remained at Perry Hall for a time, but Aunt Jane took her asthma to the coast, and she entered the lives of the Housmans very little thereafter. Aunt Mary was a well-meaning soul who took her duties with poor discrimination and too great seriousness. Her old maidishness went ill with the governess, who disliked her and took occasion to show it. Aunt Mary made the shocking discovery that the governess drank in secret, for all her veneer of extreme respectability, and she reigned with a whip hand over her after that, never missing a chance to bring her to task for her schoolroom methods, or for her management of the children. One day at breakfast, just after the morning prayer had supplicated the Father to to keep us meek and pure in heart and to bear and forbear, Aunt Mary made a particularly disagreeable remark to the governess, and the woman turned on her before the whole family in a rage.

"You nag, nag, nag all day!" she screamed.

Aunt Mary rose majestically from the table and left the room. Later in the day she sent a written request for an apology, but none was forthcoming. Although the governess remained for some time after this occurrence, Aunt Mary never spoke to her again, and the silent warfare between these two created a tension in the household that reacted unfavorably upon the children.

When Alfred was at home, he withdrew into himself more than ever, although he kept up a semblance of his old leadership and comradeship, so that none of his brothers and sisters noticed much outward change in his attitude towards them. And in fact there was no such change. He loved them as he had before, but now he felt an added sense of responsibility about them; they were a part of his charge to keep. But he no longer loved his father, and he was virtually an orphan.

Sometimes he slipped away alone and sat for hours looking at the Shropshire hills—the west country—which he somehow associated with his departed mother. Here his tensions eased and he dared to suffer. "The West" was an unfathomed, chartless unknown—the land of dreams. When the pain of looking into those pathless distances grew too great, he turned and stared at the wild flowers at his feet, or he plucked one and held it in his hand. He gazed on it and brooded about death, but like Rosetti, all he found out was "the woodspurge has a cup of three." Nothing was there for him; no secret revelation.

Nothing! He could beat upon Eternity forever, but the door would not open to the hereafter, nor would it reveal the God, benign or belligerent by moods, that he had been taught to believe in as a personal ruler over the lives of men. He became a deist, though he did not know it; for while he still accepted the idea of some vague God outside the universe—a dimly discerned creative force of an impersonal nature—he completely lost faith in the God of the

Church of England and of his fathers. Of these changes in belief he said nothing to his family for many years, and probably did not analyze himself enough to put his opinions into words, for he was only thirteen years old, and the wonder is that he pondered on such ideas at all.

With the death of his mother, the childhood of Alfred was over. He lost his happy faculty for childish play, and the main amusements he shared with his brothers and sisters afterwards were competitions he planned in writing plays, stories, and poems, activities in which he led and encouraged the others for several years. He continued his studies as assiduously as ever, but the taste of triumph over the first class honors his last year at Bromsgrove brought him must have turned to bitterness when he realized that he could never carry these honors and lay them in his mother's hand.

Katharine Housman Symons said of this time:

> Death—that cuts short both joys and sorrows—became an obsession with him, very evident in after life, but already there in boyhood, though less noticeable. We saw nothing of this then, and we never talked of our loss among ourselves. It was never Alfred's way to speak of troubles; he was sensitive and easily wounded, but wounds he bore in silence. In silence too he carried his successes, a form of modesty, or of pride, preventing ostentation or boasting.[11]

Edward Housman knew that his children were not getting the guidance they needed from Aunt Mary and the governess, but he remained in a state of shock after his wife's death, drank a good deal, puttered with photography, and was content to let things rock along at loose ends. He continued to read to his brood at night in the beautiful voice they all loved to listen to, acting out the parts in *Pickwick Papers* or *David Copperfield* by unconscious changes in inflection and expression, and it is in such scenes that his family liked best to remember him.

Because of his own loneliness, he sympathized with the bereavement of his family and occasionally showed in a very touching manner his affection for them. At that time, one of the youngest sons had to sleep with an older brother, who sometimes objected to his bedfellow and kicked him out on the floor. On one such inhospitable eviction, the child rent the night air with his outraged screams, and brought his father to the room to ask what had happened. When he saw the forlorn mite on the floor, he picked him up without a word, and carried him to his own lonely bed, tucking him in warmly by his side, and so dropped off to sleep; but the child lay long awake, full of the wonderment that he should have been signaled out for such an honor, and ever after, the comfort of that hour was remembered in gratitude.[12]

Edward missed his wife constantly; he suffered from loneliness without her bright conversation, bereft of her eyes that spoke to his so eloquently, bereft of her presence at the delightful and hitherto restful afternoon tea hour, and he still unconsciously listened for her soft silks and muslins to come rustling through the great hall and up to his side, and imagined the touch of her hand on his arm. As he mooned around by himself, he worried about his depleting fortunes, for now he lost many law cases that he should have won. His oratorical sparkle was gone. He felt as never before the financial burden of keeping up Perry Hall and its retinue of servants; for under the rather slipshod management of Aunt Mary, who often since her quarrel with the governess did not come downstairs until breakfast was long over, much careless waste and thievery was going on, which doubtless would not have worried Edward in the least if he had been able to afford it. Finally in desperation he invited his Housman cousins from Woodchester to visit him, a plan which suited Mary well, for she liked them all and probably was anxious to pour out her domestic difficulties in their sympathetic ears.

When the three Housman sisters arrived, full of vigor and affection, with boxes of clothes and presents, the children were delighted. Almost immediately the house brightened with laughter and voices; Aunt Mary was less querulous, and the machinery of living ran more smoothly. Laurence Housman remembers one incident of this visit which had particular interest for him.

Cousin Lucy had sent him up to Aunt Mary's room on some trifling errand, and he knocked at her door for admission. When she came to open it, her long beautiful hair was hanging to her waist and for the first time Laurence saw it unleashed from the severe braided rolls in which she customarily imprisoned it. Laurence was already steeped in fairy tales, and in these he had come to associate long hair with fairy princesses. He clasped his little hands in adoration.

"Oh, Aunt Mary, how beautiful you are!" he exclaimed.

This compliment was undoubtedly the best and most sincere one the austere lady ever received in her life, and forever after, Laurence was her prime favorite.

From the impressions of this visit and others to follow for some years, Laurence Housman later built one of his most delightful plays: *Possession: A Peepshow in Paradise,* in which Cousin Lucy is Laura, her beautiful middle sister is Julia, and her youngest sister appears as Martha.

Alfred's reaction to this visit from the interesting Woodchester relatives seems to have been most apparent in the strong liking he continued to develop for Cousin Lucy, the eldest of the three, whom he trusted and respected for strength of character and good sense, two characteristics he liked well in women. The youngest cousin was plain, quiet, and completely overshadowed by the other two. Alfred already knew these sisters better than did any of his brothers.

During his mother's life, Alfred had often visited these Selsley Hill cousins at Woodchester, and had explored all the lovely walks around their home. Here "Bredon Hill" (*ASL* XXI) had its scene, for this summit rises within sight of Woodchester. Also, Mrs. Wise of Woodchester, his mother's closest friend, became a trusted confidante, and her two daughters, Edith and Minnie, remained his true friends as long as they lived. He enjoyed their placidity, intelligence, and quiet acceptance of his grief at the loss of his mother. Their governess, a bright German woman by the name of Sophie Becker, possessed much the same type of mind; although she was sixteen years older than any of the young folks, she took part in their activities, and once came to visit in company with the Wise sisters at Fockbury House.

On this occasion, Edward took an interesting group picture of Alfred and his brother Basil, together with the two Wise sisters and Miss Becker. They were all costumed for the parts they had played in a charade—their favorite form of amusement. Alfred was dressed as a bishop, his head down over a book. At this time he was fourteen years old. Miss Becker is shown at the end of the group, dressed in costume too, and evidently very much a part of the activities. She was then about thirty years old.

Miss Becker happened to have been the one who broke the news of his mother's death to Alfred; he began to feel close to her for that reason, and from their Woodchester friendship developed a lifelong deep regard, which in the eyes of a sentimental world became a silly myth involving frustrated passion, of which more must be said later.

But only the Housman cousins visited Perry Hall in 1871. The family was still mourning, and Edward was in no mood for other company. Between his loss and his diminishing income, he found it difficult to keep up appearances and to conceal his depression.

Not long after the cousins went home, Edward decided that Perry Hall must be leased to bring in more income; and because Fockbury House, better known as The Clock House, was now available for occupancy, he decided to go back to the country home of his fathers, and moved there in 1873. He gave as his reason for moving that Perry Hall was damp and insanitary and had been a contributing cause of his wife's death. This opinion was ridiculous, for Perry Hall was a well-built and comfortable home, and everybody knew that his wife had died of a malignancy, but his subterfuge saved his pride and perhaps to some extent his prestige in the community.

The family move to Fockbury was not one of ease or comfort. The house had no gas, no water taps, no drainage, and it was two miles from the school, town, and office, but it was a good place for children. The whole of the country-side delighted Alfred, and he began to take the long walks which became a habit the rest of his life.

The Housmans moved to Fockbury House in the early spring of the year; and soon after they were settled in the new surroundings, Edward went to visit his Housman relatives, at which time he very solemnly proposed marriage to his Cousin Lucy.

Lucy Housman did not accept him at once, but with her usual good sense, put him off until she made another visit to Fockbury House and his children, who received her well. She had her second proposal of marriage during this visit, a heart-felt offer from Laurence, who was six and who was quite won over by her handsome face and healthy efficiency. All the children seemed glad to welcome her, especially Alfred, and she returned home reassured that she could make a success of the marriage; for her fears had been centered on the children's relationship with her. She firmly believed she could receive Edward as a husband and lover with great satisfaction to both of them. As it happened, she was not accurate in either premise, nor was she completely wrong; but such as her life turned out to be, she accepted it, adapted herself to it, and carried on a domestic program that at times seemed to require self-control and energy beyond even the unusual amount with which nature had endowed her.

Edward was facing a situation of which he was afraid; he was bewildered and troubled. He never recovered from the death of Sarah Jane. He missed the wisdom of his father, who had always offered good advice and counsel; and Grandmother Williams had slipped away from her world of rheumatism and bereavements at Perry Hall, not long before his wife had died. Edward felt utterly lost. He urged Lucy to hasten her plans for their marriage and she agreed, feeling all the perturbation and excitement that was proper for an old maid of the Victorian era, and probably a good deal more than she was willing to admit even to herself. Edward felt not the slightest excitement, only relief.

Edward Housman's second marriage occurred two years after the death of Sarah Jane, on June 26, 1873. None of the young Housmans attended the ceremony, which took place in London at the home of relatives; and after the briefest of honeymoons, Edward brought his new wife to Fockbury House, where he managed to relieve the tension of the children's meeting their step-mother by saying jovially to Laurence that he had cut his young son out in Lucy's affections. Lucy laughed, the children smiled, and they all sat down to their first meal together in an amicable mood.

At the time of the wedding, Edward was forty-two years old, and Lucy was forty-nine. She was vigorous and youthful for her age; she had led an exemplary life full of wholesome activities and much exercise. Her body was firmly built on the grand pagan scale, and her complexion was as blooming as a girl's. All her motions were quick and purposeful and she inspired confidence in the children and awe among the servants.

At heart, Lucy was apprehensive and nervous about her new family, but she gave no outward sign of this timidity. It is strange that of all the step-children, Alfred received her most whole-heartedly, for he had loved his mother perhaps more deeply than had any of the others and could have been expected to resent any-one who came to take her place. He told his step-mother in private that he was glad she had come, and voluntarily offered to do all he could to help her in managing the other children. Lucy never forgot this youthful gesture of confidence and trust, and she and Alfred remained staunch friends as long as she lived. It is possible that the complete acceptance of Lucy by Alfred was due in part to the fact that she was his father's first cousin. She was of the Housman blood, which he felt mingled properly with his own; she was cul-tured and was of the high social class that he felt her position in the household demanded. He was always extremely aware of class distinctions, and rigorously held to an autocratic standard in choos-ing his own associates. Also, his step-mother had been a close friend of his own mother, and he could not think of anyone better quali-fied to take her position in the family, a place that he instinctively knew would prove a very difficult one. It was a decided relief to Alfred to have Lucy in the household, and he felt better able to turn his attention almost exclusively to his classical studies at Bromsgrove.

3

The Land of Lost Content

THE REMOVAL to Fockbury began a life of certain limitations for the Housmans. The house itself when Lucy became its mistress was a pleasant ivy-covered establishment with sufficient rooms for a greatly reduced staff of servants, a nurse, and a governess; but it was distinctly a middle-aged, unimposing dwelling with none of the spacious grandeur of Perry Hall. A greenhouse connected with the main residence on the south, and a small dairy room and buttery in the rear suggested that the live-at-home program was the way of life at Fockbury. And such it was. Here provisions were stored; casks and butts carried meats in cure; wine, vinegar, apple butter, cider, and all kinds of jams and preserves were stored in season. Dried vegetables dangled from the ceiling; dried fruits were stored in jars. Butter was made at home; and milk and cream could be had in abundance.

The terraced lawns and gardens at Fockbury were beautiful, and commanded a view of the surrounding country for miles—a picture surprisingly satisfying, completely rural. Around the main grounds was an old wall about four or five feet high, composed of irregular hand-made bricks, mellow terra cotta in color. The wall terminated in an imposing entrance gate, with handsome brickwork at either side, and a small gardener's lodge left of it within the grounds. A tablet encased in the wall bore the date of 1640.

The interior of the main residence was sufficiently roomy for the family. A wide stairway led from a small front hall to the upper floor, and a steep backstairs with very irregular treads, some of them nearly a foot high, led directly from the kitchen to the rear upper hall, connecting closely with the apartment of the governess, and also with the nursery, which apartments were two steps up from the level of the second floor, and quite off to themselves. The back stairs at Fockbury House belonged to the children and governess as well as to the servants. The front stairs were expensively carpeted, but Lucy sternly forbade the little folks to use them for fear of wear and tear, so that they took to sliding surreptitiously down the front balustrade whenever they thought they would not be caught, and enjoyed the trick immensely.

The back stairs were continued from the second floor up to a gabled attic, which was a fascinating place to the children. It was full of relics of the Holdens. On the floor were piles of books that dated back to the time of Caxton. Here was found an emblazoned family pedigree, certified by Sir William Dugdale in 1682, showing two lines of the Holden descent for several centuries. There were old portraits and trunks with clothing to dress up in. A large botanical collection made in the seventeenth century by the Holdens interested the children, especially Alfred, who took the volume to Cambridge in later years. Later he donated it to the Birmingham City Museum, because it was originally compiled near Birmingham at the beautiful Tudor house called Woodend House, Erdington —the main seat of the Holdens.

A good deal of drama centered in the back stairs of Fockbury House, for near the top of their straight and steep ascent, about two treads below the upper hall, a small glass window had been cut in the kitchen wall, to light the otherwise dark landing. Today this window has been plastered over, though the stairs remain just as they were, with their sturdy, irregular treads. When the children lived there, they enjoyed spying on affairs in the kitchen from this secret point of vantage, and a good many courtings between the maids and their swains were observed without their knowing it. When the scene was particularly entrancing, the children by mutual agreement took turns in looking.

One evening Herbert got there first, and because the sight below was intriguing to the last degree, Herbert refused to give up his position when his turn was over, whereupon his sister Kate gave him a nudge that thrust his head through the glass.

"I'm killed! I'm killed!" he shrieked as he gazed in horrid consternation at the drops of blood oozing from his cuts on the kitchen floor below. Commotion struck the household, the children all went supperless to bed, and Lucy sternly forbade them to use the window as a spying spot in the future.

But both flights of stairs continued to have charm for the young family, and in later years they remembered how their father liked to catch their toes if they stuck them in challenge through the rails on the bannisters, and how they peeped over the top when guests were invited for tea or dinner.[1]

Over the lower floor at Fockbury were four bedchambers for the family, with interesting gabled ceilings and latticed windows which looked out on a view far lovelier than the one at Perry Hall: vast expanses of wooded hills, with higher ones in the purple distances; and in the dales between, orchards, farms, and tiny hamlets spread out in the pattern set in fast color through a thousand years.

Fockbury House, fortunately for itself, was purchased a number of years ago by Colonel and Mrs. R. K. Morcum who appreciated its charm. Colonel Morcum in 1951 was a practicing engineer of Birmingham. He made Fockbury House an estate of beauty; he restored the clock and it strikes again; many additions were added to the old house, so that its original lines melted into new ones still in keeping with the old. Today Colonel Morcum's niece, Miss Darrent, presides as hostess. To a friend of the Housmans they are most cordial and generous, showing the house, both old and new, enriched by their own collection of objects of art from all over the world.

During the renovations of the house, another secret tunnel was unearthed, together with a secret passageway into it from one of the rooms. When this tunnel was built nobody seems to know, but like the one at Perry Hall, it probably dated back to the persecution days of the seventeenth century.

In 1935, Colonel Morcum opened his house for public inspection and gave the proceeds to aid the Catshill parish church. The two pictures of the house, (one taken in 1860, with Alfred and his mother visting Grandfather Housman on the lawn, the other with the alterations made and the new owners in the foreground) were given to the visitors on this occasion. The original lines of the place were kept regardless of many additions.

Fockbury House had beautiful memories for Alfred Housman. Like his father, he was glad to leave Perry Hall where everything he saw reminded him of his mother; moreover, he loved nature with its healing solitudes far better than the environment of any town or city. His two-mile walks to Bromsgrove preparatory school in company with his brother Robert were a pleasure to him, and he supplemented them by as many other walks around the Fockbury hills as his studies would allow. The tallest of these hills was almost like a tor; and lifted its head, crowned with trees, southeast of Fockbury House, within easy walking distance up "Worms Ash

Lane." The children quickly named the hill "Mount Pisgah," and of all the promontories around them, they liked it much the best.[2]

Later, A. E. H. referred to "Pisgah" in several of his poems, notably *ASL* I and *MP* XXXIII. The first poem in *A Shropshire Lad* is titled "1887," and its inception came from the custom the children followed at Fockbury of climbing "Pisgah" to watch the beacons (bonfires) that were kindled on numerous hilltops to celebrate national or local anniversaries.

The poem "1887" commemorates the Golden Jubilee of Queen Victoria and the first two stanzas describe the "Pisgah" setting, which is placed in Shropshire by the word "Clee," (a chain of Shropshire hills near Ludlow) for the purpose of keeping the Shropshire viewpoint.

> From Clee to heaven the beacon burns,
>   The shires have seen it plain,
> From north and south the sign returns
>   And beacons burn again.
>
> Look left, look right, the hills are bright,
>   The dales are light between,
> Because 'tis fifty years to-night
>   That God has saved the Queen.

Again in 1897, on the celebration of the Queen's Diamond Jubilee, A. E. H. journeyed the distance from London to Fockbury to watch with apparently the same delight that characterized his childhood the brilliant burning beacons to commemorate his monarch's amazing reign. That night, he wrote to his sister Kate that he counted over sixty such beacons burning, in addition to the one on "Pisgah," and spoke of it as a glorious sight. He was then thirty-eight years old.

Housman's love for the Fockbury hill which was called "Mount

Pisgah" appears again in *More Poems* XXXIII. Although the later poem is not as powerful as "1887," it deserves attention as an illustration of the poet's tragic viewpoint in later years. "Pisgah" is definitely the "foreland" mentioned, and the view described in the last stanza is the one that he looked at with his brothers and sisters, who are "my friends" in the poem.

> On forelands high in heaven
>   'Tis many a year gone by,
> Amidst the fall of even
>   Would stand my friends and I.
> Before our foolish faces
>   Lay lands we did not see;
> Our eyes were in the places
>   Where we should never be.
>
> . . . .
>
> I see the air benighted
>   And all the dusking dales,
> And lamps in England lighted,
>   And evening wrecked in Wales;
> And starry darkness paces
>   The road from sea to sea,
> And blots the foolish faces
>   Of my poor friends and me.

Before this poem was completed (Notebook E, sheet 1 in the rough drafts) the faces of Herbert, Robert, and Basil had been blotted out by death, and A. E. H.'s personal struggle for happiness was long past.

In 1874, however, life was young and hopeful. All the children liked Fockbury House—its location, high on a hill overlooking Bromsgrove church tower and the town, was healthful and full of delights to be explored. The high gardens, contoured because of the steep slope, were particularly decorative for this reason, as they are today; outside the wall, the old farm buildings, such as stables, barn, and rick-yard, were wonderful places for investigation and play. Cryptomaria, deodar cedars, and willingtonia yews, marked as trees in the survey of 1777, shaded the lawns. These very trees are there today. The two miles to Bromsgrove was farther than it seems now because of lack of swift transportation, and necessarily the children lived a restricted and quite self-dependent existence; outside their own family, they had few playmates or acquaintances.

Their closest neighbors were yeomen, or else tenant farmers, and although the children liked most of them, at Fockbury they first realized the meaning of class distinctions. They noticed that at Catshill parish church, where they worshiped now on Sunday, the neighbors took off their old beaver hats when they passed by, and sat at respectful distances behind the Housman pew. The farmers were dressed in clean Sunday smocks, which they would wear at their duties throughout the week. It was a very different church from the one at Bromsgrove and much less interesting. The walls were plain whitewashed; the music came from an old harmonium, and the vicar was unconscionably dull and dour. But their grandfather's memory was vivid and they felt much at home.

Lucy brought different religious standards to Fockbury from those of the high church code to which the children had been accustomed. She was distinctly "low church," and she dispensed with the curtsey before the Gloria, and thoroughly disapproved of crucifixes. She thought the entire family should wear gloves to church, but that they should remove them after arriving; in this plan she never succeeded, for the Housmans went gloved and stayed gloved as their own mother had taught them.[3]

Hats at church were of course required, but the boys must remember to take them off on the doorstep; if a forgetful one left his on, the Argus-eyed governess snatched it off as if it had caught on fire, and marshalled the brood to the front pews with more than usual asperity. The girls were more docile under this ready-made religion they had inherited than the boys were; yet Alfred said in later life that the "Church of England was quite the best religion ever invented." The word "invented" shows exactly what his opinion of the origins of religion really was. He once wrote to an inquiring literary admirer, Maurice Pollet, in France, that "Lempriere's Classical Dictionary, which fell into my hands when I was eight, attached my affections to paganism. I became a deist at thirteen, and an atheist at twenty-one."[4]

Alfred disclosed none of his skeptical doubts to his stepmother or other members of his family during his youth. He continued to conform to the ritual of the church, and partook of communion with the rest of them. Years after, when he was with his stepmother or other women of his family, or with the Wise sisters at Woodchester, he still took communion with them, although it certainly had lost its significance. He probably did it to keep from hurting their feelings, going on the theory that participation did him no harm, and non-participation would have given his companions unhappiness.

But Lucy failed to carry her religion into the kitchen, for she took the attitude that the servants had only nominal social rights. Much as she enjoyed her own marriage bed, she refused the request of a house servant to sleep out in the village with relatives when her husband came from away to visit her. The children felt the tension in the house caused by Lucy's anger when she discovered that the woman had slipped out to the stable and spent the night there with her husband in the straw. What was so terrible about it, they wondered. What had happened out there? But Alfred did not wonder. He knew with deep revolt.

Lucy had brought a great assortment of her own furniture to use

at Fockbury—pieces redolent of the influence of the Great Exhibition of 1851, and she put Sarah Jane's time-worn antiques in the
attic, or used them as catch-alls in bathroom and kitchen. These
changes meant nothing to Alfred, for never at any time in his life
did he care to gather furnishings of beauty around him. Probably
the change from high church meant nothing to Alfred either; for
by the time he moved to Fockbury, church attendance with him
had become a purely perfunctory affair, and though he always
despised dull homilies, he was able to endure them by putting his
mind to thoughts far removed from the droning voice at the altar.

The children were withheld as long as possible from the so-called
facts of life, and what they found out they discovered for themselves. Sex with its mysteries was a forbidden subject, and naturally
this secrecy suggested that like the processes of nature at the toilet,
it was a shameful visitation of providence upon mankind—something deplorable and nasty. The reaction against these imposed sex
taboos was very strong in the Housmans, especially so in the lives
of Alfred, Clemence, and Laurence, the most intelligent and imaginative of the children.

To illustrate the ignorance about sex that prevailed in the Housman family during the adolescence of the children, Laurence Housman recalled one amusing incident. One summer night, a young
maid who was employed by the family, and slept in, tried in the
wee small hours of the morning to get in bed with one of the boys
(not Alfred) when he was in his early teens. Not knowing her
purpose, and believing she had come to rob him, (which she certainly had, but not in the way he suspected), he pierced the night
with scream after scream, whereupon the maid fled in ignominious
defeat, and lost her place soon afterwards.[5]

Whether their own mother would have brought up her children
in the shadow of such ignorance is open to conjecture. Probably

she would have liked to do otherwise, but outwardly would have remained true to her false Victorian codes, and kept silent. Privately, sex life to Sarah Jane was a dramatic, vital, and satisfying reality; but publicly, she followed the ritualists, withal a feeble brood, laden under their own burdens of shame and fear, lacking the stamina to confront instincts honestly, and basing their code of morals on the "shall nots" of ignorance and cowardice. The Housmans, moreover, lived in one of the most "cultured and refined" areas of rural England. A current English joke today, repeated with a relish, is that the people around Birmingham still think sex (pronounced "sax") is something to carry coal in!

Lucy was always an old maid mentally, not physically, and would have shrunk with horror at the idea of mentioning the word "sex" to her closest female friend, let alone to young and innocent children sprung from the chaste hand of God! Edward, who disciplined the children very little, probably never considered the possibility of educating them about their most insistent instincts, although he was firm in his resolve they should all be masters of the classics. So sexual matters were hidden under the veneer of silence which propriety demanded, and since the proprieties made proper things highly improper, life must have been very confusing.

Early after her marriage, Lucy had requested the children to call her "Mamma," a habit that only Alfred adhered to: for most of them soon shifted in private to an appellation that suited her best— "The Mater"—applied to their stepmother humorously rather than derisively, so Laurence Housman said, because of her Roman rule and majestic bearing. When Lucy overheard her new name, she took it good-naturedly, and before long she was the "Mater" in public as well as in private to everyone but Alfred, who continued to say "Mamma," a term he had never used for his mother.

In the new life at Fockbury, Sarah Jane's name was seldom

spoken, and then usually Lucy was the one who referred to her. Edward could not bring himself to mention her, and the children dared not, because of their own feelings and their intuitive knowledge that Lucy was a jealous soul. The younger ones had almost forgotten the mourning they had worn, with the horrid black stockings that scratched their legs; and now even the armbands, the final habiliment of grief, had disappeared. Their spirits rose accordingly, for life was full of youth and earnestness.

Lucy had probably married Edward with the idea of changing him, but she soon learned that her plans were the stuff that dreams are made on. She was possessive and aggressive—two characteristics never active in Sarah Jane—against which Edward rebelled, for they destroyed a part of Lucy's femininity—that quality of womanliness that had always entranced Edward in his life with Sarah Jane. Edward was afraid of Lucy. She was a stern taskmaster as well as a praiseworthy manager. Rather pathetically, she believed that by shouldering the sky domestically, she would eventually bring her wayward star into her bosom. She charted a poor course to lead that wandering planet into her orbit, and never succeeded in winning Edward over completely, either physically or spiritually. The first wife stood between them—she who had been feminine and gentle first of all, and graciously admonishing and advising afterwards. The calm beautiful eyes of her Victorian portrait seemed to follow Lucy around the house, and for a long time Lucy felt her presence in the family circle, a barrier set up by love that brooked no leaping. Only Alfred knew her tragedy; only Alfred was really understanding. Lucy would look up suddenly from her duties and find his eyes fixed upon her, warm, pitying, friendly. No word was spoken but they understood each other.

The troubled undercurrent of the new marriage relationship was felt indirectly by the younger children. Nevertheless, they played and pranced, studied and worked, or read omnivorously for their own pleasure, as the occasion arose. At night, externally the picture was one of ideal family life: Edward sat by the green lamp with his hand shading his face, either reading to himself or aloud to the children; and Lucy sat rocking comfortably near by, sometimes sewing, but often taking her turn reading to the family, for she too had a beautiful voice, and if she was allowed to read the books she liked best, she was a willing participant. Lucy did more in winning the children to herself by these evening readings than in all her other labors put together. With her, they breathlessly enjoyed the narrative poems of Scott, much of Shakespeare, *Henry Esmond,* and some of the Waverly novels. *Cranford* they decided was one of the nicest stories ever written. But they had to suffer for these evenings of bliss, for on Sunday, Lucy became the Mater again, and read them the *Life of Martin Luther* in two volumes.

Edward liked to read Dickens best; but he read Shakespeare with deep appreciation, and the works of Sheridan and Goldsmith were high on his list of favorites. With such a daily institution as well-chosen family reading to guide them, the eager minds of the Housman children unconsciously developed a taste for the best in literature, absorbed enough of the style of the writers to use them unconsciously as models, and sought to write poems and essays when most youngsters would be laboriously transcribing from copybooks.

From a card at home that pictured some twenty-four English cathedrals, Alfred developed that fondness for cathedrals and the comparison of their architecture that became one of his lifelong interests. The card, which Laurence Housman still had a year or two ago in a perfect state of preservation, was dark and large. The cathedrals were white, and the contrast in shading almost gave the effect of a third dimension. Alfred taught the children the names

and special characteristics of cathedrals from this card, and made
Laurence as fascinated about them as he was. They all liked to pore
over the alluring placard; and when Edward saw their interest, he
bought them a stereoscope with two sets of views of cathedrals,
some two dozen in all; then looking through the stereoscope became another favorite evening recreation at Fockbury House. The
children talked about the cathedrals as if they were people, fighting
for their favorites vigorously.[6]

About this time, Edward instituted a delightful innovation—the
children were introduced to a sip of wine after dinner, just before
the reading. This taste was increased by degrees until the older
children received a full wineglass, and the younger ones half as
much. Edward's wines were good, befitting an English gentleman,
and the children all enjoyed their sips of Burgundy or port, claret
or brown sherry.

Beer was common as water at the Housman dining table. Katherine Housman (Symons) says in her sketch of A. E. H.'s boyhood:
"His [Alfred's] liking for beer followed his customary drinking of
beer as a boy. He drank beer daily from his silver christening mug.
We all drank beer from our own mugs. The servants drank beer;
and so did the boarders at the School."[7]

Miraculously enough, Lucy approved of this introduction to
Bacchus, for a well-curbed acquaintance with that wayward god
had been a part of her gentle rearing, one of the social amenities of
life. From this habit formed at home with the complete approval of
his parents, Alfred derived his lifelong discriminating interest in
fine wines.

None of the children became a "wine-bibber" from these ex-
plorative bacchanalian adventures. If Edward and Lucy had
allowed the children as much freedom about the Church of England as they did with the wine cellar—tasting, rejecting, accepting

at will—Alfred might have arrived at some religious compromise. Also he might not have developed that complete intolerance of any personal interference with his private affairs which became an established characteristic.

If the children had been instructed casually in sexual matters, presented with the same frank honesty as the sips of wine, instead of having all bodily functions treated as mysterious and undesirable if not positively wicked, they might have been more uniformly normal, and certainly less subject to the dangers of inversion.

Inhibitions which less intelligent and sensitive children would either have not noticed, or would have carelessly over-ridden, took on great significance to the highly temperamental and impressionable Housmans, and created abnormal repressions which by suggestion rather than statement, made more than one of them obsessed with strange reluctances which barred them forever from the normal embraces of lovers. Of the seven children, only two, Kate and Basil, ever married, and of those Katherine alone, the least talented, had children.[8] Sexual maladjustment was to enter the lives of some of the others, and was to prove more bitter because of their sensitive and passionate tendencies.

But these matters did not shadow the happy days at Fockbury. Customarily, wine was followed first at Fockbury by the recital of passages from the Scripture and from poetry, for every day the children were required to learn a passage from the Bible and at least three verses of poetry. These had to be learned under the tutelage of the testy soul who then functioned as governess; but since memorizing was a popular part of their lessons, the children seldom rebelled and had the memory work ready for their parents several days ahead of time.

Rich, deep voices were family inheritances which remained with the Housmans into old age.[9] The voice of Clemence in childhood was considered most beautiful of all, and she recited long passages from *Isaiah,* making them great poetry; Alfred and Laurence discanted the *Psalms.* By this time Alfred had completely overcome his early habit of stammering, and was developing a gift for clear, precise expression.

While the young Housmans were busy at Bromsgrove school or with the governess at home, Lucy was energetic from sun-up to sun-down, managing household affairs so efficiently that finances were made easier for a time at Fockbury. She saw to it that farm products fed the family well and helped out the budget. Milk, butter, poultry, and pork, together with jams and sauces from the "climbing trees," made living pleasanter and also balanced the ration, an interesting fact of which Lucy was completely unaware. The children improved in health, appetites were good, and Laurence's legs, which had been weak, straightened and strengthened.

Pigs were butchered outside the wall, behind the rick-stack, probably by a nearby farmer assisted by the gardener Ben. When Clemence was eighty-eight, she wrote an account of this ritual very clearly:

> My mind goes back to childhood when we reared and cured our own pigs. They were always swealed—yes, the letter is "l," not "t,"—do you know the word or practice? It is, instead of scalding to remove the bristles, scorching on a bonfire of straw. We were allowed to look on at the blaze as a treat, but to me the blackened carcass was a horror, though I never let on, to be derided by my brothers. This treatment gives an added flavour, to the chine especially.[10]

The "Wiltshire sides" and hams resulting must have been correspondingly delicious, and small wonder that one of the worse punishments the youngsters ever incurred was to go baconless for breakfast.

Lucy supervised everything and did a great deal of the work of cooking. Her energy was tireless. The children began to develop a real liking for her, tempered with a good deal of awe, but they were always antagonized by her streaks of severity, and failed to feel as much at ease with her as they might have felt under less spartan management. Edward pursued his law practice in a more or less aimless manner, went on partridge-hunting trips, fished, and occasionally took part in Bromsgrove events congenial to his position and profession. Lucy criticized him often for neglecting his law practice, and usually made him uncomfortable after his happy days of hunting or fishing. Alfred never accompanied his father on such trips and there is no account of his ever having hunted or fished in his life. He did, at times, assist his father in horticultural experiments with trees, flowers, and shrubs. He was absorbed in his studies at Bromsgrove. In fact, he had little time for anything else. He rose first of all the children for a six-o'clock breakfast, and returned late with home lessons to prepare. It was a fourteen hour day, and only on holidays and week-ends was he able to join the family in reading, games, and glee-singing, always a welcome and beloved leader. The prizes he won in the classics came with great regularity at end of term. Certainly he cared little for the prizes themselves, for they were usually rather dull books; it was the idea of winning them that counted. One of these relics of his boyhood was a copy of Dr. William Smith's *Dictionary of Greek and Roman Antiquities,* an 1875 edition, handsomely bound in calf. In Herbert Millington's precise hand is the inscription: "Grammar School of King Edward VI, Bromsgrove. Midsummer examination prize, 1876. Prize for Classical Scholarship. To A. E. Housman. Herbert Millington, Headmaster." There is no sign that the twelve hun-

dred and ninety-three octavo pages were ever used, except that
one Latin passage had been underlined as being rather poor phras-
ing, and two exclamation points after the underlines may have
been put there by Millington, who probably enjoyed the book
himself before he passed it on.[11]

Alfred always considered scholarship as a bounden duty—his
necessity and his obligation to the field in which he had resolved
to be master. Later it represented his bread and butter and his hope
of atonement. At Fockbury the thought of fame through poetry
had not dawned on him. He took a serious satisfaction in good
scholarship, and in later life this satisfaction was to intensify into
a kind of exhilarated melancholy, like that of a monk in his citadel
passionately devoted to his laborious tome. But when the constric-
tion came to his throat, the tingle to his spine, the tension in his
solar plexus, (he once said unexpectedly that his solar plexus was
where his poetry came from),[12] it was always poetry that brought
them.

The early verses that Alfred wrote during the Fockbury period
were on three subjects, one of them artificial, the others from his
heart: classical translations, or of classical scenes and characters;
nonsense rhymes, or poems based on nature. The last two kinds
were spontaneous. The nonsense verses were usually very amusing,
and the nature poems showed promise of *A Shropshire Lad,* but
such effusions were few and far between.

At Bromsgrove School Alfred received little scientific training;
also the one-sidedness of his preparatory education gave him small
background for the supplementary readings required at Oxford in
both philosophy and history. He received training in mathematics
at Bromsgrove, and was an accurate although lukewarm student
in this science. The only sciences that ever appealed to him were
two that fired his imagination—botany and astronomy. He picked

up a good deal of accurate information about both of these subjects at home, and through his liking for astronomy, he became interested in astrology, which combination resulted decades later in his greatest Latin research project, *Manilius*.

When Alfred was about eight years old, he began reading an astronomy book in his father's library, and some illustrated botany books inherited from the Holdens captured his fancy at about the same time. From these he learned a considerable amount about common plants of the English countryside. He never made any use of his botanical knowledge except to tabulate to his precise satisfaction the names of English trees and flora, together with their growing habits, especially the time of putting forth leaves or blossoms in springtime; and for years he kept records of when these plants and trees would first leaf out, so that he could tell at a moment's notice whether the spring came a day or two earlier or later at Cambridge, and his friends got into the habit of asking him. But he could never abide to have on his walks a companion who babbled inanely about the beauties of nature without knowing anything about them, and he was quick to set such a one right with brusque corrections as to names and habits of plants he knew both scientifically and esthetically.

By 1876, four of the Housman sons—all but Herbert—were in Bromsgrove school and all were there by merit of their ability in examinations leading to Foundation Scholarships. Thus all four were able to secure a good education at less cost for the lot than was the salary of the governess at home! Nobody could accuse the school of favoritism, because all the boys had won their places fairly by their own efforts and it was known generally that the Foundation Scholarships were based on the top marks in competitive examination, and on nothing else. All the boys won these scholarships in their eleventh year and then entered Bromsgrove, which may be compared to a private junior high school going on through senior high school. The principal studies were Greek, Latin, (excellent courses in both), mathematics, French, and English grammar and literature, probably less good but adequate. The Bible entered surreptitiously under the desks of some of the pupils as an aid in Greek translation, morality supporting and aiding immorality! Alfred was able to read French well when he left Bromsgrove, and he continued to read French authors in the original all his life, and was able enough in French conversation to use it adequately on his frequent trips to France after 1892.

In the final form (year), the sixth, at Bromsgrove School, all four boys were able to pass an examination called then the "Higher Oxford and Cambridge Local" and Alfred gained an "Oxford and Cambridge Leaving Certificate" which qualified him for entrance to either of these universities. The Bromsgrove education suited Alfred better than any of his brothers, for it best fitted the particular scholastic interests and talents that endowed him; but Robert and Basil would have welcomed more scientific subjects, and they must have found their first years in engineering and medicine, respectively, rather rough sledding.

Bromsgrove was an excellent school for those days, however, and it has progressed as time has gone on, improving its curriculum and requirements to fit the rapid advancement of twentieth century education. In 1950 it had an enrollment of 231 boys at a flat rate of 200 pounds a year. Of these some thirty pupils were day students (as the Housmans always were) and their present rate of pay is ninety pounds a year. Alfred's education cost less than a third that much, but it must be remembered in 1875 a pound was worth more than it is now, and the burden of tuition was an increasing load on his father's flattening pocketbook.

For of the busy bee-hive at Fockbury House, Edward was fast

becoming, like Coleridge, "the sole unbusy thing." The profession of Solicitor seemed slowly to stagnate, and it was discouraging to have a rapidly growing family make heavier inroads on a purse that never had been very flourishing. Later on, when Laurence was ready for college, there was not a crown to send him, and Edward's property was all mortgaged.

Return to Perry Hall

Making a desperate gesture to recoup his fortunes, Edward decided to return to Perry Hall, where his law practice might benefit from a position nearer his clients. Therefore after a five-year residence at Fockbury House, the family moved back to Perry Hall in 1878, a year or less after Alfred had entered Oxford, and the same year that Robert entered Mason and Queen's College at Birmingham. Edward's ostensible reason this time for moving was that with two sons at college, and Basil to go soon, it would be advantageous to be closer to the railroad, a fact which of course was obvious.

Actually, the last family horse, dearly loved by the children, had died, and there was no money to replace him. Likewise, it was impossible to pay the staff at Fockbury any longer; because, although the country offered a better living, several times as much labor was required to gather and care for the crops and foods than Edward was able to pay; it would be cheaper to retrench and live in town. Edward hopefully expected to have more income by returning to Bromsgrove, where he reduced the household staff to one servant, and dismissed his office clerk. Thereafter Clemence was his clerk, and she added this duty, not too strenuous except at tax times, to her usual one of helping Lucy with her load of cooking and house management. The house, somewhat run down and bearing the scars of tenants, was not kept up as meticulously as it had been; that was impossible, but it was comfortable, although in winter most of it was shut off in order to reduce the cost of fuel, and family life centered during these months in the dining room.

Regardless of these retrenchments, the family fortunes steadily worsened, and by 1880, everyone at home realized the household was in dire financial straits. The fact that Perry Hall was mortgaged hurt Edward's pride, but did not shake him out of his lethargy. A little later Fockbury House passed out of Housman hands. Much of the money realized was swallowed in meeting past-due mortgage obligations and by taxes.

Not until this final Perry Hall period did Lucy completely display the courage of which she was made. She went her way calmly, proudly concealed her feelings, and still carried the Roman rule over her household. She scrimped and saved, patched and mended; she even sold vines and plants from her greenhouse to help defray expenses. She hoarded eggs as if they were diamonds and sold them for tea and sugar. The boys had to go to school in mended jackets with trousers that did not match. They were always to remember that humiliation. However, Lucy continued to entertain guests at intervals, and always managed to keep up appearances when callers descended upon her. She concealed from the children the true state of affairs as best she could, especially from Alfred, and she encouraged him to bring college friends home with him when he was on holiday.

As a result, Alfred knew less about the tragic family poverty than he should have known, and the Christmas reunion of 1879 was a happy one at Perry Hall. Alfred was home from Oxford, and Robert came from Birmingham. This Christmas was the last one that the Housmans were to remember as being full of the merry misrule of youthful exuberance. The Yule log burned in the broad hall fireplace, holly and mistletoe decorated the mantels, candles were lighted, and cakes and plum puddings, planned and saved by Lucy and Clemence for weeks ahead of time, ornamented the wide sideboard in the dining room. Stories of college experiences put sparkle in the conversation, and Edward was pulled out of his seclusion by the vivid life around him. He was proud of his brilliant sons and their records, and willing to fool himself temporarily into the idea that his affairs were going as well as could be expected. He sat in the background, smiling and nodding, with his wine glass in his unsteady hand.

Alfred, true to his leadership of old, announced a story competition open to all the children. The tales were to be finished on a certain evening when they should be read aloud to the family and the winner decided upon. Robert and Basil with characteristic scientific aloofness turned in nothing, but the others all contributed.

Herbert was awarded first place by common consent, because of the paroxysms of laughter evoked by his romantic tale, called *Why They Eloped*. The reasons proved to be a masterly exhibition of eleven-year-old innocence. The throbbing lovers in Herbert's work of art were "Richard and Eelen" (the latter misspelled for Ellen consistently), whose entire efforts from first to last were governed by a dominating passion to reach The Altar for no better reason, apparently, than to foil in necromantic fashion the equally strong passion displayed by "Eelen's" father to thwart their objective by fair means or foul.

The story revealed a few hidden but chaste meetings, when the lovers' sole topic of conversation was the best and speediest method of reaching their Sacred Goal. A series of preposterous events well suited to a modern Wild West movie thriller climaxed in an elopement on horse to the church door with the outraged and apoplectic father in close pursuit.

But bang! The lovers had reached their haven, slammed the church door and locked it in the very faces of their pursuers; the vicar was conveniently waiting, the vows were read; and Virtue, hand in hand with Romance, whose head must have been bowed and her mouth dry by this time, prevailed forever after. The story was read aloud by Alfred amid shouts of laughter. Herbert, rather shy about its reception, had to be dragged out from under the sofa, where he had secretly ensconced himself to listen, in order that he might receive the ovations of his elders.

Alfred's contribution—his only short story either before or after—was titled *A Morning with the Royal Family* and was printed later in *The Bromsgrovian,* the publication of his preparatory school, without his consent, probably because Basil was then editor of the school magazine during his final year at Bromsgrove. Alfred was ashamed of his story afterwards, and said it deserved to be burnt, but this could hardly occur after it had been printed and circulated. Because of his antipathy for this single bit of prose fiction, it has never been published since *The Bromsgrovian* edition of 1880, but Laurence Housman granted permission to quote the first chapter and the final nonsense verse at the end. It illustrates well the rollicking pleasure that Alfred got out of his unleashed liberty with the English language at home, and illustrates the whimsical humor that still brightened a great part of his outlook on life in the year of 1879.

A MORNING WITH THE ROYAL FAMILY
By A. E. Housman

"Pigs on the front lawn again!" cried the King, "Give me a cannon, somebody!"

Nobody gave him a cannon, so seizing a teaspoon from the breakfast table, he rushed from the apartment.

Pigs on the front lawn were an old nuisance at the palace. The reason probably was that the Royal Drive was so much wider and finer than the road into which it opened that all the pig drivers mistook it for the main road, and drove up it accordingly. The King had long ago determined to stop this, but his efforts had not been successful. He had first written with his own hands and fastened upon the drive gate a placard bearing these words:

"I'll cut off your head if you do."

This notice, however, no one seemed to understand, though many had their heads cut off—not that they understood it any better after that—and the King therefore resolved to compose a notice about which there could be no possibility of mistake. He composed the following:

"This is to give notice that any person, or indeed, any nurserymaid, found trespassing on these premises in company with pigs, cows, peacocks, antelopes, serpents, perambulators, or any other kind of poultry whatsoever, will be taken to the lock-up and put to death, or otherwise executed."

Even this catalogue of livestock, however, was not found sufficient, and the King took down this notice and put up a number of others in succession. The one which was up at the present time was the simple announcement: "Trespassers will be vaccinated!"—which had hitherto worked very well; but it had failed at last.

His Majesty, therefore, as I have said, seized a tea-spoon which was a thing he always seized when the thing he wanted was not at hand; in fact, it was only that very morning that he had brushed his hair with a tea-spoon, having previously thrown his hairbrush out of the window at a partridge; he seized a tea-spoon and rushed out of doors.

He had just reached the foot of the door steps when a cedar tree blew down on him, in the fifty-third year of his age and the twenty-eighth of his reign. He was municificent, affable, and loquacious, and was succeeded by his son, Henry X.

This Alice-in-Wonderland kind of nonsense reeled along for eleven chapters, with an ebullient spontaneity which testified to the fact that Alfred thoroughly enjoyed his temporary release from Horace and Ovid. The punctuation is given exactly as he had it.

The story ended with a hitherto unpublished nonsense rhyme, supposed to have been written by the poet-laureate of the King on the death of a friend of his who was a dancing dervish:

Let us play on the pianner in a melancholy manner,
Drinking ipecacuhana while you listen to my songs;
Let us play the bag-pipes mellow, and the flute and violin-cello
And the tea-tray and the bellows, and the poker and the tongs.

His dancing made me giddy, and I said, "Oh do be steady
Or your wife will be a widdy, and the tears will fill her eyes;"
But in spite of all my cautions, he continued his contortions,
Till he broke himself in portions of an unimportant size.

Oh good-bye! good-bye forever! You were truly, truly clever,
Although you almost never did appreciate my songs;
But it didn't make me jealous, and I'll dig your grave most
    zealous,
With the pick-axe and the bellows, and the poker and the tongs.

The King and his escapades offered welcome relief to the Bromsgrove pupils after Greek translations, and even Herbert Millington enjoyed the story. Before circulating the issue containing it, however, he caused two expressions to be deleted and hidden by bits of paper pasted over them, in order that the parents of his charges would not be shocked, and thus recorded an unconscious commentary on the religious taboos of the period.

In the second chapter, the princess took a cup and scooped out a huge serving of marmalade for her morning bread and butter.

" 'My dear, how *can* you do it?' the Queen protested weakly.

'God helps those who help themselves, Mama,' replied the princess, calmly spooning down her marmalade."

In the magazine, "God" was covered by the over-slip "Heaven."

The other example was near the end of the story.

"The Queen . . . made an attempt to say the Lord's Prayer backwards, but fell over into the flour bin."

The words "The Lord's Prayer" were covered by the over-slip "abracadabra."

Thus was the face of Deity saved, and decorum preserved.[13]

Alfred enjoyed writing nonsense rhymes occasionally during his later life, but the larger portion of them were written before 1881, and with a few exceptions, the earlier ones were the best. They were often based on the novel use of words, and usually constituted a part of family contests to see who could best combine in verse a series of totally unrelated nouns. A delightful account of some of these efforts can be found in Laurence Housman's *My Brother, A. E. Housman*,[14] and the poems themselves are for the most part in the last pages of that volume.

Alfred's sense of humor never deserted him, and though it became less effervescent and much more cynical in the days when he was called A. E. H., it still was a balance wheel for the melancholy and introspective bent that altered him in maturity as if witchcraft had struck him.

After the happy Christmas of 1879, trouble bore down fast and hard on Perry Hall, and throughout 1880 the Mater had a distressing time as she tried to make ends meet on almost no money. Her character was a strange mixture of tyranny and courage,[15] so that when the darkest of financial afflictions fell on them, she was staunch in her duty as she saw it. Laurence became closer to her then, and she sometimes called him "her comfort" and knitted woolen socks for him. But her innate will to manage everybody forced him (as well as others in the family) to put his foot down and insist that she stop treating him as a child. When she had learned that, with difficulty, their relations remained comfortable and friendly.

Lucy and her sisters were interesting studies in personality; Lucy all imperialism and courage; her middle sister all grace and poise; and the youngest, no grace, unattractive, not at all intellectual, but with a heart of gold, and most faithful in her affections. Those three sisters all lived to be eighty years old or more and not one of them ever needed as much as a false tooth in her head. They were monuments to Victorian vitality, which in Edward's family was inherited more by Clemence and Laurence than the others, although Alfred lived to be seventy-seven.[16]

As finances became hopeless, Edward failed in health rapidly. He retired constantly into a dream-like world of his own, and ambled around the house and garden without purpose or plan, often mumbling to himself about nothing. He drank now because he had to. He wanted to become oblivious to the family straits; he wanted to be blind to the penury, the retrenchments, the stretching of shillings. The Mater was amazingly calm about it all; and when Alfred brought his college friend, Alfred W. Pollard, home with him for a summer holiday, she managed to have the comforts at hand that the social amenities, always so important to her, demanded; and on the surface life ran in fairly smooth waters. She planned the visit for weeks ahead, conserving her resources, so that when the time arrived, there was fine wine in the decanter and delicious ham on the table. Afternoon tea was served in the drawing room on the best rose-colored Worcester china, and leisurely games of croquet followed on the beautiful lawn. Alfred and Pollard went on long walks in the morning and carried biscuits and cheese for lunch, with ale at some distant "pub."

Again Lucy tried too hard, for again Alfred left for Oxford not realizing that hopeless poverty had struck Perry Hall. He thoroughly appreciated his stepmother, but became increasingly withdrawn from his father, whose condition could not be concealed.

His chagrin about the change in his father was manifested best by the fact that after his return to Oxford, he wrote no more to Edward, but preferred to send him occasional messages in letters to his stepmother. One of them was to thank his father for having written to him. Their area of communication had narrowed to nothing.

Winter came on, with the cold and snow of 1880. The Christmas season rolled around, the season of carols so dear to the hearts of Englishmen, each song filled with the spirit of peace and good will toward men. It had been customary for decades that the village carolers would sing in groups before the houses of the local great, and receive a silver offering in return. The Housmans were always first on their list, but this year a strange incident occurred.

When the carolers began the first sweet notes of "God Rest You, Merry Gentlemen," at Perry Hall, the Mater's pride suddenly gave in to despair, for there was not even a half-crown in the house to reward the singers. Tight of lip, she told Laurence to go out in the snow and stop the carols because they could not afford them. Her bitterness and her pride overflowed in that brief statement. Naturally Laurence hated to do it, but he finally complied, and the next day everybody had heard the story. Here was sad news, thought the villagers. The Housmans were unable to pay a half-crown for Christmas carols! There was a vast amount of shaking of heads over this, but nothing malevolent; for the Housmans were well-liked, and poverty made them no less the "gentle folk" to the community that had looked up to them for generations.

There is no account of the Christmas of 1880 that is authentic, but it must have been spent very austerely, and probably was shadowed by the impending cloud of greater trials yet to come. Laurence remembers one incident about Alfred during this Christmas visit. Just after the arrival of Alfred, when he came to the dining

table, the Mater mentioned that she disliked the cut of his moustache.

"Why in the world did you have it cut like that?" she demanded.

"Because it's *my* moustache!" he flung back at her. His intolerance toward interference is well illustrated by this incident, which
Laurence remembered because it was such an unusual outburst.

The decisive blow fell in the spring of 1881, when Edward was
stricken with an illness that broke him completely. He recovered
enough to walk around with a cane, but thereafter he never could
take on his duties of Solicitor with any degree of regularity, and
finally gave up so much of his practice that Clemence could not
carry on as his clerk. His deterioration went on for over ten years;
he died at Perry Hall November 27, 1894, at the age of sixty-three.
Lucy and Alfred, who helped her pay for the funeral, buried him
in the Catshill parish churchyard, in the presence of all his children.

There is no doubt that Lucy mourned a man that she had sacrificed for and had loved sincerely, but never had been able to win
over to herself. Her willful insistence had worn down a nature best
suited to gentle encouragement, but probably too indecisive to
have made much of a success under any regime.

Perhaps in order to preclude the meeting of Edward and Sarah
Jane in Paradise before she arrived, Lucy had these words inscribed
at the top of his tombstone:

Here rests *waiting for the Resurrection Day* Edward Housman of Perry Hall.

She left a space between the graves of Edward and Sarah Jane.
When she died in November, 1907, in her eighty-fifth year, at
Hereford, she was buried in the vacant "bed of mould" that she
had picked out between Edward and his first wife, so that while
Sarah Jane was a barrier between Edward and Lucy in life, Lucy

perhaps planned to be a barrier between them in death. She left clear and determined instructions as to her burial and the words to be cut in the stone on Edward's marker, below his inscription:

Also Lucy Agnes
For more than 21 years his wife
To her may the Lord give felicity and make her glad with the joy of his countenance.

And if Lucy could be happy in a world where, by her own interpretation, God would be ruler instead of herself, perhaps her prayer was realized.

Two

Shadow of the Mask

The troubles of our proud and angry dust
Are from eternity, and shall not fail.
Last Poems

4

Grey Stones of Oxford

THE ENTIRE later life of Alfred Housman would have been changed if he had gone to Cambridge University instead of Oxford. Whether for better or worse cannot be predicted, but his future would certainly have been very different. Necessity decided where he was to go. Oxford offered the scholarship (100 pounds per annum) which was essential if he was to go at all; Cambridge offered nothing, although it had the Classical Tripos which would have been much more appropriate to his talents. Edward wanted him to go to Oxford, where his father and grandfather had gone, and luckily, here was the scholarship! Alfred had nothing to do with the decision, although if he had, he would probably not have contested it. It was Oxford or nothing.

Lucy sighed with relief when the matter was settled. She loved Alfred the most of all her ready-made family; she wanted him to have every chance he deserved. She clapped her large, capable hands with joy when the good news came that the scholarship was his; also the children were delighted and already fancied their brother an Oxonian with first class honors. Lucy did all possible to fill his bags with a comfortable if simple wardrobe, and Edward had the money for his hat and black coat, his books and his miscellaneous needs which were few by habit. Alfred went down to Oxford alone, and under the blue rare sky of autumn, he beheld for the first time the spires and towers of the ancient university pointing to the heights.

Alfred was sensitive, shy, and alone, but not afraid, for he had resourceful courage. Oxford did not particularly impress him then, or later. When he remembered Oxford most pleasantly, in later years, his memories centered upon the beauty of the curving High, or the innumerable clocks on the college towers that disagreed about the time every fifteen minutes with charming dissonance.

Dr. Alfred W. Pollard says in his reminiscences of Housman:

> Alfred Housman and I won open scholarships at St. John Baptist's College, Oxford, at Midsummer 1877, and started residence on the same "stair" in the second quad the following October, 1877; thus Housman and I, from the first were thrown much together.[1]

The solemn Latin ceremonial of matriculation, however, Alfred sensed as a sham, and hence found very amusing, as he wrote to his step-mother next day:

> At a quarter to five all the freshmen of this College, twenty-two in number, were collected in Mr. Ewing's rooms and were then instructed how to write our names in Latin. . . . Then he marched us off to New College, where we found the Vice-Chancellor seated in dim religious light at the top of the hall. . . . We one by one inscribed our names in a large book, in this wise:
> Alfredus Edwardus Housman, e Coll. Di. Joh. Bapt. Gen. Fil, Natu max.
> Which is, being intepreted, A. E. Housman, of the College of St. John the Baptist, eldest son of a gentleman.
> Then I wrote my name in English in a smaller and less dignified book, and then paid 2 pounds 10 shillings to a man at the table . . . then an attendant brought in 22 copies of the Statutes

of the University, bound in violet, and piled them on the table, hiding the Vice-Chancellor from the eye. Presently his head appeared over the top and we got up and stood in a sort of semicircle in front of him. He called each of us by name and presented us with a copy of the Statutes, and with a paper on which was written in Latin, or what passes for Latin at Oxford: "At Oxford, in the Michaelmas term. A. D. 1877 on the 13th day of the month of October: on which day A. E. Housman of the College of St. John the Baptist, gentleman's son, appeared in my presence and was admonished to keep the laws of this University, and was enrolled in the register of the University. J. E. Sewell, *Vice-Chancellor.*"

You may judge what a farce that is when I tell you that one of these laws is that we are forbidden to wear any coat save a black one, or to use fire-arms, or to trundle a hoop, among other things.[2]

Immediately, the well-known Oxford system of education descended upon him together with the before-mentioned black coat; and the monastic walls of old St. John's became his residence for the next two years. Housman at eighteen found it easy to be a monk in his citadel, and so he must have appeared to most of his mates, for he had never given the heart out of his bosom, and had kept his fancy free. His sister Kate, in writing of his early youth remarked: "He was singularly free from amorous entanglements";[3] at Bromsgrove school he had been satisfied with the society of his brothers and casual acquaintance with the other students; his tremendous capacity for intense emotion in human relationships had never been tapped, let alone tested. His life had been remote from cities; although when he was fourteen, Edward had taken him to London where under the guidance of relatives he had been decorously introduced to Trafalgar Square, Westminster Abbey, the British Museum, and a Shakespearean play.

However unsophisticated he was, he had learned to stand off and view people and life in general with an appraising eye, quite objectively and with a good deal of cynical amusement. His early letters home are full of this witty type of amused observation, and were usually addressed to his stepmother. His naturally mature and cautious viewpoint made him better able to enter a world of which he knew little, but his intense craving for love and affection, which he did not know he possessed, made him particularly vulnerable to the influence of the few close associates that he soon gravitated toward as naturally as a plant turns to the sun.

From the twenty-two men to enter St. John's that autumn Housman soon singled out two for his main companions, Alfred W. Pollard and Moses J. Jackson. Pollard was a student in the classics, as was Housman; Jackson was a scientist. Both men were brilliant in their particular fields, and genuinely interested in university life. Of the two, Jackson surpassed Pollard in grades, but Pollard was destined to take a higher place in the world of scholarship. Jackson's father was principal of The Vale School, Ramsgate, Kent. Pollard was a delightful young fellow of rare good taste and judgment. He remained a close friend in later life of Laurence Housman as well as Alfred. He became a bibliographer in the British Museum and later went to Cambridge in the field of bibliography.

Housman never wrote of Jackson in his letters home and never took Jackson to visit there, but he referred often to Pollard and invited him twice to Perry Hall. In the family album there is no picture of Pollard, however. There is one—strangely enough—of Moses Jackson; it was taken when he was about twenty-two years old, and is placed on a page with Alfred's portrait of the *Shropshire Lad* period, when he was thirty-five. The portrait shows that Jackson was a good-looking wholesome man with strongly masculine features. His eyes were dark and his straight black hair was parted on the side. His forehead, nose, and mouth were well-formed and determined, and his general appearance was practical and matter-of-fact. Such, indeed, he was: there was nothing of the dreamer or poet about Jackson. Extrovert, unable to comprehend those who were not, magnetic, he had the ability to give his companionship freely and constantly, almost indifferently, without concentrating upon any of those friendships, or in any way making them essential to his existence.

The three young men, Pollard, Jackson, and Housman, continued to be congenial, and at the beginning of their fourth year at Oxford, they moved into an apartment in St. Giles, where they remained until the end of their college course. Dr. Pollard says:

> When Housman was in the mood he could recite to very restricted audiences humorous stories of his own making which were doubly humorous by his prim method of telling them. We had from the first taken many walks together and continued to do so in our third year, and began also to play lawn tennis together in the College garden; otherwise I saw rather less of him as I had moved into the other quad.
>
> In our fourth year, however, when we had to go out of college, he and I and Moses Jackson took five rooms together in a picturesque old house in St. Giles', nearly opposite the college, now long ago displaced by academic buildings. . . .[4]

By 1881, Pollard was gradually withdrawing from close intimacy with Housman and Jackson—a change from earlier Oxford days—although Canon J. T. Nance wrote in his recollections of his undergraduate days at Oxford: "I had very little to do with Alfred Housman as an undergraduate at St. John's. He lived a quiet student's life, reading hard. . . . His great friend was A. W. Pollard."[5]

Housman's friendship with Pollard was life-long; from 1880 through 1881, however, Housman centered more and more attention upon Jackson, and Pollard chose to absent himself from both of them, and concentrate upon his readings for Greats. Whether any other reason prompted him was never disclosed.

In describing their college life during the final year Pollard says:

> After we had returned from dining in Hall, and had our coffee (neither Housman nor Jackson smoked), I mostly retired to work by myself in the sitting room, leaving the other two on the first floor. Jackson's was an absolutely safe first in science in the schools and he had no need to read much in the evening. What and how much Housman read I don't know.[6]

Of the tutors that Alfred had at Oxford little is known, for although he casually mentioned a Mr. Warren and a Mr. Ewing as advising him in that capacity his first year,[7] these men apparently had little influence on him, nor is there any account of any Oxford professor making friends with Alfred, or affecting his life one way or the other. His morning hours were spent at lectures, either prescribed or optional, and in essential readings or essay writing.

Housman wrote to Maurice Pollet, February 5, 1933: "Oxford had not much effect on me, except that I there met my greatest friend." Grant Richards adds his own footnote at the bottom of the page: M. J. Jackson."[8]

The courses were planned to prepare the students for Moderates, which would occur at the end of the second year, an examination which for Housman would be on the classics alone. Therefore during the first two years at Oxford, Alfred had a happy time of it, delving into the Greek and Latin he liked, and doing more reading than was required of him. He got into the habit of spending long hours working in Bodley, translating and studying Propertius, and doing more work in Horace than was demanded.

He avoided college athletics, but in addition to his tennis with

Pollard he took long walks for his exercise in the afternoon, when most of the students were punting on the Thames or playing cricket. During these walks, occasionally a line of poetry flashed across his mind—a different kind of verse from that which he had composed before. He had fallen under the wanton sway of Swinburne, and most of these lines were embellished with Pre-Raphaelite ornamentation.

Two of Housman's earliest poems were written during this period about the year 1879. One of them distinctly Swinburnian in style he named "New Year's Eve";[9] the other, a much better poem, was "Parta Quies,"[10] three lines of which are carved on his memorial tablet at Ludlow.

"New Year's Eve" was his verbal rejection of religious faith. The poem is interesting not for its value as poetry, but to show that Housman during his second year at Oxford not only became an atheist, but also prophesied the dawn of a new era that would break with Victorianism completely.

Housman was twenty when he wrote "New Year's Eve." It was published soon after in *Waifs and Strays,* an Oxford magazine. After the printing in 1881, he consistently ruled the poem out of subsequent publications, but finally it appeared in the "Additional Poems" section of *The Collected Poems* after his death. No manuscript was found for it. Probably Housman barred it from publication again because he had emerged from the influence of Swinburne and his over-sensuous imagery.

"Parta Quies" discloses three of the poet's growing preoccupations in style and thought: his desire to renounce romantic embellishment for a condensed power and brevity to which the classics had led him; the conception of death as a deliveress from the plight of living; and the belief that there is no conscious personal existence in the hereafter.

Death was to be the polyphonic background of Housman's poetry, with many variations in the foreground of his compositions —deviations in mood according to whether the theme dwelt on the death of soldiers, or lovers, or suicides, or criminals—a fugue developed in minor keys that sang of the silence of the grave; its darkness, its immobility, its remoteness; relieved by interludes interpreting it as a healing peace and eternal balm for the pain and dearth of living.

In 1881 Housman purchased two Dürer etchings which were to be the only decorations of his room at Oxford; later they were on the wall at Byron cottage, and finally his suite of rooms at Trinity College. The choice of these highly tragic, haunted figures that were cherished all the rest of his life is significant proof that Housman's viewpoint on life had darkened during his third year at Oxford. One Dürer sketch was the crouched figure of mad-eyed *Melancholia*; the other was the better known and less dreadful *The Knight, Death and the Devil*. Both of these tragic etchings, worn and specked by time, are today in "Elbow Room" at "Longmeadow," Laurence Housman's garden study.

Little outward sign of these altered opinions colored Housman's life during 1880-81. The clouds were forming around his head, but they had not broken. He took a genuine interest in almost everything at Oxford, regardless of his predilection for long solitary walks. He was called "House" by Jackson, and his nick-name for Jackson was "Mo"; there is no account of what Pollard may have been named. But in these early years the three had good times together, and were full of tricks they played on each other. The "apple pie bed" was one of their favorites. It consisted of the lower sheet being folded in the middle, and pulled up, so that the victim had no place to put his legs until he laboriously made his bed over. There is an account of the three men playing this joke on each other many years later in Dr. Pollard's Kensington home, amid gales of laughter, this when two of them were staid university professors, the other head of a school in India.[11]

"House" took a lively interest in "Mo's" prowess on the Oxford rowing team, and usually attended the boat races. He also participated in campus political meetings which he described with cynical amusement in letters to his stepmother.

Housman was more faithful to his early teachings about politics than to those about religion. He was always a regular old Tory in his political opinions. He supported the belief that war was necessary for the survival of the English race and the crown, and that it would always be so. It was an essential part of British living. The English soldier therefore became to him the greatest of all patriots. Later in life he had no use for pacifism, and deplored the rise of liberalism and the labor party; the one because it represented vague idealism; the other because it opened the way to unleashed power of the lower classes. His political beliefs were based upon the Tory background of his father and forefathers, and on the social distinctions in the air he had breathed at Perry Hall and Fockbury. He was an aristocrat by nature, and firmly maintained to the end of his life that social gradations were necessary in a well-organized government. Once he went so far as to assert that slavery was essential to a well-governed civilization! He was intensely English; he believed in maintaining the extreme prerogatives of the crown to the day of his death. He attended all Tory meetings at Oxford, and took an amused interest in campus scraps at times of elections, but he never ran for office.

By the end of his second year at Oxford, Housman had tried unsuccessfully to win the Hertford Scholarship, and also the Newdigate Prize for an essay-poem on the set subject of *Iona.* On the morning the winners' names were announced, Housman was cynically amused at the choice of text for the chapel sermon: "We have toiled all night and have taken nothing." "How true," he said wryly to Pollard.

There are no other accounts of his attempts to win prizes. At the end of his second year, however, he won a First in Moderates, which high rank more than compensated for his loss of prizes and delighted his family at home. At this time, a rejoicing relative came to his financial aid with a quarterly allowance.

By the time he was twenty, he was a strange mixture of the old and the new, of Toryism and conservatism on one hand, and on the other, liberalistic rejection of creeds and insistence on man's individual self-assertion and independence. His later symbolism in poetry was to emphasize the latter struggles; gales against Nature symbols of the storm and stress of life; stinging nettles as the symbol of temptation, and the pain of preserving decency; hangings and suicides as the symbol of man's injustice to man; "The West" as death—the land of freedom from these miseries beyond the boundaries of dreams. The recurrence of cherry blossoms and the fading of cuckoo flowers were symbols to him of the beauty and the tragedy of life; the stars in the sky and the salt of the sea were symbols of the changeless universe, indifferent to man and his doom, a creature destined to exist in a world pattern he never made and could not alter. Alfred was changing rapidly into a withdrawn and melancholy man consciously beginning to enact a tragic role.

Defeat at Oxford

His last two years at Oxford[12] were marked by less congenial required courses which led to the examinations at the end of the final year and which demanded lengthy readings in philosophy, economics, and history. These assignments were required in order to broaden the knowledge of students in correlated fields of research closely associated with the major classical subjects, leading to the degree in the Final School of *Literae Humaniores*. Through the second year, Housman had been required to read nothing but Latin, Greek, and literature, with emphasis on translation and composition.

The reasons for the indifference of Housman to these added requirements involved psychological changes that were far more complicated and devastating than his dislike of the requirements themselves. It is true that his intellectual arrogance made him despise prescribed readings that he was not doing at his own volition; it is true that he was spending more and more time on his self-assigned studies in Propertius, Ovid, and Horace; and it is true that the disquieting news of his father's serious illness came to him just before Greats were given.[13] None of these obstacles, formidable as they were, would have kept a man of Housman's caliber, with his natural passion for achievement, from reaching the goal he had set for himself in 1877. Those closest to him have given these deterrences as the sole reasons for his failure. But none of these drawbacks could have caused Housman with his retentive mind, studious nature, and natural ambition to turn in a number of almost blank papers at that tragic examination. Yet that is what occurred. He said later: "There was nothing for them to do but fail me."

To understand the bitter secret that tortured Housman's last years at Oxford increasingly, and shadowed all the rest of his life, excuses put up by his protective friends for his failure must be discarded. Physically he was sound and normal, but mentally he was the product of inheritance plus a childhood environment that stressed false creeds and inhibitions. Added to that, the death of his mother shocked him and completed his youthful disillusionment.

How much her death contributed to his morbid slant on sex is conjectural. Since he shrank from the idea of normal sexual relations from about the time he was fourteen years old, when he first began to think about them, it is probable that as he matured he felt his mother's death was untimely, and brought about by childbearing that was far beyond her strength—an opinion which is no doubt true, for she bore seven children in the nine years between 1859 and 1868. He must have pondered long about the stages of her sexual response, from the happy early surrenders, to the quiescent times, then the tolerant, then the sacrificial. His firm belief in the inequality of love between man and woman grew from these introspections, and he usually represented the love of woman for man as being expressed through pity rather than passion. When pity was not strong the woman repulsed her lover:

> Be kind, have pity, my own, my pretty,
> 'Good-bye, young man, good-bye.'
> —*ASL* XI

> Night should ease a lover's sorrow;
> Therefore, since I go tomorrow,
> Pity me before.
> —*ASL* XI

> 'I shall not *vex you* with my face[14]
> Henceforth, my love, for aye:
> So take me in your arms a space
> Before the east is grey.'
> —*ASL* LIII (The True Lover)

His natural compassion was so great that he unconsciously was revolted by the idea of imposing passion and its inevitable sexual penalty of childbirth on a woman, or ever being the perpetrator of that sorrow himself.

> When the lad for longing sighs,
> Mute and dull of cheer and pale,
> If at death's own door he lies,
> Maiden, you can heal his ail.
>
>   . . . .
>
> Buy them, buy them: eve and morn
> Lovers' ills are all to sell
> *Then you can lie down forlorn:*[15]
> But the lover will be well.
>   —*ASL* VI

As he grew older, he regarded the inextricable mix-up of love and lust as one of God's most deplorable mistakes, his brother told the author,[16] if this was normal love, he wanted no part of it. Passion was to torture him, but never passion for a woman. He possibly never attempted relief for his tension within the walls of a prostitute's den. One poem, however, expresses a revulsion resulting from such an experience (*ASL* XXI). In this poem, the ironic contrast between the sweet freshness of morning and the sour taste of dawn in the brothel, with its guttering candles dying out like the spent flame of passion is indicative of Housman's opinion of that kind of attempt at release. The poem was not written before 1890, but possibly it does not refer to autobiographical facts. The rough draft shows one erased stanza. This lyric is associated closely in thought with *LP* XXXV; in fact, part of the latter poem was written on the same page as *ASL* XXI. A study of these poems answers the question that the average person asks as to why Housman could not have thrown off his obsession in an orgy of sensual release so easily found on the midnight streets of London.

Repulsion and disgust had caused him to shrink from his father

after his mother's death, and to choose his feminine friends carefully and cautiously. He narrowed them down to three—Edith and
Minnie Wise, who were more like sisters, placid and uninspiring;
and Sophie Becker, their governess, old and sensible enough not to
allow him to be bothered sexually so far as she was concerned—but
willing to take the place of mother and confidante in his life for
over fifty years.

Before Alfred went to Oxford, the channel of his adolescence
flowed through a dream world of self-interest and introspection
that resulted in a harmless narcism quite apart from the rest of his
life save in the development of reserve, shyness, and a feeling of
greater ease either when alone, or in the company of men. Connected with his inevitable discovery of sexual impulse and relief
there was probably a strong sense of guilt. An interesting biographical poem devoted to narcism is *ASL* XV, the final stanza of
which mingles with another kind of passion nourished on hopelessness as great as that of Narcissus when he fell in love with his
reflection.

The date of this poem is unknown, but was very early, for its
rough draft is in Notebook A, sheet 27. It clearly links together
the early period of narcism with a shift to passion centered on a
person outside himself. Normally such transferences concentrate
on a woman, but with him a much more intricate transposition
developed. In 1880, Housman was ripe for a tragic obsession which
was to alter his life. All his boyhood he had been unconsciously
preparing for this tragedy. The most significant words his sister
wrote of him were these:

The little eccentric habits that he had, and occasional moodiness, we were accustomed to. Many things he did with an inner
intensity that was obvious. . . . When lost in thought he would

contort his features, or become oblivious to what was going on around him. His sense of some pleasures was acute, and seemed exercised best alone.[17]

During his third year at Oxford, when Pollard had moved out of his quad to another one, a disturbing change developed in Housman's affection for his friend Jackson. Housman discovered with despair that he was capable of a strange abnormal love which all the stern upbringing in him abhorred. During those months his early struggle—the initial rending of his mind between his desire and his hatred for the irregularity that caused it—tore him to pieces emotionally. Jackson's words, expressions, gestures absorbed him; they came between him and the textbooks he tried hopelessly to read. He lost weight, consumed by the intensity of his craving.

He felt himself to be a condemned sufferer, but he determined to save himself before the world. He dreaded disgrace and ridicule and covered his feelings as best he could by increasing moodiness and taciturnity. He was of a mind then that neither Jackson, nor his close friend Pollard, nor anybody ever should discover the truth about him. That view was later to change drastically.

Outwardly he kept the leash on himself, strengthened by his natural restraint which helped him to disguise the tragedy that had befallen him. In lesser men, a personality twist of this magnitude frequently proved a complete tragedy, as with Oscar Wilde. Even so, all that saved Housman from suicide in the spring of 1881 was his fierce pride and courage.

He analyzed himself with the same precision and accuracy which later he would apply to *Manilius*. The results were both infuriating and devastating. That this "cursed trouble" must fall on him! His life stretched out in imagination to a miserable future. Not because he felt shame . . . he had not made himself abnormal, and how it happened he did not know. He was no criminal, but a victim on one hand of "the laws of God," on the other hand "the laws of man."[18] He could escape neither, in spite of his rebellion against them.

> And how am I to face the odds
> Of man's bedevilment and God's?
> I, a stranger and afraid
> In a world I never made.
> They will be master, right or wrong,
> Though both are foolish, both are strong.
> And since, my soul, we cannot fly
> To Saturn nor to Mercury,
> Keep we must, if keep we can
> These foreign laws of God and man.
>
> —*LP* XII

The first unquoted six lines of this poem date back to Notebook A, or to earlier lines destroyed, and prove that the idea for the completed one (written in 1900) was put in words many years earlier. The word "must" is of course highly ironic and the entire poem expresses angry rebellion and intolerance against the moral code. The first six unquoted lines express the idea he will not keep the laws; the quoted ones at the end reverse the earlier decision. Contradictions and turmoil seethed within him.

Housman from first to last entertained no hope of changing the laws of God and man; therefore he believed that he had better try to cut his cloth to fit the pattern insofar as he could. Compare this poem with the one he wrote about the Oscar Wilde trial: "Oh who is this young sinner with the handcuffs on his wrists?" (*AP* XVIII). "The nameless and abominable color of his hair"—given as the reason for society placing the handcuffs on the sinner —is homosexuality. Its victim is egregious in the self-righteous crowd with its accepted patterns of conventional inflexibility. This mental twist is represented as born and bred in "the young sinner's" personality as much as the color of his hair. Bitter cynicism against the injustice of society toward such abnormalities is expressed in these lines which suggest an attempt at concealment:

> Oh a deal of pains he's taken and a pretty price he's paid
> To hide his poll or dye it of a mentionable shade. . . .

The poem was published after A. E. H's death, but was written in rough draft long before the turn of the century. There are three rough drafts extant, with many erasures and changes, and Notebook E shows a fair copy, which fact suggests that Housman may have contemplated publishing it in *Last Poems* and decided against it.

The growing intensity of his interest in Jackson was concealed in part by his great ability for restraint, but also because of his fear of discovery which would make him ridiculous before the world, and most of all, before Jackson. Housman was stunned that his friendship had insidiously turned into a torture that he dared not name even to himself. He brooded over it in long, solitary walks in the daytime and at night it kept him awake. "Happy are those who love when they are loved in return," said Bion in his eighth Idyll. Then he gave three examples of happy loves: Theseus and Pirithous,[19] Orestes and Pylades, Achilles and Patroclus.[20] Housman thought of the countless men who had been tempted, and who had suffered:

> Others, I am not the first,
> Have willed more mischief than they durst;
> If in the breathless night I too
> Shiver now, 'tis nothing new.
>
> More than I, if truth were told
> Have stood and sweated hot and cold,
> And through their reins in ice and fire
> Fear contended with desire.

• • • •

[93]

But from my grave across my brow
Plays no wind of healing now;
And fire and ice within me fight
Beneath the suffocating night.
—*ASL* XXX

There is no way of knowing when the first lines of this poem were written, for the notebook discloses only one greatly erased and amended rough draft, Notebook A, sheet 23. Written under pressure, its emotion is strong to the point of havoc. The undercurrent of shock and amazement at his predicament has stunned him; he wonders at his own manifestations of passion, and recounts them as a kind of horrid phenomenon. In line three, "breathless" was emended from "sunless," "smothering," and "stifling."

The word "reins" (line 7) did not refer to restraints, but was used in the old Biblical sense, relating to the affections, and especially to the sexual ones. Therefore, in a poem about youthful temptation, it is particularly applicable.[21] The most provocative and revealing emendation was the one in line 15, which came from the obvious sexual meaning. "And fire and ice within me fight" was in the first draft stark and bare: "And fire and ice stand up to fight," a line in which there are no concealments.

Housman at no time wrote more tragic lines. The mood of the poem is frustration, but not self-pity. It is not weakness to make an agonized rejection of natural impulses, and that is what this pagan Victorian was attempting. The poem is not only enlightening but as it finally appeared is one of Housman's best lyrics, and one of the most frankly revealing in the entire world of poetry. Probably it was one of the poems that caused George Meredith, then imperturbable and cool-blooded in old age, to call *ASL* "an orgy of naturalism."[22] Yet Meredith himself had suffered from passions no less consuming.

During the long nights of temptation that Housman experienced then, he began to doubt affection, and actually never trusted it afterwards, fearing it might play him the cruel trick again that it had dealt him in 1880. To the end of his life he held at arms' length the men to whom he was especially attracted. But the Jackson episode was far from over.

There is no doubt that during his last years at Oxford in the apartment in St. Giles', Housman succeeded in concealing his passion for Jackson from both Pollard and him. He probably appeared moody and inexplicable, but outwardly the relationship remained much as it had been. That Housman was afraid of himself and fighting his bewitchment becomes evident in the fact that it was Pollard not Jackson whom he invited home for summer holiday. Another reason for his effort to conquer himself was his distaste for violating "the fitness of things." He was naturally refined and fastidious to the point of niceness, and he hated to admit to a role which his higher senses told him was deplorable.

Pollard certainly at that time would have been horrified to know of his friend's obsession, and Jackson probably would have been irked, but not at all scandalized. Such was the difference in the two men.

The last months at Oxford were a nightmare to Housman. The bald fact remains that Pollard and Jackson pursued their scholastic goals unimpeded by their friend in any way, so that with no difficulty they both graduated with first class honors. Canon J. T. Nance in a letter to Grant Richards (1937) said: "I think the only matter of interest to you will be my interview with T. H. Grose of Queen's after Housman had failed to secure a degree. He showed me his marks, one paper being marked F . . . his answers . . . were practically no answers at all."[23] Housman was ploughed in Greats, packed his bags in proud misery, and returned in silence to Perry Hall.

Three

The Mask Drawn Down

Those who want a mask have to wear it.
Oscar Wilde, *De Profundis.*

5

Proud and Angry Dust

WHEN ALFRED returned to Perry Hall, silent, morose, and without his graduation certificate, he met a family completely stunned by his failure. Every one of them had expected him to graduate with first class honors, but their congratulations froze on their lips in the icy silence of his proud withdrawal and intolerance of questioning. His explanation was one terse sentence:

"There was nothing else for them to do."

He was a wretched stranger in the family circle, and his sufferings grew more intense as he began to realize that financial affairs at Perry Hall were much worse than he had expected. The horror of what he had done to his family as well as to himself stung him bitterly, as he saw his father's helpless condition, Lucy's hurt disappointment, and his brothers' curious glances cast askance at him across the wall he had set up between them.

His remarkable sister Clemence, always blessed with poise and efficiency, was too busy trying to keep up the little law business that still trickled into her father's hands, combined with the cooking and housework she plunged into when not in the office, to pay very much attention to Alfred. His more sympathetic sister Kate was the only member of the family who seemed unembarrassed in his company; she was still able to talk freely to him. She took it for granted that his failure had been caused by worry over his father's illness; hence she tried to reassure him on those grounds. He had always been her favorite brother, and now she wisely comforted him without intruding upon him. Laurence was busy helping with the garden, clipping hedges, reading prodigiously, and fuming for a chance to enter an art school in London. The Mater planned and regulated everything with an eye to economy, often at her wit's end to keep the household running. She still was devoted to Alfred but hurt that he did not confide in her. She actually had no time to devote to him nor did she try to conceal her desperate financial straits. In the midst of this undisguised struggle against poverty Alfred felt like a miserable intruder. His comprehension of the true state of affairs shocked him into bitter remorse for what he had done to those who had loved him and sacrificed for him. The relative who had furnished Alfred with his money for incidental expenses during his last two years at Oxford withdrew the sum to show his disappointment and displeasure.

Alfred appreciated the well-bred silence of his family about his deplorable failure, for after their first shocked outburst, they said no more. He made the firm resolution to do what he could to atone for their sacrifices made as he knew only too well, in order to afford him the chance that he had blamably thrown away. His first move was to go to Bromsgrove School where he had a talk with Herbert Millington, fortunately for him, still headmaster; and Millington gave him the opportunity to teach Latin to the sixth form that winter and spring.

He kept this post for approximately eighteen months altogether, and won a recommendation from Millington for being a "faithful, sympathetic, and conscientious" teacher. He brought papers home to correct, and during his spare hours he studied, took solitary walks, and pondered on what his next move should be. Laurence Housman aptly calls this time "The Purgatory Period."[1] However, in his brother's long journey of atonement it was to lead neither to paradise, nor completely to hell.

Housman's inner struggle was smoldering; the flame was still there. Letters passed constantly between Jackson and him. Jackson loved Housman, had been concerned and grieved at his friend's failure, and he sensed lonely discouragement in Alfred's letters. He finally suggested in a letter that "House" might prepare for the Civil Service examination, as he had done, and get a job in the Patent Office Division in London with him. Jackson was using his money from his Patent Office post to get his doctor's degree, and taking studies at the University of London towards that end. The post of Jackson was not unpleasant; it was somewhat suited to his scientific interests, a position of Examiner of Electrical Specifications; and this was so easy for him that he had enough time left to prepare the readings and experiments for his doctorate. Housman knew his obsession was strong as ever, that it was a consuming flame, and that tragedy would strike should he accept Jackson's offer.

But the longing to be with Jackson again, the lure of his personality and his presence was too strong for him. He suddenly announced to his family that he was preparing to study for Civil Service and a position in London. This news they accepted, too, in silence, and for months they watched him concentrate at night on the boring material he must master for the Civil Service examination. Again his powers of concentration came to his aid; in the midst of the activities centered upon the large dining room at Perry Hall—now the only room in the house heated at night in the winter—with his brothers and sisters talking around him, he apparently lost himself in study, at what expense to his taut nerves one can imagine. Again his memory and will came to his rescue, and he passed the Civil Service examination successfully.

Meanwhile, a legacy of 200 pounds was left to each of the children by Uncle Tom, and Alfred immediately turned over his share to Lucy. He also contributed nearly all his stipend at Bromsgrove School to the family budget, and so relieved considerably the difficulties of paying mortgage interest and taxes.

In the early fall of 1882 he left Perry Hall for London, and thereafter Bromsgrove was never his residence again. He settled himself in his dull job at the Patent Office, where he had a pittance to live on, 100 pounds a year, a sum so small that Jackson and his younger brother, Adalbert, invited him to move into their little apartment in Bayswater so that he could meet expenses. He was to pay his share of the rent.

It was a generous and well-intentioned offer. Jackson like Pollard had been stunned at his friend's Oxford failure, and he was eager to be of help to him. Housman knew he should not accept the proposal, but he was not strong enough to refuse. He was bitterly lonely, very poor, and too shy to make new friends easily. But the temptation he could not resist was the fascination of being with Jackson again.

He moved into the Bayswater apartment occupied by the Jackson brothers at 82 Talbot Road in November, 1882. Adalbert turned over his small room to him and moved in with his brother. The two welcomed "House" whole-heartedly. Their frank acceptance of him and genuine interest in his welfare made Housman warmly grateful. They gave him renewed self-confidence, for they trusted his integrity and admired his great mental powers. Housman's position in the group was not a dubious one. The Jacksons accepted him without question, and treated him like another brother. Housman liked Adalbert Jackson at once and got along with him easily, for he was warmly sympathetic, though very different from his brother. Adalbert, who was an undergraduate student at University College, was planning to be a classical master; scholastically he shared Housman's interest; and probably the first time Housman ever entered University College was an occasion when he attended a lecture there on the classics with Adalbert, who spent most of his day there and often read in the library there until late at night.

A few months after the Bayswater move, Clemence and Laurence Housman completed plans to start their art studies in London, aided by their legacies from Uncle Tom. Alfred met them at Paddington Station, and directed them to rooms he had found for them in Kensington, a section of south London some distance from his own lodgings. He was kind and considerate, yet seemed preoccupied, and with a shade of embarrassment he asked them not to call at the Bayswater apartment. Hurt and surprised, they obeyed his injunction, but they nevertheless asked him to visit them. He occasionally did so, but Laurence remembered an unaccountable strain between them. Alfred appeared like a stranger with a barrier set between him and them. Clemence, who possessed a forthright and practical nature, was definitely embarrassed. The brother of Perry Hall was only a fond memory. No connection joined the beloved "Wa-Wa" in her alert mind with this silent, tense substitute. She could only surmise his troubles, for he disclosed nothing whatever. A wall arose between them and their brother that was never broken down, and never crossed until old age partly destroyed it.

Alfred treated his brother and sister no differently from the rest of his family. He never invited any of them to visit the Bayswater apartment, though Lucy hinted for invitations. It is quite certain that from 1882 to 1886 he was almost completely cut off from his relatives. He did not go home and he wrote few letters. Such as he did write were short and impersonal.

These years are obscure because Housman kept them veiled in secrecy, but they emerge today as the most crucial ones. They involved the only ecstasy of his life and the bitterest adjustments to an existence he deplored; they gave him the basis for belief that "the world has still much good, but much less good than ill" (*ASL* LXII). He had passed from the thesis of mere living into the dramatic antithesis of struggle.

Financially Housman was groping in the dark; he was plunged into the uncongenial life of an obscure clerk with an unpromising future. He was secretary to the Comptroller of the Patent Office for a period, but was too independent to suit the job and was transferred to another department which supervised the trademarks on various patents—drudgery of the most boring kind—consisting largely of looking over new applications and determining whether the symbol chosen for a trademark had ever been used by anyone else. A high school graduate could have done the work, and the humiliation Housman incurred must have been almost overwhelming to a man of his mental powers. To all outward appearances, he was lost in the maelstrom of London, submerged and commonplace, with small chance of ever developing the talents that his stars had given him. After ten years in the Patent Office, his salary was only 213 pounds a year.

A compensating fact was that the hours at the Patent Office were mercifully short. Housman did the filing of patents and tabulating of illustrative symbols used to advertise patents as neatly and methodically as his patience permitted, but according to Alan Ker, Housman was said to have been the worst clerk they ever had.[2] The truth is that Housman could hardly wait to rush from his filing cabinets to the companionship of Jackson. He worked long hours, when Jackson was busy, on the critical notes dealing with Propertius and Horace that he had started at Oxford. His unprescribed labor at Oxford on these Latin writers stood him in good stead now, and he rigidly adhered to the writing of essays based on his findings. He let nothing interfere with his classical research, not even Jackson. He became a familiar figure at the British Museum.

The power of his will to retrieve himself was strong enough to keep him at a task that seemed almost hopeless. How could a humiliated Oxford failure expect to regain a place in the world of scholarship by his own efforts alone? Who would give him an ear, a nobody, an inefficient filing clerk? Destiny mocked him; obscurity enveloped him, he told himself a dozen times a day. Yet his bitterness acted as a counter-irritant; he was all the more determined to succeed. He was accomplishing a grim change in the way of his preparation for poetry—he was through with romance, fully able to call a spade "a bloody shovel."[3] He considered the ability for endurance to be the best quality of man, and decided to "quit himself like stone" (*ASL* LI).

This poem dates to the time when Housman made a habit of haunting the British Museum, and occasionally looking at the Greek statues lodged there, as the first lines of the poem show:

> Loitering with a vacant eye
> Along the Grecian gallery
> And brooding on my heavy ill,
> I met a statue standing still. . . .
>
> Years, ere you stood up from rest,
> On my neck the collar pressed;
> Years, when you lay down your ill
> I shall stand and bear it still.
> Courage, lad, 'tis not for long:
> Stand, quit you like stone, be strong.

[105]

But it was not a pretty prospect, and he needed all the "blood, boots, and bones" of the ancestral Drakes to stiffen his spine for the ordeal. Meanwhile, he clad himself in the armor of his destiny (*LP* II), accepted what tools it gave him—will power, his superior intelligence, an unshaken interest in the classics, and an ability to accept trouble if it came (*MP* VI).

He could not deceive himself about his private physical miseries; he had at once discovered that the proximity of Jackson complicated his task immeasurably and produced an insufferable unrest and trouble. He tried to keep away from him. His effort was made easier by the fact that Jackson was tremendously busy at his double job of clerk and student. The two men left early in the morning, and were not often together during the day. Jackson went to classes in the late afternoon when Housman went to the British Museum. They usually met at a restaurant to dine at night and walked home together. When Jackson was not attending night classes, they habitually were together at the apartment, Jackson always relaxed and at ease, Housman inwardly tense and disturbed, pitifully eager to serve Jackson in small ways.[4]

> The brisk fond lackey to fetch and carry,
> The true, sick-hearted slave,
> Expect him not in the just city
> And free land of the brave.
> —*MP* XXIII

The two men were of completely opposite temperaments. There was nothing imaginative or abnormal in the affections of Jackson, which were based on reason and common sense, although we know now that he had "intimate relations" with Housman during this period. He was so matter-of-fact and self-centered that his own affairs, especially his satisfactory progress in his conquest of the young woman he had picked out for his wife, completely occupied him; Housman no doubt offered a sexual satisfaction to him which he could easily throw off for a normal one at marriage. But Jackson was not bisexual, he merely drifted casually into the Housman affair.

Housman, on the other hand, was the most imaginative and sensitive of men; he was melancholy by temperament, an invert, a throwback, mentally, to the primitive parthogenetic. Heredity as well as training had made him what he was; a man capable of love of an exclusive and subjective nature which fed itself by being unshared, and nourished its roots on the obstacles that lay in the path of its fulfillment. Although all love partakes of these qualities to a certain extent, this particular type of emotion, of which only a very passionate yet restrained person would be capable, increases in proportion to the hopelessness of ultimate happiness.

The breath of scandal is worse than scandal itself; innuendoes are far worse than truth; and the mass of conjecture that has made Housman an enigma has done him a disservice far greater than an honest facing of the facts could do. The facts are extraordinary. Housman was no Wilde nor yet a Gide; if Wilde had possessed half the stamina and self-respect of Housman he could have died one of the literary elite of London instead of a miserable exile in Paris. Though by desire a pagan, Housman was a stiff Victorian by birth, and he was by ingrained self-discipline destined to reach that brilliant inner circle, and to know on equal basis many of the most significant minds of the twentieth century. He had to climb his ladder of achievement round by round, however, and in 1883-85 he was on the lowest rung.

Whether Housman ever participated in other sex experiments is open to conjecture; there was possibly one in Venice, which will be discussed later.[5] There may have been some other explorations of this nature, and it would be strange if there had not; but of these, if they existed, nothing is known. The matter is one which does not concern us at all. If experiments occurred, it is not necessary to cover them with whitewash; all that concerns us is to understand the man's natural bent which made him and his poetry what they were.

There are almost as many kinds of inversion as there are inverts, every one is a law unto itself. They have been produced under conditions of heredity and environment of infinite variety. The typically passive type is that expressed usually between women of high intelligence, who are often quite content to live together and be all in all to each other without any physical longing or morbid manifestations.

The gradations are legion from the passion of the mind alone, that psychologically feeds love on impossibility of realization, to the degraded type of perversion that too often the average person interprets as the only kind of inversion, since he knows nothing about any other. It is now an accepted fact that eroticism between members of the same sex is a common condition, and some psychiatrists, as well as physicians, seem to think that it is Nature's way of diminishing the population. There is positive proof that the sublimated type, in which the energy of procreation is directed finally from its primitive aim to one that is culturally and ethically higher, has existed in the lives of a great many men of genius and has been the incentive for creation among all the arts: painting, music, poetry, drama, novel, and even dissertation. Such men are not always unhappy; others, like Housman, achieve a kind of serenity of detachment after years of struggle. Usually they attain periods of comparative emotional calm after the release of sexual tension through the struggle of the subconscious to successful expression by some form of creative art: Tschaikovsky by means of his music, Gide and Proust by way of their novels and essays. With

Housman such release came in part through his creation of *A Shropshire Lad*.

During 1883-85 Housman's depression from his sense of failure to subdue his passion for Jackson was at the peak of its morbid control, and often overcame his resolutions. He wrote in poetry of vows he had not been able to keep that would cause his day to end in despair:

> . . . .
> Today I shall be strong,
> No more shall yield to wrong,
>   Shall squander life no more;
>
> . . . .
> Days lost, I know not how,
> I shall retrieve them now;
> Now I shall keep the vow
>   I never kept before.
>
> Ensanguining the skies
> How heavily it dies
>   Into the west away;
> Past touch and sight and sound
> How hopeless underground
>   Falls the remorseful day.
>   —*MP* XVI

The rough draft discloses the following phrases in the margin but unused: "aims missed"; "sinks like a stone"; . . . "to pave the very floor of hell." Such poems, published posthumously, were among the ones that aroused the storm of curiosity about the secrecies in Housman's life, and often resulted in cruel and unjust premises, for even in this period, his restraints, if not always successful, were certainly attempted.

In another poem published posthumously he gives the year when he was twenty-four, 1883, as the period of his complete spiritual blackout:

> The world goes none the lamer
> For ought that I can see,
> Because this *cursed trouble*[6]
> Has struck my days and me.
>
> . . . .
>
> Oh worse remains for others,
> And worse to fear had I
> Than here at four-and-twenty
> To lay me down and die.
> —*MP* XXI

That he did not "lie down and die" is significant testimonial of his character. He had no thought, then or later, of solving his problem by marriage, or by submitting a woman to his moods and broodings, or by leaning upon her virtues, as did Gide in the sad marriage to his long-suffering Emmanuele.

That Sophie Becker was a kind of platonic Emmanuele at a distance was a great comfort to Housman. During this period he wrote to her in Germany very often, and her sensible letters were a comfort to him. It is probable that she destroyed his letters as he did hers; after Alfred's death, Laurence Housman found only one letter from Miss Becker among Housman's possessions, a letter which she had written when the poet was past seventy and she nearly ninety. It began "My dear boy," and was signed "Your affectionate old friend." Her watchful fondness was needed for many years; then it was not needed, but the friendship continued to the end of her life when Housman was seventy-five.

Housman knew nothing of what dark labyrinths his maze of passion would carry him into—yet he had the stab of warning from his repugnance for his abnormality. Was he to go through life a slave, torn between a pathetic desire to please Jackson, and a desire to rid himself of it all by death? His tragedy reflects itself in

MP XXIII, which was planned and partly written in 1886; finished before 1922, and published after his death by Laurence Housman.

In the midst of this Bayswater period, torn by alternate moments of rapture and despair, he veiled his misery when he wrote to his stepmother by moods of biting but witty cynicism and mockery. These letters[7] always began "My dear Mamma" and were signed, "Your loving son, A. E. Housman."

> 82 Talbot Road
> Bayswater, W.
> '29 March '85.

. . . I was delighted to get your long letter on the 26th:[8] it was quite the best epistle I have ever seen, with the possible exception of the second of the apostle Paul to the Corinthians. The violets also were very sweet: I don't know whether St. Paul used to enclose violets. Also please thank my father for his letter. Clemence and Laurence sent me a post card with a very lovely drawing on the back, representing Cherubim and Seraphim continually crying, and an inscription in Spanish or Portugese, I think.

I saw the boat race yesterday, from the Thames boat house at Putney this time, so that I saw the start. . . Palm branches seemed to be the commonest decoration among the lower orders. The blue which they wore was a very artful shade, which could be made out to be either Oxford or Cambridge with equal plausibility, whichever might happened to win. . .

The juvenile son of a friend of mine at the Office[9] has the loftiest ambition I ever heard tell of. When he goes to heaven, which he regards as a dead certainty, he wants to be God, and is keenly mortified to learn that it is not probable he will. However his aspirations are now turning into another channel; it has come to his knowledge, through the housemaid, that the devil has horns and a tail; and in comparison with these decorations the glories of heaven have lost their attractiveness.

An elaborate new Index of Trade Marks is being compiled at the Office. It goes on very remarkable principles which I do not quite understand. Under the head of 'Biblical Subjects' is included a picture of an old monk drinking out of a tankard; and the Virgin Mary and St. John the Baptist are put among 'Mythical Figures'.....

10 June '85

You would never guess what I was doing on Tuesday week: serving on a Coroner's Jury. This comes of having one's name on the register of voters. Civil Servants I believe are exempt from serving on ordinary Juries, but not on Coroners'. Of course for once in a way it is rather amusing, and it is not likely to happen oftener than about once in four years. We sat on five bodies: one laundryman who tied a hundred-weight to his neck and tipped over into the water-butt; one butcher's man who cut his throat with a rusty knife and died a week after of erysipelas (moral: use a clean knife on these occasions); one old lady who dropped down in a fit; one baby who died of convulsions; and one young woman who died of heart disease after eating spring onions for supper. I really do not know what is the good of a Jury or of witnesses either; the Coroner does it all: his mind seemingly is lighted by wisdom from on high, so he tells the Jury what their verdict is and the witnesses what their evidence is: if they make mistakes he corrects them. The butcher's man had a brother-in-law: he looked radiantly happy: a member of his family had distinguished himself, and he was revelling in the reflected glory.

I think if there were an Inquest held on this Government of ours the verdict would have to be deliberate suicide: there does not seem to have been the least reason why they should have been beaten unless they wanted it. I should say whether they go out or not the whole affair will do a lot of damage to the Conservatives, because if they take office before the election they will have a fearful muddle to deal with, and if they do not, everyone will call them unpatriotic. . .

There was a mild sort of scare at the Office the other day: a loud bang which collected quite a crowd. Civil Servants in these days of course live in hourly expectation of being blown up by dynamite for political reasons, and the Patent Office has the further danger of the ingenious and vindictive inventor of explosives, who might try to lay the place in ruins if his patent did not go smoothly. The room I sit in is considered the likeliest place, because it has a charming deep area outside, which looks as if it was made to drop dynamite into; so when this explosion was heard, several people came trooping into the room in hopes of finding corpses weltering in their gore. However they had to go empty away: I believe the noise was really the firing of a charge of powder in a neighbouring chimney to bring the soot down. . . .

To avoid a haunting desire for suicide, Housman kept himself at his task in the British Museum. With precision and exactitude he read and compared various manuscripts of Propertius and Horace, and made exhaustive studies of what previous critics had said about those Latinists; then he launched forth in his own original brilliant style, and separated, dissected, criticized, and emended with a firm assurance that was convincing and illuminating. He began studies of Aristotle, Aeschylus, Euripides, Isocrates, Sophocles, and Ovid, in addition to the research he was doing already in Horace and Propertius.

The fact that he was equalizing his study between the Greek and Latin poets and dramatists proves that he was preparing himself to be a professor of either Greek or Latin when the opportunity opened. He never expressed any especial fondness for the Latin over the Greek, but said later that he had accepted the chair of Latin, knowing full well that he was unequal to becoming an authority in both. He could have successfully taken the field toward either goal, but since the Latin offered itself, he then concentrated on it for the remainder of his life.

It is significant to notice that from 1883 to 1887, Housman published little or nothing. This fallow period was the black time when he was paying the penalty for his torturing companionship with Jackson, toward the end of which their final severance occurred.

The cause for the parting was unexpected and quite accidental. It happened that Housman and the Jackson brothers were invited to a large afternoon art exhibit and reception sponsored by people who had also invited Laurence and Clemence Housman. Alfred Housman declined such invitations habitually; the Jacksons accepted, and in the course of their intermingling with guests they were introduced to Alfred's brother and sister. Moses Jackson was surprised and puzzled.

"Is it possible you are related to my friend, A. E. Housman?" he asked with some hesitation.

"Rather!" Clemence said promptly. "We are his brother and sister."

Jackson's amazed expression deepened.

"But—does Alfred know you are here? How long have you been in London? Where are you staying?" he asked.

"About two years. Yes, Alfred knows all about us, and has visited us from time to time," replied Clemence, puffing away at her cigarette with a good deal of amusement.

Clemence and Laurence then told Jackson of their studies in engraving and illustrating, of where they were lodging, and how much their interest was growing in their art classes.[10] The meeting passed off pleasantly enough, but for Jackson it was an unpleasant revelation. From this inadvertent discovery it became obvious to Jackson that Housman's attitude toward their relationship was not reciprocally casual, and that, indeed, Alfred was ashamed of it. What other reason could he have for not inviting his brother and sister to the Bayswater apartment? Jackson was not the sort of man who could allow a situation like this to go unresolved, and it is safe to assume that he and Housman "had it out" that very evening. What was said can only be guessed at, but very soon after the ill-fated art exhibit, Housman found other quarters, and the two men saw very little of each other during the following years. The posthumously published *MP* XXXI, which undoubtedly refers to

their farewell, indicates that Jackson demanded relief from the
burden of a love misplaced, and Housman agreed to break off the
connection with Jackson and forget him.

> Because I liked you better
>   Than suits a man to say,
> It irked you, and I promised
>   To throw the thought away.
>
> To put the world between us
>   We parted, stiff and dry;
> "Good-bye," said you, "forget me."
>   "I will, no fear," said I.
>
> If here, where clover whitens
>   The dead man's knoll, you pass,
> And no tall flower to meet you
>   Starts in the trefoiled grass,
>
> Halt by the headstone naming
>   The heart no longer stirred,
> And say the lad that loved you
>   Was one that kept his word.
>   —*MP* XXXI

The lyric takes on a ballad note in the last two stanzas. "If this
poem had been written in the ballad form," commented Laurence
Housman, "the 'tall flower' (l. 11), would actually have sprung up
from the grave to show that even in death his love was faithful."[11]

The rough draft of these lines marks them as autobiographical,
because the handwriting shows great inner tumult, and because the
erasures and side jottings are revealing. There is no doubt, however, that this is one of the poems whose first draft was destroyed
when the extant rough draft was finished. There is no way of

knowing when the destroyed copy was written, but there is not a shadow of doubt that its inception was some time before 1890;[12] the same is true about several more of the most personal poems in the posthumous publication.

The single rough draft of *MP* XXXI gives the first stanza thus:

> The heart by nothing stirred . . . .
> Because I liked you better
> suits a man to say,
> Than ~~friends in liking may,~~
> It irked you,
> ~~I tricked you,~~ and I promised
> To throw the thought away.

The lines struck out are much more revealing than the final ones. The second line tells of a love beyond the boundaries of propriety; the third line confesses that Housman was willing to deceive Jackson about his constancy in order to save the friendship. The fact that Alfred gave his brother Laurence free permission to publish any of his poems posthumously, provided that they did not fall below a certain standard, suggests that he did not care what posterity discovered about him after he was gone. Laurence Housman wisely gave to the world the collection called *More Poems* as a result of the freedom of choice his brother invested in him, and for his generosity the literary world has cause to be grateful.

A letter sent me by Laurence Housman on October 7, 1956, disclosed knowledge of an even more revealing unpublished manuscript of his brother's. It reads in part as follows:

About the manuscript at the British Museum—A. E. H. had told a Frenchman that he had once intended to write one accounting for himself; but had decided *not* to.[13] But what I have now lodged at the British Museum to be made public at the centenary of his birth in 1959 is a remarkable diary which reveals the most intimate relations with his friend Moses Jackson. . . . It will shock some people, and make them very angry; but I believe that A. E. H. wished it to be known after his death that he was what he was—a man who gave more devoted love than he ever received: and as a result was a *lonely* man to the end of his days.

I had no knowledge of this diary when I visited Laurence Housman in 1951. I now believe he was on the verge of showing it to me several times. After we had discussed Alfred's tragedy, he would sometimes flush and get up and pace the floor, very excited. He would stop at the great filing cabinet, and mutter, looking at the floor. Tears would come to his eyes. He often left me alone in this study to work for hours, but not once did I trespass on his privacy— I never opened a drawer. He had told me I could browse around among the books at will.

After Housman moved from the Bayswater apartment, he had no open break with Jackson; in fact, the removal saved a friendship which was grounded on loyal sympathies. He and the Jacksons continued to dine at the same restaurant together, and Adalbert's delightful presence lessened the tension between the other two men. Jackson was glad that "House" had left the lodgings, his fear of scandal was allayed; Housman had the stiff pride that concealed his inner distress sufficiently for Adalbert to suspect nothing unusual in his departure.

Byron Cottage

Not very long after the removal from Talbot Road, in the autumn of 1886 Housman leased rooms on the ground floor of Byron Cottage,[14] 17 North Road, Highgate Woods, later known as Highgate after the area had been shorn of trees and patterned after the plan of the Mayor and Commonalty and Citizens of the City of London.

[117]

The apartment was exceedingly pleasant, and when Housman first lived there, it was in open country innocent of axe or scythe; a new section with trees, birds, irregular paths for long walks, and suitably distant from his previous environment.

Byron Cottage was a comfortable three-story residence, with the width of a good-sized hall and living room, and the length of three such rooms, like many other houses in the area. It had no distinguishing characteristics other than an air of extreme respectability. Housman went up three impeccable steps to a correspondingly immaculate oaken door with a polished brass handle and knocker. He turned the key, entered an equally blameless front hall, turned directly left, unlocked his own door, and there he was, in a very comfortable sitting· room. A blue-tiled fireplace faced the door; flanked right and left were built-in bookcases and comfortable chairs. A table for books was near a lounging chair, and a desk stood between the long windows which faced the street. Opposite this desk was another table, two small chairs, and the door that led to the bed chamber.

Byron Cottage marks the beginning of Housman's rebirth. Here was the first place he could call his own that he had ever possessed; it was peaceful and in no way distracting. In fact it was the most congenial lodging he ever had up to the time he was seventy-five years old.

By the autumn of 1886, Housman was making a somewhat better wage at the Patent Office, and with strict economy he was able to pay for the peace and comfort that were to aid materially in his restoration. His landlady, Mrs. Trim, was his bed-maker, and she also at times served his afternoon tea. When the Mater descended on him for her first visit of inspection—a visit which Alfred had planned and prepared for—she was delighted with the new location, and demanded at once to see Mrs. Trim. Alfred refused point

blank; in part because he would not have the good soul submitted
to the indignity of inspection, but also because to invite her to his
rooms to meet his relatives would have broken down the class barrier socially which he was always meticulous in observing. Already
he insisted upon privacy, and Mrs. Trim soon learned not to inter-
rupt him unless necessary.

Byron Cottage remained his home from 1886 to 1905. Here he
grimly organized a new program of living; he set himself with
distracted concentration (if such is possible) to his research in the
British Museum; he began to produce papers again, and to make
plans for his life as a college don more definite. His printed output
in learned periodicals after his removal to Byron Cottage is indicative of his returning adjustment to life and his acceptance of things
as they must be for him.

During 1887 and 1888 he published four papers on Aeschylus,
two of which were in the *Classical Review* on the *Persae* and the
Agamemnon; and two appeared in the *Journal of Philology*, one
on corruptions of the *Persae*, the other on the *Agamemnon*.

In 1887 he also published a commentary on Sophocles: *Electra*,
564, in the *Classical Review*. In 1888 he presented in the *Journal of
Philology* the first of a series of papers on Propertius, followed in
the 1890's by five more papers on the manuscripts of this poet. In
1888 he had a paper of critical notes on Latin poets in the *Classical
Review*, followed by two other such papers the next year. Also in
1888 he did a treatise for the *Journal of Philology* on *Horatiana*,
followed by two more in 1890; in 1888 the *Classical Review* published a paper of his on *Paneg. 40 of Isocrates*. The first of a long
series of critical works on Ovid came out in the *Cambridge Philological Society, Proceedings*, in 1889. The first paper was a brilliant
group of emendations in Ovid's *Metamorphoses*. In 1889, a study
of *Persius* iii, 43, was in the *Classical Review*. Studies in *Euripides*

began in the *Classical Review* in 1890, and were continued at intervals.

Not all of Housman's early papers are included in this list,[15] but a sufficient number are given to prove that a change had come over his life like an invigorating wind, infiltrating new mental energy. He was encouraged by the dramatic success of his papers that showed a rarefied scholarship awe-inspiring to his German contemporaries. For example, the famous German scholar Wecklein, of Munich, was impressed by Housman's work to the extent that he read his commentaries with delight and amazement, and wrote Housman a glowing testimonial when he tried for the University of London professorship. Famous men of letters spoke of "differing from him with reluctance!"

Housman's failure at Oxford has been described as a revolt against a prescribed program of readings. Such an explanation is ridiculous and blamably misleading. Housman never revolted against necessary mental discipline, witness his study to pass the wretched Civil Service examination, and later, to do the prescribed Oxford readings for his pass degree, and at Highgate to dedicate himself to studies which were by their fruits to alter his entire life.

The peace of Byron Cottage was making him over. In addition to his work at the Patent Office, plus his arduous studies at the British Museum, which have been shown to have been profound and original enough to shake the dry-as-dust world of scholarship, he found time in 1890-91 to sandwich in the acquisition of his Oxford pass degree. This necessary connection with the university having been established, he soon afterwards, aided by his writings in the *Journal of Philology* and the *Classical Review*, gained his M. A. from Oxford, and thus he was ready for the opening that came in 1892.

A. W. Pollard, who knew Housman and Jackson far better than

anyone else during the final year at Oxford, when they all had rooms together, vaguely laid Housman's failure to his willingness to waste time with Jackson, to follow him around in his activities, and to be with him rather than attending to his own affairs. A. S. F. Gow, who of course never knew Housman at this period of his life, discloses that Jackson had a pronounced and outspoken contempt for the classics, quite natural for an electrical engineer to possess, and Jackson's good-natured scorn for the work Housman was laboring over Gow suggested as a reason for his failure.[16] But Housman did not fail in the classics! He failed or made poor showings in ancient history, political economy, logic, and philosophy, subjects which Jackson had no contempt for, although he may not have known much about them. These subjects, although distasteful, could have been mastered with ease by Housman provided he could have concentrated on them, as is proved by the speed with which he completed them for his pass degree later, in addition to his Patent Office grind, his research and his brilliant publications (1890-1892).

Housman should not be measured by his temptations, nor by his failures, but rather by his resistances; he appears strong when viewed in the light of his resistances. Fabrications about his failures are vague and muddled; the truth is clear. Biographical truth is something of granite-like solidarity which is called upon to grasp and disclose personality—a thing of rainbow-like intangibility. To grasp personality in the grip of truth is bound to be a difficult task, but unless truth is achieved, the effort is useless. The truth about a man is the man himself. There is a virtue in truth; it has mystic power, for like radium, it gives off grains of energy, atoms of light. Housman's life, made up of many days, strung together in the chain of months and years, was colored from irregular facets cut by slow time and hard experience; the effect of the whole might blind and deceive one if the lodestar of truth did not illumine those facets.

When Housman struggled out from the Jackson obsession and began to plan his life without his friend, he renewed his research interests and scholarly pursuits with intensity, as his classical publications and the acquirement of his Oxford degree prove. He also began to resume normal relationship with his family again, and although he was a totally different man—and a very unhappy one from this time to the end of his life—he made his personal sorrow secondary to his passion for achievement.

In 1887, Moses Jackson received his Doctorate in Science from the University of London, and also became a Fellow of the University of London. That same year, he went as far away from England as he could. He became president of Sind College, Karachi, India. He and his brother visited Housman before he departed. It was the first time they had entered Byron Cottage. They shook hands with good will and God speeds, the usual formal words. Externally, the episode was over but it was to rankle in Housman's heart for years, and to darken his outlook forever after. The character of the man strengthened, so that he was able to emerge from the influence of the affair, and to build his contribution to immortality on a sound though slow foundation. His loyalty to Jackson remained unshaken always and he never spoke of him without flushed emotion. Their parting when Jackson first went to India was later the theme of several poems:

> He would not stay with me, and who can wonder?
> He would not stay for me to stand and gaze.
> I shook his hand and tore my heart in sunder
> And went with half my life about my ways.
> —*AP* VII
> (Written about 1887)

His sense of loss when the ocean separated the two comes out here:

> Oh were he and I together,
>   Shipmates on the fleeted main,
> Sailing through the summer weather
>   To the spoil of France or Spain.
>
> Oh were he and I together
>   Locking hands and taking leave,
> Low upon the trampled heather
>   In the battle lost at eve.
>
> Now are he and I asunder
>   And asunder to remain;
> Kingdoms are for others' plunder,
>   And content for others slain.
>   —*AP* II
>   (Written about 1887)

These poems are great biographical material, tragic evidence of the truth. At their final meeting Jackson again earnestly asked him to forget the turn their friendship had taken. Housman's reply reached the world after his death:

> I promise nothing: friends will part;
>   All things may end, for all began;
> And truth and singleness of heart
>   Are mortal even as is man.
>
> But this unlucky love should last
>   When answered passions thin to air;
> Eternal fate so deep has cast
>   Its sure foundation of despair.
>   —*MP* XII

Another posthumous lyric, obviously an early one (*MP* XXX), dates either to the time when Housman moved from Bayswater, or the year 1887 when Jackson left for India. The rough draft with emendations is displayed as first written.

~~No, no, all's over, I'll try no longer~~
                              use to try
~~Shake hands forever, no more's to say~~
Shake hands, we shall never be friends, all's over;
    I only vex you the more I try
~~I have but vexed you and all for nought~~
                    I've done or said,
All's wrong that ever ~~I did or said,~~
    And nought to help it in this dull head:
                    here's luck, good-bye.
    Shake hands, ~~past friend, good-bye, night.~~
            come to
But if you ~~chance on~~ a road where danger
    Or guilt or anguish or shame's to share,
Be good to
~~Think of~~ the lad that loves you true
    And the soul that was born to die for you,
    And whistle and I'll be there.

            So east and west away (Unused line at bottom
                            of the page)

Here Housman voiced not only guilt, but also fear that the friendship with Jackson was to end with the separation, a fear that dates the poem before 1889, when the attitude of Jackson was completely sympathetic and friendly at the time he returned to England and insisted that Housman come to his wedding that summer. The unused line with its "east and west" clearly refers to Jackson in India, Housman in London. The seventh and eighth lines suggest that there was no shame, guilt, or anguish in Jackson's parting, but that should he ever experience these emotions, he could remember the man who had felt them all in his love for him. Housman's

"Epithalamium,"[17] a marriage hymn, was the result of his presence at Jackson's wedding (1889).

During a visit to A. E. H. when the poet was past seventy, his brother Laurence noticed on Housman's study wall two framed pictures of men. One Laurence knew. It was the bewigged portrait of their Holden ancestor whose proud pedigree traced the two lines of Holden descent from the days of Henry II. The other was of an attractive middle-aged man whom Laurence had never known. "Who is that gentleman?" he asked. In a voice full of repressed emotion, Alfred said:

"That was Moses Jackson, my greatest friend, and the greatest influence in my life."[18]

Jackson died at the age of sixty-three years in British Columbia, when Housman was sixty-two. The last letter Jackson wrote to Housman was upon his death bed in Canada. Housman traced over the wavering pencil lines with ink to preserve them, and wrote on the outside: "Mo's last letter." Laurence Housman discovered it after his brother's death, among a few keepsakes in his desk. He destroyed it.

The effect of Housman on the life of Jackson was relatively small. His life centered upon his wife, four fine sons, and his positions. The fact that Jackson was matter-of-fact and neither emotional nor imaginative makes him less blamable for keeping Housman with him so long in London. He accepted Housman's devotion with little thought of what it meant, and with no sense of obligation. Although he must have hurt Housman deeply, even tortured him by consistently keeping just out of his spiritual reach, he had allowed the relationship to drift on, without any detriment to his own poise. Engrossed in his studies, his job, and his courtship, combined with interest in a much larger circle of acquaintances than Alfred possessed, he had found it for the most part pleasant to come back to Bayswater and Alfred, who was loyal, quiet, understanding, and above all in Jackson's sight, intelligent.

In 1889, when Jackson came home on schedule to marry his betrothed, he was merely completing his level-headed pattern for living which had been built with mathematical precision over a ten-year period. Housman was better able to accept the marriage when it came; he was learning stoicism, and was tasting first fruits of success. Nothing Housman ever said about himself was more frank than these words, once penned to Maurice Pollet of France: "The emotional part of my life was over when I was thirty-five years old."[19]

But he should have added one more word, the word "externally." For under the constant restraint with which he disciplined himself from 1886 onward, he was often rebelling within; passions shook him that were allayed only by the writing of *A Shropshire Lad*; then only temporarily—for until the end of his life, occasionally the old pain and grief for what he had lost would sweep over him like a devastating flood, and wring his heart with the same bitter twist that cursed him in the early days.

In 1892 Housman's opportunity toward which he had labored and sacrificed finally arrived. Dr. Alfred Goodwin, who had been professor both of Greek and of Latin at University College, London, died; and the post that he had held was now to be replaced by two professors, one in the chair of Greek, the other in Latin. Housman applied for both, stating a preference for the Latin, and with his pitiless frankness directed as impartially against himself as against lesser commentators, he said in his application:

"In 1881 I failed to obtain honours in the Final School of *Literae Humaniores*."

With the application there went seventeen testimonials in his behalf, beginning with that of his old teacher Herbert Millington. Herbert Millington had come to Housman's defense once before in an article published February 11, 1888, in the *Journal of Education*. One of the questions that Housman had answered in the Oxford Local Examination at Bromsgrove School in 1877 was: "Compare Horace and Juvenal as writers of satire." Herbert Millington published in comment on this part of his great pupil's answer:

> Now it will tend to illustrate the truth of the Professor's charge [Professor Tyrrel] against modern Oxford, if I state this: I was told after the examination by one of the examiners—a Fellow and Tutor of his College—that this candidate's [Housman's] essay on this question was particularly good. I smiled to myself, but I did not reveal that the candidate in question had not read at that time a single Satire of Horace. That, this being the case, his essay should have been selected for special praise while no word of comment was bestowed on his translation or composition, which was, I know, full of promise, does indeed substantiate in a measure the truth of Professor Tyrrell's charge.
>
> I should like too to state that a young man of acute classical sensibilities was not likely to be attracted to the philosophies of the Oxford Greats School by hearing the college tutor who took the Greats candidates in philosophy, while preaching in the College chapel on the text, "See then that ye walk circumspectly," mispronounce the original Greek of the emphatic adverb. After that, I am not altogether without a sneaking sympathy with this young man's "plough" in Greats.
>
> I can only hope that there are still in Oxford men of influence who read the *Journal of Philology,* and that, having read a certain article therein on the *Agamemnon of Aeschylus,* they will speedily take steps to call this wandering son of theirs, who wrote it, home.
>
> I am, Sir, your obedient servant,
> A Headmaster.
> [HERBERT MILLINGTON]

This letter was re-published in the Oxford magazine, November 11, 1937, in an article by A. S. F. Gow.

Noted linguists of Germany and America, as well as of England, sent letters to University College which gave high recommendations to Housman. As a result of his own tremendous effort, and the effort of his supporters, he was finally recognized by University College, and his days of oblivion were over. He was appointed to the chair of Latin there, and in 1892 Laurence Housman had the satisfaction of hearing his brother's Introductory Lecture from the platform of that college, which was at that time not affiliated with the University of London.

The lecture was based on the value of knowledge for its own sake. Housman went back to his Oxford ideal in this proclamation and, like Cardinal Newman in his *Idea of a University,* declared that knowledge was capable of being its own end. The lecture was an almost fanatical defense of "sweetness and light," and publicly allied Housman with the men he chose to call "fellow soldiers who strove to determine which one can most victoriously achieve the common end of all." His main emphasis was on the necessity of arriving at the truth through scholarly research, and expressed contempt and intolerance for anything less than truth. He was like the Grammarian of Browning expressing himself. He stressed the necessity for accuracy that is the special province of the linguist, and foretold the savage treatment which later he was to mete out to slovenly commentators: attacks that were to be so merciless that for many years they retarded his influence among European men of letters. Portions of the lecture were autobiographical, if one had the wit to discern them:

> Our business is not to live, but to live happily . . . our true occupation is to manufacture from the raw material of life the fabric of happiness. . . . For knowledge resembles virtue in this, and differs in this from other possessions, that it is not merely a means of procuring good, but is good in itself simply; it is not a coin which we pay down to purchase happiness, but it has happiness indissolubly bound up with it. . . .

Fortitude and continence and honesty are not commended to us on the ground that they conduce, as on the whole they do conduce, to material success, nor yet on the ground that they will be rewarded hereafter: those whose office it is to exhort mankind to virtue are ashamed to degrade the cause they plead by proffering such lures as these. And let us too disdain to take lower ground in commending knowledge: let us insist that the pursuit of knowledge, like the pursuit of righteousness, is part of man's duty to himself. . . .[20]

In these words Housman sentenced himself to celibacy in a citadel. His declaration that hereafter his life was to be devoted to building a monument in the world of scholarship, also suggests the possibility that the attainment of his goal might bring him peace. But like others who have striven and won, he discovered in the end that the pinnacle was hardly worth the climbing. Honors and admiration usually bored him; and virtue, which having committed himself to follow, he rigorously practiced, proved to be a cold bedfellow. Housman was made for love and affection, which he desperately needed all his life, but which after 1886 he willfully pushed from him when the opportunities for warming his heart at the fire occurred.

One of his short exquisite lyrics, published posthumously, testifies to the fact that the Cambridge Sir Percival perceived the Holy Grail through a darkened veil:

> He, standing hushed, a pace or two apart,
> Among the bluebells of the listless plain,
> Thinks, and remembers how he cleansed his heart
> And washed his hands in innocence in vain.
> —*MP* XXVIII

These tragic lines suggest a knight in armor, the armor being the pursuit of knowledge and virtue, splendid and shining accoutrements, but not capable of protecting the heart of the wearer. Victory is as transient as bluebells on a spiritless, monotonous landscape— hence the terse confession in the last two words: "in vain." The thought of the verse centers in the word "thinks." If Housman had not been capable of profound and introspective thought, he would have been much happier:

> Could men be drunk for ever
> With liquor, love, or fights,
> Lief should I rouse at morning
> And lief lie down of nights.
>
> But men at whiles are sober
> And think by fits and starts,
> And if they think they fasten
> Their hands upon their hearts.
> —*LP* X

Housman had no personal temptation about drinking to forget his sorrows; he had established a contempt for such weakness because of his father's downfall. Drinking to excess he scorned as a temporary hypnosis, because in sober hours men must think and suffer. He believed man to be too complex a being to be capable of solving his troubles in liquor, love, or fighting. If he were less complicated mentally, how gladly could he lie down at night, and how willingly rise in the morning! This poem is an interesting sidelight on the poet's main reason for melancholy—his predilection for memory and recall, which in him amounted to tragic brooding.

Possessed of passions more demanding and intense, because more spiritual, than those of most other men, Housman repressed them so sternly that his outer life was a perpetual paradox of his inner struggle, and he indeed had the reputation of "standing hushed, a pace or two apart," from the rest of his fellows to the last of his life. The final line is based on Psalms LXXIII: "Surely in vain have I cleansed my heart, and washed my hands in innocency." The Victorian in him never conquered the pagan.

University College

From 1892, when Housman took the chair of Latin at University College, he began rapidly to fit into an assured position of honor and authority. He had escaped at last from the slavery of the Patent Office; he was doing the Latin research in which he was eminently able to excel, and he was surrounded by an earnest and highly gifted group of professors who soon became his friends. The teaching of Latin required a considerable amount of his time, although the classes were small and most of the students were immature. About ten hours a week of actual teaching were required, and in addition to these, Housman gave every year a special course of lectures in the spring term, usually eight or nine in number. These were offered to the post-graduate school, and were catalogued under this heading. From 1892 to the end of his life he found time to be constantly engaged in research, some fruits of which he employed in the seminar courses for advanced students, but most of which he published in learned journals, or as volumes of textual criticism.

In addition to this constant labor he also prepared and delivered papers before the Literary Society of University College, whose capacity for making demands on the faculty was so great that Housman wryly compared it to a Minotaur, a monster preying on helpless professors. The addresses that he read before the Literary Society he rated so low that he destroyed some of them, and refused to allow them to be published. One he dryly tore up page by page as he delivered it. The subjects of these essays included Matthew

Arnold, Burns, and Campbell—(this lecture inspired one of the most amusing cartoons ever made of Housman in action, with the ghost of Campbell cowering in the background, and the caption: "Mr. Thomas Campbell begins to wish he hadn't"—by Sir R. E. Mortimer Wheeler).[21] Housman also read papers on Swinburne, Tennyson, and the "Spasmodic School." Housman particularly loathed the pretentious and feverish compositions of Alexander Smith, Gerald Massey, and Sidney Dobell, and did his share in laughing them into oblivion.

Housman always disclaimed the title of critic of literature, and preferred not to perpetuate his modest efforts of that nature. His opinion of the critic, the real critic, was so high that he once said not more than one in a century could reasonably be expected to criticize adequately his particular branch of the arts. The falsity of sham critics he abominated, and hurled his wrath upon them at every provocation. Rules of criticism he declared were framed by the benevolent for the guidance, support, and the restraint, of three classes of persons: *"They were leading-strings for infants, crutches for cripples, and strait-waist-coats for maniacs. . . . Of course you can have hard-and-fast rules if you like, but then you will have false rules, and they will lead you wrong."*[22] When Housman uttered this pronouncement, he had arrived at a position of such eminence in the group of linguistic scholars that he was unimpeachable, though not always impervious to attack.

University College was already a leader in the study of philology when Housman was added to its faculty in 1892, for as far back as 1828 the evolutionary point of view regarding language had been recognized by Professor Friedrich August Rosen, who came to University College in that year as Professor of Oriental Languages. In the short time before his death at the age of thirty-two he had trained three of his colleagues to the new philology, Professors Key, Long, and Malden, all recruited when they were about thirty years old. Key held the chair of Latin, and Malden of Greek. They were soon aided by the great Henry Morley, who came to University College to remain as they did, loyal to its interests as long as he lived.

These earnest linguists, by means of association with Richard Garnett, Edwin Guest, and other philologists of London, managed to found and publish a periodical purely philological in nature called *The Proceedings.* From this time on, the department of English identified itself with the amazing work of that linguistic genius of Germany, Grimm, (who combined his research in ancient languages resulting in Grimm's Law, with the writing of children's fairy tales)! The aims of the department changed from stress on moral development as fostered by Dr. Dale, the head of the English division at the University in 1828, to an emphasis on linguistics, especially the study of comparative languages from about 1850 on, based on Grimm's Law, Verner's Law, and Grassman's Law.

Therefore linguistic emphasis upon Latin in 1892 was most favorably received, and the type of scholarship that Housman had to offer, together with his superior knowledge about the evolution of Latin and his brilliant comparative studies of manuscripts in that language, fitted the program University College was sponsoring, and immediately gave him a group of congenial acquaintants with whom he could good-naturedly argue and with whom he deigned to disagree at times. In this circle of earnest authorities, Arthur Platt and W. P. Ker were the most brilliant; this triumvirate— Housman, Platt, and Ker—because of the depth of their scholarship and their ability to present public addresses and papers, combined with their interest in their students as individuals, made the study of linguistics notable at University College; in fact, it may be safely said that at the turn of the century University College was more advanced than most universities in its evolutionary linguistic offerings.

Of the three men, Platt, professor of Greek, was the most lovable; Ker, professor of English, the most capable in administration; and Housman the most challenging and provocative. He fascinated his students by his cold and clear deductions; he alarmed them by his caustic comments in lectures and public discussions; he reassured them in personal conferences, when his sympathy and interest became apparent; he stirred them to loyal awe by the glimpses he gave them of a profundity of knowledge that lay in depths of which they only skimmed the surface. He had great tolerance for youth and its mistakes, a saving grace which precluded any possible clashing with his students. Although he sometimes left his women students in tears because of their errors, they always admitted the justice of his comments, and several of them in after life occupied chairs of language with honor.

The majority of Housman's University College students were rather ordinary, but where it was possible, brilliance was recognized and fostered assiduously. Several of Housman's students later made names to be reckoned with in the classical world:

Gerald Gould, editor of University College magazine and classical scholar, graduated A. B. with First Class Honors in Classics.

Sir R. E. Mortimer Wheeler, at present in the Institute of Archaeology of the University of London, as professor of Archaeology of the Roman Provinces, C.I.E., N.C., D. Litt., F.B.A., who used to draw the amusing cartoons of his Latin teacher, graduated M. A. in classics in 1912.

G. F. Forsey, Professor of Classics at University College, graduated M. A. in Classics in 1912.

F. A. Canenaugh, Professor at King's College, London, graduated M. A. with distinction in Classics in 1909.

Ethel Mary Stewart graduated B. A. with First Class Honors in Classics in 1908. Later she was a scholar and Fellow at Girton, and thereafter a Headmistress in a girls' school. She dedicated her *Annals of Quintus Ennius* to A. E. Housman, her "honoured teacher."

However, R. W. Chambers, one of his friends and colleagues at the college, who had also been in his classes, wrote: "So far as I know, he never had any student at University College worthy of his scholarship. But three things we, his students got from him. They were things which even those who were not exact scholars could learn."[23] These, to sum up what Chambers elaborated, were first, the sense of having come in contact with a mind of extraordinary distinction; second, Housman's love of truth, a love so intense as to make Housman say over and over, "Accuracy is a duty and not a virtue"; third, his grim courage in meeting the world.

Sir R. E. M. Wheeler remembered Housman as a professor:

Housman I knew then [1909-'10-'11] as the austere and aloof Professor of Latin. He had very little liaison with his students, who came and went at their own individual discretion. He had, if I remember rightly, something of a special dislike for female students, but his tongue could on occasion be as biting to all of us as his published prefaces. In spite of this, we all liked him in a kind of way, and felt a certain awe of him as a man of mystery and of manifest ability. The Shropshire Lad never emerged: but when he interpreted a page of a Latin text, his precise and incisive translations, free from all ambiguity and humbug, are remembered still. No one, I think *knew* him, and I doubt very much if he knew very much about himself. Somewhere, however, I have a copy of the *Shropshire Lad* which, greatly daring,

I asked him to sign on my last day. He did so with his usual matter of courseness but with a slight unwonted twinkle in his eye.[24]

About 1900, the interest in the Arts Dinners at University College, long an annual function, became accelerated. Students filled the tables to listen to Platt, Housman, Ker and occasionally guest speakers read papers or give informal discussions on literature. It was a delight to watch these brilliant minds break lances against each other, and the listeners always left with a doubt as to who was the final victor, for the discussions were dignified, full of humor, and never acrimonious. These Arts Dinners were formal and carefully planned, and Housman thoroughly enjoyed them. They resulted in an amusing form of perpetuation: the clever cartoons which Sir R. E. Mortimer Wheeler liked to "scribble" (the word is Dr. Wheeler's modest depreciation). Housman appeared in a number of these cartoons, and some of them found their way into books and periodicals. One of them had in some way been previously overlooked although it is one of the most amusing. It was drawn as a result of the Arts Faculty Dinner held on December 13, 1909, and was presented to me by Laurence Housman, who found it among the papers of his brother. Of the cartoon, Dr. Wheeler wrote to me on October 17, 1951:

. . . I had completely forgotten the poster but recognize the handiwork of a very junior under-graduate (I suppose I was 18). The personages at the high table I recognize: A. E. Housman in the centre, with Professor W. P. Ker (Professor of English) on his right (left to the spectator) and Professor Arthur Platt—the professor of Greek—on his left, with the long hair streaming out behind. At the table on the right I recognize only two figures: the furthest is myself, with the extended hand, and, next to me,

[136]

is the late Lawrence Solomon, then assistant in the Classical Department. The other two I completely forget. . . .

Apparently the young cartoonist had some kind of artist's cap
on the back of his head, from which bristled his drawing pencils.
Evidently the side table in the picture was the first one of several
tables, the second of which is visible in the lower right hand corner
of the poster. The ice cream, molded in the form of geese, is worth
noticing. The poster gives some idea of how the three professors
conducted these dinners, and suggests the type of informal conversation by which they educated and stimulated the students and
lesser faculty.

The Dining Club at University College was another social outlet
in which Housman participated. It was a long established organization composed of leading professors, who met for the pleasure of a
good dinner, good wine, and good conversation. Housman was its
treasurer, and kept accurate accounts of its expenditure and income.
He also chose the wines, and had a chance to display that discrimination which was to make him known later as a connoisseur. Ber-
gundy and port wine were the usual ones for these Dining Club
collations; the vintages sparkled in the glasses no more brightly
than the repartee across the board. When women were added to
the faculty, the question of whether to elect them to membership
in the Dining Club came up and was favorably considered until
Housman squelched the idea with some of the most sarcastic in-
vective he was capable of.

Housman's ability as an after-dinner speaker became known at
University College by accident. Professor Oliver had arranged with
Sir Henry Roscoe to be the principal speaker at a faculty dinner,
and to everyone's consternation, he telegraphed a refusal at the
last minute. Mr. Oliver had heard from a friend at Oxford that

Housman kept his "lamp of public speech under a bushel," and prevailed on him to display it in the open; his speech turned out to be the success of the evening. After that, the planning of formal dinners fell upon him, and he organized a number of them and took part in them, to the great enlivening of the guests. He had an odd way of speaking which Mortimer Wheeler caught successfully in his cartoons: a strange way of "looking down his nose" when talking; a dry manner, which got drier as he reeled off his provocative turns of words in rich humor; a slight twitching of his wrist when he was about to send forth his lightning thrust of sarcasm or cynicism.

He dressed most carefully at all times, and was a pattern of formality at the public functions. Students liked to watch him because there was nobody in the least like him, and although he never looked at them in either dinner speeches or classroom lecturing, they stared at him in captivated awe. He once gave as the reason for his detachment in the lecture room that he could not keep his mind on the names of his students and his Latin endings at the same time! But they soon learned that, concealed by an outer shell of austerity, the real man was reachable in personal meetings, when his generosity and kindness to the students were willingly exhibited. His grimness was actually an expression of his own courage; he knew no better way of meeting the temptations and terrors of the world.

> To stand up straight and tread the turning mill,
> To lie flat and know nothing and be still,
> Are the two trades of man; and which is worse
> I know not, but I *know that both are ill*.[25]
> —*MP* XXVII

Yet the man that wrote those lines disclaimed pessimism, and said that he was not a pessimist but a pejorist—one who depreciates life.[26] His outlook was more like that of the ancient Norsemen: a brave assertion of individual freedom against a world hopeless and antagonistic, an absolute resistance against powers impregnable and unchangeable.[27] The bravery of Housman was recognized by his compeers and students alike; he carried heavy programs, devoted himself to his scholastic labors, and flagellated sham scholars unsparingly.

In 1905, Housman's landlady, Mrs. Trim, who had faithfully served him for a period of nineteen years in Byron Cottage, found that she would have to move, and Housman chose to move with her. Her new address was 1 Yarborough Villas, Woodridings, Pinner; and here Housman had rooms until he left for Cambridge in 1911. It was a bother and discomfort to Housman to move, but he preferred not to change his landlady, who suited him exactly because she never intruded on his privacy. From Byron Cottage he had traveled by train to University College every day, but after the change to Pinner he was relieved of this nuisance which he always had abhorred.

Mrs. Trim once remarked to Professor Platt that Housman was an ideal roomer, but that she wished heartily he had more social life, and she was happy that University College furnished him with contacts he had almost entirely lacked before his professorship. She knew that he was a lonely man, almost without social contacts while at the Patent Office, and she soon discovered that he was less melancholy after 1892.

Ten years before the removal to Pinner, however, in the sanctuary of Byron Cottage, Housman revised and completed most of the poems that made up his first volume. Explanation has already been made that the inception of many of these poems began ten years before the publication of *A Shropshire Lad*. Housman once said that it took him twenty-three years to write *A Shropshire Lad,* and although this was as provocative a deception as was the Shropshire milieu, it had a kernel of truth in it. At the bitterest moments of The Purgatory Period, there is no doubt that many lines were set down that ten years later made their way into *A Shropshire Lad*; that the poet chose not to say so was an attempt to conceal his tragic love. Probably at the time the lines were put on paper he had no idea of publishing any of them, and certainly a number of the most personal he never published in his lifetime.

Obviously the events told in *A Shropshire Lad* were not events of 1896. By Laurence Housman's testimony and by the content of the poems themselves, they dealt with events in A. E. H.'s life from the time he started writing poetry up to 1896. It would be ridiculous to suppose that after the poignancy of passion was long past—ten years after—Housman should suddenly be flooded with the emotions that produced *A Shropshire Lad*. His life as a staid, remote professor precluded those emotions, and was a complete antithesis of the seething torture and passion which had wrung his heart. He himself told Percy Withers that the poems went back as far as 1886.[28]

Why did Housman decide to put the poems together and publish them in 1896, after, in his own words, the emotional part of his life was over?[29] The comments that Housman made about his poetry were often said for purposes of concealment, and could at times be completely misleading. "The Shropshire Lad," he once wrote, "is an imaginary figure, with something of my temper and view of life. Very little in the book is biographical."[30] This statement was deceptive for self-protection.

The main reason that Housman decided to devote the period of convalesence from a severe throat infection in February, 1895, to poetry was his desire for fame. He knew the work he had done was unfinished, but good. He was always sustained by personal pride at crucial moments in his life, and since pride had helped him to renounce strange love, "a love surpassing the love of woman,"[31] pride directed him to replace love by fame. His pride was not conceit; it possessed a more manly element. It was an attempt at self-justification based on a guilt complex; it represented his old struggle to gather the antitheses of his life into a synthesis. He did not seek personal admiration but he wanted fame in a general way, devoid of personal advances which he disliked and mistrusted.

He was ashamed of his desire for fame, although he rejoiced in it when it came to him. His likening himself to T. E. Lawrence, who described his desire for fame in *The Seven Pillars of Wisdom* (one of Housman's favorite books) is well known. The similarity of feeling was so close that Housman wrote in the margin of his copy: "This is me."[32] Lawrence's paragraph disclosed two things: he wanted to be liked so much that he dared not be friendly for fear of disappointment, and he wanted fame so much he was ashamed of it.

The fact that Housman's lyrics are autobiographical is emphasized by the title he first gave his volume: "Poems by Terence Hearsay." He believed that by publishing his book anonymously, he could conceal his authorship, and thus conceal the biographical element.

Now two reasons for publication had materialized: the desire for fame, and the assurance that his own life would be concealed by the Shropshire setting and the fabrication of Terence Hearsay.

A third reason for publication in 1896 was the time element. The episodes of his strange love were ten years past; he would never live them again. Now he was able to get a perspective on himself, to view himself objectively. As a man looks at a painting down a long portrait gallery, so he viewed himself down the avenue of years. He was now able to integrate in smoother phrases what he could not express so well when emotion had made him dumb with suffering; the shock was over, and he could recover from it by the medium that all such geniuses have used: the method of confession through creative art. But the confession was not Housman's alone; it was the confession of all men, expressed in images that few men are able to put into words:

> They say my verse is sad: no wonder;
>   Its narrow measure spans
> Tears of eternity, and sorrow,
>   Not mine, but man's.
>   Epigraph, *More Poems*

Grief is a form of exhilaration seldom recognized as such, says Professor Cleanth Brooks, and it was that type of exhilaration that made *A Shropshire Lad*. Housman's most intense excitement came at moments of almost unbearable sadness, not for himself alone, but for mankind. His poetry was a series of passionate outbursts against the frustrations and disorders of his own experience, which he generalized as the common fate of all.

The year and a half (1895-96) that brought forth *A Shropshire Lad* from finished poems, fragments, phrases, and lines, in addition to some completely new poems, was a period of renewed inner excitement for Housman. He was tense with reminiscence, gripped by passion for creation, and stimulated by a sudden desire to complete lyrics which he knew were better than most. Virginia Woolf's comment that to be able to write well, one must have five hundred a year (in pounds) and a room of his own was substantiated in the experience of Housman. For the first time in his life he was independent and had the privacy he needed to complete and polish the oddments of verse in his desk.

The process of creation he found always to be exhausting, and he could take only so much of it at a time. When its sway gripped him he fell under its domination to the extent that sometimes whole new poems came to him during afternoon walks. Later he said in *The Name and Nature of Poetry* (1933) that he was seized by sudden emotional images while he was shaving in the morning, or preparing for bed at night. When the waves of creative emotion came, with words to articulate them, they inundated him; he shook and trembled; he says the hair rose on his head, and gooseflesh pricked him. Poetry was to him a distinctly physical experience as well as a mental one, and he felt the depth of nervous reaction in the pit of his stomach. At such times, the lyrics were produced, but not altogether spontaneously, and the pangs of creation were as much as he was able to bear.[33] Housman's method of bringing forth poetry involved a strange mixture of masculine and feminine creation; it came after a physical travail that almost prostrated him, and having arrived in the world, it was his child.

6

About That Shropshire Lad

THE COLLECTION of fragments that went into *A Shropshire Lad* were first written because Housman could not hold them back. Many of them were founded directly or indirectly upon his passion for Jackson. Others were put down at moments of fierce anger and revolt about certain social injustices. Some were the result of his longing for the landscape of his birth, its changing seasons, its bells and hills, its blossoms. And some few came from God knows where. The disguise of the country yokel was loosely thrown over them for purpose of anonymity, but through the veil shone crystal lyrics—clear and salty as tears.

After eighteen months of revision and addition, the poems were as nearly right as Housman could get them, and they had become so much a part of him that he shrank from showing them to anyone. After several weeks' delay that resulted in a rejection slip, he invited his friend Pollard to visit him. Following luncheon in Hall the two returned to Byron College, Housman in a mood of depression. With the greatest difficulty he thrust the manuscript in Pollard's hands and asked him to read it. Then he went for a walk and left his friend alone. Hours later he returned, abashed and ill at ease.

Pollard quickly rose from the desk and held out his hand.

"Alfred," he declared solemnly, "those poems will be read two hundred years from now."

A warm color flooded Housman's face. "I have to thank you for reading them," he murmured rather formally. "There is no one I know well whose opinion I value more. You know, I think, better than most, that they contain somewhat of my own viewpoint on life." Pollard was gratified at this confidence, but quickly veered off it. There were some things that he would much rather not know.

"And so you want to conceal that fact by calling them *Poems by Terence Hearsay!* Horrid possibility! That title is not worthy of the lyrics," he said warmly.

"I don't like it much myself," Housman admitted.

"It's really unworthy," said Pollard. "Doesn't go with the spirit of the thing at all. I've been thinking—presumptuously, of course. . . . You already have the Shropshire milieu—a good enough disguise. And Shropshire lads are speaking. Why not call the book *A Shropshire Lad*, and acknowledge your authorship?"

"It's true that title and setting would make it purely objective. I'll think about it," Housman replied. "But you may be mistaken about the value of the thing. I must tell you that the book has already been rejected by the Macmillan Company. John Morley was, I believe, their reader."

"Don't be depressed by that," returned Pollard. "Have you thought of submitting the manuscript to another firm?"

"Not definitely. I wanted to get your opinion first."

"My opinion is that the poems are so good they must find a publisher at once. Of course, it's hard for a new voice to get a hearing. There is one publishing firm in London that I am familiar with, Kegan Paul. Let me introduce you to them."[1]

The introduction was made, and an agreement was drawn up

that Kegan Paul would publish the book at Housman's expense! Pollard's title was to be used. Also, Housman insisted that he would receive no royalties. He would have no more thought of selling his poems than he would have considered putting his heart on the market. It was not a satisfactory arrangement, but the best that Housman could do. Kegan Paul was lukewarm, ventured only five hundred copies, and asked Housman for thirty pounds to publish it. The volume had blue-gray boards with vellum spine and paper label, and was printed by Ballentyne, Hanson and Company. Housman must have liked the looks of it for he wrote dryly to his brother Laurence:

"The binding seems to me so extraordinarily beautiful that I cannot bear to lose sight of it by opening the book."

The original price was half a crown. This edition, which sold so slowly that Laurence Housman at the end of two years bought up the last few copies, created little excitement in the literary world at first. But if you ever find a copy in your grandmother's attic, you can exchange it for a Cadillac or a year's trip to far away places.

The United States liked the book better than England did, where most of the criticisms were lukewarm or adverse.

Two years later, after the fabulous old Queen celebrated her Diamond Jubilee, and retired weary and happy to the privacy of her last years, a new chance came to Housman and fame was around the corner. On the verge of the twentieth century, he met an enthusiastic young publisher, Grant Richards, who had recognized the genius of *ASL* and now asked to publish a second edition. Housman liked Richards and found him easy to know; so began a business relationship that was friendly as well. The feelings of Kegan Paul were not in the least lacerated when Housman transferred rights of publication to Richards in 1897. The edition came out attractively bound at Richards' expense, five hundred copies which sold much better than the first. Housman steadfastly refused royalties, and Richards realized a profit from the edition.

Richards published the third edition of *ASL* in the spring of 1900, this time a thousand copies. At the end of 1902 he issued another edition of two thousand copies. The fame of Housman advanced, but in England he was still unimportant as a poet. America began to publish pirate editions of *ASL* that sold rapidly; but against the advice of his brother, Housman still refused to take out an American copyright. "They have a perfect right to publish the poems if they want to," he said with some hauteur.[2]

Meanwhile Richards was busy putting out new editions, two of which were illustrated, against Housman's better judgment. They sold like hot cakes, and now the books were being ordered from Europe. Writers asked Housman for permission to translate them (often in poor English) and Housman threw such requests in the wastebasket with venom.

Conflicting statements about the immediate reception of *A Shropshire Lad* were numerous. Sir William Rothenstein, head of the Royal Academy and master of portraiture, was a personal friend of Housman for many years, and one of his enthusiastic readers. He states:

> Few men—how words are abused by use!—have *taste*; can savour the flavour, the aroma, of man's precious vintages. Most are deceived by the label, the market price, or their habits have dulled their palates. Yet now and again a man's work is assessed at its true value; A. E. Housman's *A Shropshire Lad* became, almost at once, an English Classic.[3]

R. W. Chambers, his contemporary at University College writes: "The world knew little of Housman in those days (*circa* 1898-1900) but we felt a possessive pride in him. We knew (when most people did not), 'The lads in their hundreds.' "[4] This comment suggests a slower public recognition than Rothenstein's. A. S. F. Gow has nothing to say about its reception at all, but this omission is natural, for Gow dealt with Housman primarily as a scholar.

Laurence Housman in his memoir of his brother has this comment:

> Though the literary world had become aware, within the first month of its appearance, that a new poet had arisen, only three hundred and eighty-one copies of the book had been sold, at half-a-crown each, by the end of the year (ten months); and two years after, finding that six copies of the first edition still remained unsold, I bought the lot. . . .[5]

Grant Richards discloses that the volume had small notice at first: "It is certainly true that a small book, *A Shropshire Lad,* with the name of A. E. Housman on its title page, came out in 1896 from the house of Kegan Paul without attracting much attention."

After the slow stream of Housman readers from 1896 to 1903, the momentum of popularity increased rapidly. During this period *A Shropshire Lad* had been reviewed in thirty-three periodicals with both praise and condemnation. Controversial opinions aroused curiosity, and Richards had the satisfaction of selling thousands of copies of *A Shropshire Lad* and getting out several attractive editions.

The fame of Housman as a poet finally was established, and if he had known it, his immortality; for while he was fuming over his first and second volumes of *Manilius,* his monumental Latin work, he was slowly but surely becoming appreciated as a poetic genius not to be imitated. *A Shropshire Lad* was Housman; it contradicted his aloof disguise. When his sister Clemence first read *A Shropshire Lad* she cried out with a mixture of sorrow and relief: "Alfred has a heart!"[6]

"There are degrees of impossibility of reading Housman into his poems, just as there are degrees of possibility in the other direction, but the outstanding lyrics which it was impossible for any Shropshire Lad to have conceived, let alone written, are the ones in which A. E. H. is most himself."[7]

Even his poems that deal with the love of man and woman are not objective, for they reflect his personal viewpoint, usually cynical, always based on the inequality of love, or the faithlessness of lovers, or the faithful "lover of the grave." In his sex philosophy, A. E. H. regarded the human alliance of love with lust to be inescapable and one of God's most damning errors. He expressed his opinion with cynical repugnance in "The True Lover," *ASL* XIII:

> The lad came to the door at night,
>   When lovers crown their vows,
> And whistled soft and out of sight
>   In shadow of the boughs.
>
> 'I shall not vex you with my face
>   Henceforth, my love, for aye;
> So take me in your arms a space
>   Before the east is grey.
>
> 'When I from hence away am past
>   I shall not find a bride,
> And you shall be the first and last
>   I ever lay beside.'
>
> She heard and went and knew not why;
>   Her heart to his she laid;
> Light was the air beneath the sky
>   But dark under the shade.
>
> 'Oh do you breathe, lad, that your breast
>   Seems not to rise and fall,
> And here upon my bosom prest
>   There beats no heart at all?'

'Oh loud, my girl, it once would knock,
　　You should have felt it then;
But since for you I stopped the clock
　　It never goes again.'

'Oh lad, what is it, lad, that drips
　　Wet from your neck on mine?
What is it falling on my lips,
　　My lad, that tastes of brine?'

'Oh like enough 'tis blood, my dear,
　　For when the knife has slit
The throat across from ear to ear
　　'Twill bleed because of it.'

Under the stars the air was light
　　But dark below the boughs,
The still air of the speechless night,
　　When lovers crown their vows.

Actually, this poem is a ghost story! Housman told his brother
that the true lover is dead before he begins to speak; he has already
cut his throat, and it's only a ghost that whistles, and it's only a
ghostly throat that bleeds from a ghost body whose heart no longer
beats. It is a ghostly copulation that occurs, not a physical one, and
he has to get through with it "before the east is grey," because
ghosts then have to disappear. The girl had rejected him; had failed
to "pity him"; and straightway he cut his throat and became a
painfully true lover, "the lover of the grave." He thereby got rid
of "the folly that has no fellow beneath the blue of day," (*ASL*
XIV), or the black night either. "A. E. H. in his dislike for the
woman, projects his imagination into a macabre narrative of what
he would like to have happen to her—namely a thoroughly nasty
bit of haunting, a visitation from the suicide that she has flouted
to his death."[8]

The love Housman had for soldiers as expressed in *ASL* poems on soldiery was not sexual. Half-truths often result in whole untruths, and the whisperings about the sex life of Housman have resulted in such gross misinterpretations of a spartan-like man and his poetry that there is need for facts to testify in his behalf. Nothing could be more ridiculous than the rumors that his soldier poems were based on sexual experiences. Most of these falsities are insecurely grounded on total ignorance about the simplest facts in A. E. H.'s life—facts which any encyclopedia could straighten out if one took the trouble to look them up.

One notable example of such ignorance would be quite amusing if it were not so blamable. An English lecturer in a western college wrote triumphantly in a 1951 letter to Laurence Housman (who charitably wishes her name withheld) that with the aid of an equally clever masculine associate professor, she had solved the Housman mystery! And she did it in this fashion: that there was a young soldier at the time of the Boer War with whom Alfred Housman was "in love"; he was killed, and Alfred's Muse died with him! But the poems under discussion, those of *ASL,* were published three years before the Boer War! To anyone who knows the historical facts about the Housmans, it is apparent that the soldier referred to in the Boer War (*LP* and *MP*) was A. E. H.'s favorite youngest brother Herbert, who died in battle.

The same professor goes on to say that at the time of World War I, there was another young soldier, so much like the first that he might have been a re-incarnation. So A. E. H. "loved" again, and again burst into poetry when his second "love" was killed. Thus she accounted for *Last Poems,* 1922! The plain truth out of which this hatch-up was evolved is that the soldier killed in World War I was number three of Housman's four nephews, the son of his sister Katherine, Clement Aubrey Symons. Housman took a tremendous interest in all of her children, and when his nephews were called to the service of England, Housman contributed a considerable sum to provide them with the proper outfitting and greater comforts which he felt was all he could bestow on these boys he loved. One of them, Victor Noel Housman, lost a hand in battle, and his uncle provided the money to secure for him the best possible artificial substitute. On the death of his brother and the death of his nephew, Housman wrote commemorative poems, "Illic Jacet" especially to his nephew, but a number of others directed to his brother. Mrs. Symons wrote in *The Bromsgrovian Memorial*:

> On his human side he was ready to humble himself before the man who chose to go out and fight and risk his life in doing so. It is true that he sent £100 to help in equipping three nephews who had joined the army, and all the rest of his bank balance he sent to the Exchequer. . . .[9]

Housman generalized his emotion to include all British soldiers:

> They sought and found six feet of ground
> And there they died for me.
>   —*LP* XXXII

Housman had written many of the verses in *Last Poems* and *More Poems* before either the Boer War or World War I occurred (twenty-six soldier poems, in fact), as a sequence study of the original manuscripts proves: there was no temporary death and resurrection of his Muse. A great many lines and stanzas published in *Last Poems* and in *More Poems* antedated *ASL* but were withheld because of their personal note. As has already been emphasized, for the more discerning there are poems which tell of that friendship which gave him so much more sorrow than joy, but they are not soldier poems, not one of them.

Knowing the 1886 beginning of the poems and the facts that led

to their writing, we understand why *More Poems* is no more revealing than *ASL* or *Last Poems,* and Laurence Housman certainly is
of this opinion. The single exception is "Because I liked you better"
(*MP* XXXI), which has been explained previously in connection
with the circumstances that led to its writing.

In *A Shropshire Lad* the tensions of Housman's own life are always on the surface. One poem which dramatically expresses those
struggles is "On Wenlock Edge," (*ASL* XXXI) in which the terse
starkness of the lines is a paradox itself with the world of passionate feeling that colors the mood of the verse.

> On Wenlock Edge the wood's in trouble;
>   His forest fleece the Wrekin heaves;
> The gale, it plies the saplings double,
>   And thick on Severn snow the leaves.
>
> 'Twould blow like this through holt and hanger
>   When Uricon the city stood:
> 'Tis the old wind in the old anger,
>   But then it threshed another wood.
>
> Then, 'twas before my time, the Roman
>   At yonder heaving hill would stare:
> The blood that warms an English yeoman,
>   The thoughts that hurt him, they were there.
>
> There, like the wind through woods in riot,
>   Through him the gale of life blew high;
> The tree of man was never quiet:
>   Then 'twas the Roman, now 'tis I.
>
> The gale, it plies the saplings double,
>   It blows so hard, 'twill soon be gone:
> To-day the Roman and his trouble
>   Are ashes under Uricon.

In powerful monosyllables Housman creates an image of the
eternal struggle of man and nature with the gale of destiny as sym-

bolized by the Romans and the trees in battle and tempest. He becomes one of the Romans on Wenlock, their brother by heredity and struggle. The trees bent double in the gale are images of his own twisted personality, torn by the irregular nature of his stormy desires.

The poem could hardly be better located in order to give the proper background for a conception which is deceptively simple. Wenlock Edge, a wooded chain of hills ten miles east of Shrewsbury, Shropshire, stands as an important historical landmark. Traces of old British camps lie along the summit of the Wrekin. Both the Wrekin and Wenlock rise above the River Severn. Uricon, the third geographical location referred to in the poem is actually *Uriconium*, an ancient Roman stronghold of early Britain, the site of which is four miles east of Shrewsbury. It existed from the first century of our era, about 700 A.D., as a Roman fortress, and later as a city which was sacked and burned by the West Saxons in the sixth century.

The Roman on Wenlock Edge stands for strength and courage against onslaught, and the trees on Wrekin in their savage war against "the old wind," symbolize the same thing. The gale of tragic Fate blows through the tree of man with the same havoc that "the old wind" wreaks on Wenlock Edge. The Roman, with his four hundred and fifty years of living in those hills, fused himself with the history and the life of the island, and the nineteenth century yeoman—the Shropshire Lad himself—is a related outgrowth of Uricon. Not the yeoman alone, but his entire past is joined in one long everlasting struggle with Fate and her final triumph over man, of which Uricon is a symbol.

"Yonder heaving hill" typifies the confused, angry world that man must face, then and now. That slow line, " 'Tis the old wind in the old anger" has fateful power. How desperately the forest of humanity struggles against Fate is disclosed in the metaphorical expressions "riot," "heaves," "threshed," and "plies the saplings double."

Wind of hurricane force is suggested by the lull in the next to the last stanza; then comes the renewal of cyclonic ferocity at the beginning of the last stanza, which suddenly resolves itself into the dramatic calm of ashes and peace on the last line. Time has done his worst, the battle is over, and the Roman has found his solution of life in the same way that all men have discovered— death.[10]

No reader could be censured if he placed *ASL* XXVIII, "The Welsh Marches" above "On Wenlock Edge" for both are superlatively good poems, but in restraint and finish, "Wenlock" is the better lyric. In "The Welsh Marches," which is more biographical, A. E. H. links his personal battle against his inheritance with the conflict between the Saxons and the Welsh, and with the instincts that resulted in their struggles. Just as the two warring nations fought to a finish on the border hills along the Severn centuries ago, so the "marches of his breast" are invaded by two warring natures—two personalities fighting for the victory over his body. He voices the ceaseless conflict in his blood, and "blood" is inheritance. "My father and my mother" refer to the generations of parentage behind him, as well as to his immediate inheritance.

A picture of savage invasion, ruthless torment, followed by careless procreation emphasizes the idea that we are not very far now from a semi-heathen heritage. In 300 A.D. "the Saxon got me on the slave (*ASL* XXVIII). In another poem published in *LP* he wrote: "The night my father got me his mind was not on me."[11]

Housman affiliates himself with the "ancient wrong" because of his inner warfare, and he believes that the spiritual battles of mankind are much the same now as in the days of the Welsh Marches.

The clearest reference Housman ever made to his mental twist is found in these lines from "The Welsh Marches":

> None will part us, none undo
> *The knot that makes one flesh of two,*[12]
> Sick with hatred, sick with pain,
> Strangling—when shall we be slain?

Biographical value is found in "Be Still, My Soul," (*ASL* XLVIII), certainly one of the noblest poems in the book. The crescendo element in this poem is very strong; the poem has four movements; the first one conveys almost indifference; the second, endurance; the third, indignation, as the plight of man and his colossal tragedy impresses itself on the poet; and the last, a mood of complete helplessness against the injustice of the eternals. Here is a Prometheus bound indeed.

"To An Athlete Dying Young," (*ASL* XIX), is another of the great poems which by no stretch of imagination could a Shropshire yokel have written. It has become highly popular in American anthologies of late, possibly because of the magic word "athlete," sacrosanct in the college world.

The poem starts on a tempo of glorious vitality which is abruptly arrested by the immobility of death. In no other lines does Housman glorify death as much, and yet show in the moment of its glory, the hopeless inertia of the grave.

Housman once said that his "effort as a poet was not so much to find the right word as to reject the wrong word."[13] His rejections were numerous enough in this poem to make it worthy of special study in rough draft. The work sheets show the process of revision which led to the rejection of a number of wrong words and the substitution of exact ones in their places. For instance, the word "wise" as first written in line nine, lacked dramatic quality, and was not appropriate to the world of racing on the village green. So the phrase "well-done" was second choice, with its hint of approbation. But, though this is improved in one sense, it is too general; it does not compliment the runner in the vernacular of his onlookers. The phase "smart lad" was finally the right tone of compliment —a hint of the language of the green—for the boy who has brought his life's race to an end at the right time. Housman had to be careful not to over-do the vernacular. Lines 17-18 read at first:

> Now you will not join the throng
> Of lads that live a ~~spell~~ day too long.

Finally came the exact language needed:

> Now you will not swell the rout
> Of lads that wore their honours out. . . .

"The sill of shade," line 22, has proved difficult of interpretation. The obscurity lies in the fact that Housman suddenly steps out of the vernacular. The portion of the poem that no Shropshire Lad could possibly have written begins with the twenty-first line. "The sill of shade" is not the threshold of the grave, but of Hades, and the poetic image is abruptly transferred from the village churchyard to the scene of death as interpreted by the ancient classical writers in their conception of death. The ghastliness of the words "gaze" and "strengthless" suggests the staring wraiths of the lower world. Since Housman did not believe in a conscious hereafter, he resorted to the Greek conception of life beyond the grave as justification for the continuation of his contrast between the living and the dead.

If Housman had believed that his athlete could ever sense the fearful difference between life and death in that split second of border-land transition, he could not have written those lines. The fact that he did use them proves his alteration of viewpoint to Greek philosophy in the final stanzas. The poem is really consistent with Housman's atheistic avowals elsewhere. Almost a Mercury, the shade of the boy stands poised, but still active, at the door of Hades, carrying his hard-won cup above him, and his laurel of victory about his brow—a powerful symbolism justified only by the Greek viewpoint. The last stanza is not an anti-climax if one understands that the maiden's wreath of flowers at the festival was by legend a token of virginity, and that the moment of fame and fortune typified by the laurel, is as transient as her maidenhood.

Greek influences in "To An Athlete" are strong enough to remind us of specific Greek classics: the idea of "the strengthless dead" is strongly conceived in the *Odyssey,* Book XI, and other Homeric ideas of the powerless shades in the after-world. Also, the poem may have been somewhat influenced by the funeral oration of Pericles: Housman knew it by heart. Likewise, the "smart lad" may be compared in thought with this translation from Thucydides:

Thus choosing to die resisting, rather than to live submitting, they fled only from dishonour, but met danger face to face, and after one brief moment while at the summit of their fortune, escaped, not from their fear, but from their glory.

The thought of "Is my team ploughing?" (*ASL* XXVIII) illustrates Housman's belief that true love between man and woman is possible only in a state of monogamy—a lifelong devotion to one mate. Joan Thomson wrote of Housman from Trinity Lodge, Cambridge, to Grant Richards, in substantiation of Housman's opinion:

Professor Housman argued that a really great man is not also a great lover, because he can shake his life free from the troubles of love. He would not tolerate the idea that it was possible for a man truly to love more than one woman in his life; anyone who considered that he had done so had simply really never loved at all. It was perhaps because his emotional nature went so far deeper than that of ordinary men that Housman instinctively felt lonely with most of his contemporaries, who would be even less capable of imagining the intensity of his feelings than of rising to his intellectual level.[14]

"Is my team ploughing?" was set to music by Dr. Vaughan Williams, but he cut out the football verses, and Housman objected strongly. "How would he like me to cut two bars of his music?" he asked belligerently!

Laurence Housman made it plain that "If truth in hearts that perish" (*ASL* XXXIII) was not a tribute to Sophie Becker, as has been affirmed by Percy Withers, Grant Richards, and others.[15]

Mr. Withers' picture of Miss Becker as A. E. H.'s "lost lady of old days"[16] is a false presentation, due in part to Mr. Withers' sentimentalism, and in part to his naïve determination to center Housman's affections on a woman. Miss Becker could not have given A. E. H. the soothing, comfortable friendship upon which he counted, if he had been in the least in love with her, in the ordinary interpretation of the word. Like his mother, Miss Becker was unselfishly interested in him and had a remarkable ability to understand him. These two women, his mother and Miss Becker, were the women that Housman loved and trusted most during his lifetime; he loved them in something of the same manner, a love based on confidence and complete detachment from sexual excitement. As Housman grew older, his natural unhappiness and loneliness poured out in letters to Miss Becker, but he said when she died that he was glad. "She is the last of my great friends to leave this unsatisfactory world," was his comment when she passed away at ninety.

"If truth in hearts that perish" is found in three rough drafts, all from Notebook A. Marginal words not finally used mark the mood and theme of the poem better than the final draft. At the bottom of the page, these apparently unrelated words appear: "sighing," "grieving," "endless toil," and "hopeless pain." These are not words connected with friendship, but with hopeless and tortured love.[17]

Because A. E. H. considered sex his greatest trial, he would certainly have preferred not to have any dealings with it. Its disturbing effect on the life of the intellect he regarded as an extreme inconvenience, and certainly he would have been much happier if he had never allowed it to trouble him. He had many objections to life, both social and sexual, as "some brute and blackguard" had made it, but of these, sex was worst.

Mr. Laurence Housman is of the opinion that his brother's meaning in speaking of "the primal fault" was the initial mistake in creating the world at all, and in some of the poems there is much reason for this opinion; but in *ASL* XXXIII, the cause of unhappiness—the curse of man—is clearly linked with an unfortunate type of passion that induces a guilt complex towards sexual relations. The whole body of Housman's poetry proves that the poet's interpretation of "the original fault" was in one way or another connected with sex, and in this opinion Housman resembled Gide. But Housman suffered from none of Gide's exhibitionism and his desire to turn a spotlight on himself by using his creative work as a confessional. Gide believed, as did Housman in his innermost heart, that certain abnormalities in sexual expression due to mental attitudes are to a great extent not abnormal, but natural. Gide declared openly that since the nature of abnormal people is not "normal" according to conventional standards, nevertheless these so-called "abnormals" are really a part of the natural scheme of things, and should be considered as such.[18] These affirmations are clearly opposed to "the laws of God and man," and therefore hostile public opinion has operated against the "abnormals" who represent these unconventionalities. Social opprobrium has made them warped and secretive, having always to pretend to be what they really are not. In this opinion Gide was influenced as much by the Greek philosophy, centering upon the *Corydon* of Socrates, as Housman was, but he was much more outspoken about it than his English contemporary, for he had not been raised in the lap of Victorianism.

Both men believed that if these victims dubbed "abnormals" had been allowed to enjoy the same freedom as that practiced by the Greeks of old, they might in their own way work out a harmony of living which would be no less bearable than that achieved by the "normals." Since in their opinion all life was not very desirable, no matter how it was lived, they thought every man had a right to strike a compromise with his own fate, and to adapt himself to his private scheme of living.

Housman's pity for "abnormals" comes clear in the poem that he wrote during the Oscar Wilde trial, which occurred while Housman was finishing *A Shropshire Lad*. This poem was published as *AP* XVIII, "Oh, who is that young sinner with the handcuffs on his wrists?" The poem appears in Notebook B, sheets 16 and 17, in pencil drafts with many erasures and changes. Notebook E, sheet 8, shows a fair copy in ink, which fact suggests that Housman considered it for publication in *Last Poems,* but even then, in 1922, could not bring himself to include it.

More than ten years before *Si le grain ne meurt* was published by Gide (1911) A. E. H. had written "Oh, who is that young sinner . . . ?" The sinner was an "abnormal" like Oscar Wilde, and the theme of the poem is the reason for his imprisonment. The horrible curiosity of the crowd at the Wilde trial, feasting on the perversions of which Wilde was accused; the humiliation and tor-

ture to which Wilde was subjected for his "nameless and abominable" abnormality; the manner in which Wilde recklessly uncov-
ered himself in the deplorable trial—all of these Housman knew
by heart, and they made him even more compassionate than he
otherwise would have been.

But in one respect he did not portrary Wilde truly; the lines "Oh
a deal of pains he's taken and a pretty price he's paid/To hide his
poll or dye it of a mentionable shade" (l. 9-10) unconsciously iden-
tify Housman, not Wilde. Wilde was notably flamboyant and
defiant in defense of his actions that involved Lord Alfred Douglas,
and for his recklessness he paid the penalty not only in the trial, but
in the years of imprisonment in Reading Gaol.

Unlike Gide, Housman had no hope of altering public opinion
towards "abnormals." He was convinced of the impossibility of it,
and he never chose to take on the role of a preacher, a thankless
job, he believed, as when he said in "The Carpenter's Son" (*ASL*
XLVII):

> Oh, at home had I but stayed
> 'Prenticed to my father's trade . . .
> I had not been lost . . .

Housman was never convinced in his own mind that abnormalities were sufficiently justifiable to fight for. Never in his life could
he escape his dour Victorian conscience. His early reading prescribed by his father and grandfather—the Bible stories and the
Psalms and Isaiah; Milton, Shakespeare, the ritual of the Church
of England—all were too deeply rooted in his innermost soul ever
to be superseded by a wholehearted espousal of liberties outside
the law. It was his own struggle against personal temptation to
live his own life in his own way that made him compassionate for
the men whose resistance was not as great as was his own. To

understand the abnormals he thought a new world would have to be created:

> And since, my soul, we cannot fly
> To Saturn nor to Mercury,
> Keep we must, if keep we can,
> These foreign laws of God and Man.
> —*LP* XII

Housman had returned alone to Shropshire—Ludlow, Shrewsbury, and Wenlock Edge—just after *ASL* was published in 1896. He had taken a peculiar delight in gazing long at the landscapes with which he was forever after to be associated. He also visited Wenlock alone in 1907, after his stepmother's funeral, and once more took a melancholy pleasure in imagining himself with the Roman of old that roamed its heights. Such solitary musings seemed necessary for him, helping him to overcome the waves of depression that engulfed and all but overwhelmed him at periods throughout his life. During his Wenlock journey in 1896 he wrote to Laurence:

> 5 Oct. 1896
> ... I ascertained by looking down from Wenlock Edge that Hughley Church could not have much of a steeple. (*ASL* LXI) But as I had already composed the poem and could not invent another name that sounded so nice, I could only deplore that the church at Hughley should follow the bad example of the church at Brou, which persists in standing on a plain after Matthew Arnold has said that it stands among mountains. ...

He dryly added:

> ... A new firm of publishers [Grant Richards] has written to me proposing to publish "the successor" of *ASL*. But as they don't also offer to write it, I have had to put them off. ...

Housman's fearful depressions moved him to agitated compassion for suicides. Because of his depreciation of life, he knew too

[163]

well why there were men who could not bear it at all, and said (*ASL* LXI) that he would not be lonely if he slept on the north side of Hughley Steeple (where the graves were set apart for slayers of themselves). The same compassion comes out in "Shot? so quick, so clean an ending" (*ASL* XLIV). During his "Purgatory Period," Housman had been almost overwhelmingly obsessed with the desire to kill himself, but was saved from it by native courage and ambition. The desire for death followed him all through life, though less insistently, and he told his friend A. S. F. Gow, that he wished he had never been born.[19]

Two tragic deaths darkened the life of Housman during the turn of the century. His youngest brother, Sergeant George Herbert Housman, was killed in the Boer War in 1901, and buried in the Veldt in South Africa. At the time, the Housman family received only the shocking news of his death, and it was not until the second World War that the pitiful and heroic details were found out by a nephew in a Paris hospital. Some of Housman's best poems resulted from this heartbreak, notably "Astronomy," *ASL* XVII.

Robert Housman, the companion of Alfred at Bromsgrove School, and the brother closest to him in age, died in 1905 as the result of an accident which would not have been fatal to a stronger man. Robert, who by 1905 was a brilliant professor of electrical engineering, went for his spring holiday in April to the ever hospitable home of his sister Kate at Bath, where her husband was headmaster of King Edward's School. Robert took her young sons fishing of mornings, and on one of these expeditions he slipped and fell into a cold stream. He reached home with a severe chill, followed by a high fever made worse by his asthmatic chest. The doctor recognized that pneumonia had developed, and in spite of Kate's frantic efforts, Robert died in three days.

Alfred was present at the burial of his brother, and at this time he helped Kate to select a family lot in Smallcombe Cemetery at Bath-wick, on the outskirts of Bath. The family monument was chosen later by means of a number of letters between Kate, Laurence, and Alfred, and the idea of having a sundial in the center of the plot was decided upon.

The sundial at Alfred's request was to be circumscribed by a passage from Ecclesiastes XII more notable for its pagan beauty than for its orthodoxy. The names were to be inserted on the face of the dial, with birth and death dates. But since the vicar had to be consulted as to the propriety of each new monument, it became necessary to submit the proposed dial for his approval. He objected to it as pagan and agnostic, but agreed to it, provided it was sur-mounted by a cross. This concession the family accepted, but when the monument was finally erected the cross was placed on the face of the dial, not standing perpendicular and hence not very notice-able. Probably the vicar did not like this, but so it stands, and will so remain. A. E. H.'s letter quoted here refers to this monument:

> 1 Yarborough Villa
> Pinner
> 26 May, 1908

My dear Laurence,

I enclose cheque for five guineas which Kate has asked me to send you towards the sundial in Bathwick cemetery. I was down there last Saturday: the stone looks well enough, but the dial is conspicuously marked with an advertisement of the Birming-ham Art Company, or whatever it is, which will have to be erased. The sign of our redemption, which has also been added, is less obnoxious, except that its addition is due to a lying priest. . . .[20]

Housman never wavered from his atheism, as this letter shows, but during the University College years he was ripening under the warming influence of success. He was remarkably tolerant to his students outside the classroom, under the compulsion of a growing compassion for them. He was developing deep sympathy for humanity, although he had not reached the place where he was willing to admit he needed it for himself. Mr. Eugene Davidson expressed well the new color of Housman's feeling:

> One thing characterized him more than love of beauty or bitterness, or stoicism—that was compassion. Compassion for the lad who thought the fair was held for him, and for the army of mercenaries who saved the sum of things for pay; for courage and cowardice; the suicide, and the young men playing games they would not play for long.[21]

In November, 1907, Alfred's stepmother died at Hereford after a two-year illness made comfortable by family donations. Alfred had helped with her medical expenses and he attended her funeral at Catshill. His home circle was not broken by death again until 1931.

As the twentieth century lengthened, the fame and occasional notoriety of Housman increased, for the many reviewers of his poems fought their usual pro and con battle. Highly controversial statements about *ASL* were printed: "false pastoralism,"[22] "the filthiest book I ever read,"[23] "triteness of technique equalled only by banality of thought,"[24] "an orgy of naturalism,"[25]—and on the other side, "All the great machinery of Greek purgation gathered into a dewdrop,"[26] "a devotee to the great Housman,"[27] "sparkling gems,"[28] "as nearly perfect as lyrics can hope to be,"[29] "the shadow of a great rock in the weary land of modern verse, so boundless and so bare."[30]

Housman was eager to read what everybody had to say about

him, though probably he was not much affected by their adverse criticisms. In 1936 when his belongings were gone through after his death, Laurence Housman found a large collection of clippings about his brother that dated as far back as the first edition of *ASL,* showing that these had been gathered and probably read with more or less cynical amusement; in fact, he had paid an annual fee to have them sent to him.

The close of the first decade of the twentieth century marks the end of Housman's crucial struggles. He had suffered and conquered a strange love, he had achieved an honored position at University College, and had won world recognition for two strongly opposed reasons: cold, keen scholarship, and passionate poetry. He was cruelly critical of himself even in the midst of emotional waves that battered him, and doggedly plotted his paradoxical course along an angry main where male warred with female, Cyrenaic with Stoic, Church of England creed with atheism, common sense with purple passion, and Latin scholarship with poetry.

Christopher Morley once said: "Poetry is the log of man's fugitive castaway soul upon a doomed and derelict planet."[31]

Nothing could describe more accurately the poetry of Housman than this definition. It fits his hopelessness, his anger at man's predicament expressed in his own "log"—his biographical poems— which read like a struggle charted against bleak tempest in a fruitless endeavor to find harbor and weigh anchor at last. All he could offer as a panacea for the bitterness of the voyage was its deliveress, death. Yet this philosophy was paradoxical to the real life he lived. He had adopted towards himself and his natural instincts an habitual attitude of the "normally minded." He felt overwhelmed with remorse when he thus viewed himself objectively, and he hid the flames of his passionate desires in solitude. Marcel

Proust's unpublished notebooks contain sections that describe Housman quite as minutely and fairly as Proust described himself:

When one is young, one is no more aware that one is homosexual than that he is aware he is a poet, a snob, or a bad lot. A homosexual is not a man who loves homosexuals, but merely a man who seeing a soldier, immediately wants to have him for a friend. Every man, in his beginnings, is centrifugal, eager to escape from himself, turning his gaze outwards, contemplating his dreams, and believing he receives his stimulus from outside himself. His eyes are fixed on some object far removed from himself . . . and he prefers to believe that his propensities are governed by its charms rather than by some defect in his own nervous make-up, some twist in his own temperament. Only when the thought that eddies about his *self* has come full circle, only when his intelligence has come into the open so that he can see himself from the outside as he sees other people, do the words, I am a snob, I am a homosexual, take form in his mind, even if they do not always find a way to his lips—for in the interval he has acquired sufficient hypocrisy to learn to speak a language which is more successful in deceiving the world about his true tastes than were the confidences which, at an earlier stage, when he did not know what they meant, he was led so imprudently to make. . . .[32]

But Housman, when his thoughts about himself had come to full circle, did not shut himself in a cork-lined room for the rest of his life, nor did he turn with feelings of repugnance from the society of average married men, nor did he look at men to find one with a shared taste for ardent friendship. He lived on alone in Byron Cottage, and concentrated upon the language of Latin instead of the language, venerable and strange, that has no words, is beset with difficulties, and so sadly hampers those who speak it.

Slowly and by painful degrees, the sexual vigor that harrassed him became diluted in the whirlpool of his daily activities and habits. But it was not actually lost; it was merely transferred elsewhere. With Housman it was concentrated in the Shropshire Lad, in his love for his nephews and his younger brothers, Basil and Herbert, and in his changed love for Jackson, a love which at last was refined into a chaste affection, of which he could speak, not without tears, but without embarrassment, in after years.

7

A New World Opens

AFTER THE PUBLICATION OF *A Shropshire Lad,* Housman began a long series of European trips which occurred during almost every year of his later life. They varied in length from two weeks to a month, and they were planned some time ahead. They furnished relief from the monotony of his routine and brightened the otherwise rather drab existence of a college don. Housman's happiest life, as well as his saddest, occurred in the world of his imagination, where he pondered over maps and routes of travel, and dreamed of the places he wanted to visit. France and Italy he explored thoroughly, and went as far east as Turkey. His first trip of importance came in the summer of 1897. Upon his return, he wrote to his stepmother his earliest impressions:

> 17 North Road, Highgate N.
> 22 Sept., 1897
> ... I came home yesterday after having been just a month away, at Paris, Rome, and Naples. ... What strikes one in Paris is the countless number of handsome streets, any five of which would constitute a fine town in England: imagine a place as well built as Edinburgh or Bath and practically about as large as London. Notre-Dame is hardly equal to Westminster Abbey, and none of the modern churches are anything like St. Paul's, but

the number of such buildings, interesting or beautiful, is much greater than in London; and London has nothing at all equivalent to the Louvre. . . . They make a great deal more of their river than we do of ours; it is all edged with handsome quays and crossed with handsome bridges.

When I got into Italy the weather was very hot, and remained so all the time I was there. . . . I went to Pompeii, which is more extensive than I thought, and to Vesuvius. . . . When you get to the cone you begin to hear an angry sound such as water will sometimes make in pipes, as if the mountain were gargling, or trying to talk but had stones in its mouth; which indeed it has. . . . It is much the highest hill in the neighborhood, so you see all the country, vineyards and olive yards and woods of young trees, dotted with white or pink houses: into this green carpet the lava runs out on every side in long grey tongues, as if you had spilt an inkpot. There had been an overflow about a month before I was there. . . .

Here I have said nothing about Rome, which I liked much the best of the three; but I have to go into town this morning, so I will stop here for the present. . . .

The European trip made in 1897 began a long series of holidays that became Housman's main recreation and may have saved his sanity. It was his custom to spend three weeks or a month of every summer in France, choosing each year a new district, exploring it by car, and studying the architecture, the local dishes and the local wines. When air travel came later he usually flew to Paris and went back to London by plane.[1] His first plane trip occurred October 3, 1920, and he wrote an entertaining account of it to his sister Kate:

3 Oct. 1920

. . . Well, I flew there and back all right, and am never going by any other route in future. Surrey from overhead is delightful, Kent and France less interesting, the Channel disappointing, because on both days there was too much mist to let both shores be seen at once. It was rather windy, and the machine sometimes imitated a ship at sea (though that is due to differing densities of atmosphere and not to wind) but in a very life-like manner. Members of your unhappy sex were sick, however. The noise is great, and I alighted rather deaf, not having stuffed my ears with the cottonwool provided. Nor did I put on the life-belt which they oblige one to take. To avoid crossing the 60 miles of sea which a straight flight would involve, they go from Croydon to Hythe, Hythe to Boulogne, Boulogne to Paris. You are in the air $2\frac{1}{2}$ hours: from Leicester Square to your hotel in Paris you take little more than four; though on the return journey we were 2 hours late in starting because the machine required repairs, having been damaged on the previous day by a passenger who butted his head through the window to be sick. My chief trouble is that what I now want is no longer a motor and a chauffeur but an aeroplane and a tame pilot, which I suppose are more expensive. The weather in France was beautiful, though I read of storms in London. Unfortunately I got poisoned at a restaurant and was out of action for the best part of two days. . . .[2]

For nineteen years now, Mrs. Trim had brought Housman his morning *London Times,* and after a discreet knock, had fled back to her kitchen. One cold foggy December day in 1910, the paper carried a piece of news that was destined to alter this comfortable routine. When Housman turned the pages in front of his cozy fire, he discovered that Professor J. E. B. Mayor, who had succeeded Munro in the Latin chair at Cambridge and held it for thirty-eight years, had died. He may not have thought of standing for the post, for he required encouragement before he would stand, and his election was not inevitable. However, to the future delight at any rate of the younger scholars of the University, he was appointed!

Housman, who habitually "trained himself for ill, not good," was surprised when he got the appointment as if a bombshell had struck him. Again he was torn by inner struggle. Should he remain, as happy as he ever expected to be, in this fixed area of calm, where he had learned to find satisfaction in a tolerable adjustment to the routine of living, an adjustment that had grown on him and become familiar? Or should he break away and challenge a new environment, new faces, new living quarters, and certainly new opportunities?

Again he faced a struggle of paradoxes: his reserve and dislike of change warred with his ambition and desire for fame. He was rather indifferent to the handsome increase of salary Cambridge offered, but highly responsive to the position of authority in the classical world which the Kennedy Professorship assured. The post was named for "old Dr. Kennedy," long-time professor of Cambridge University, who wrote a famous Latin Grammar, and who died in 1889.

For nearly a month Housman struggled to make up his mind, and characteristically discussed his dilemma with nobody. In early March, he wrote his letter of acceptance with one proviso: that he should not take up permanent residence at Cambridge until autumn. Cambridge agreed, and Housman wrote to his brothers Laurence and Basil and sister Kate that he was to go to Trinity in October. They were unreservedly delighted at the news, although Basil had his doubts. He wondered if his brother was making a mistake. He believed that so far as Alfred's private life was concerned, he would be happier to remain in the comfortable niche he had cut out for himself in London.

The ovations which Housman received before he left University College were sincere and numerous, but mingled with regret. His Latin students dined and wined him, and presented him with the "Malt does more than Milton"[3] silver cup which he always treasured. He was entertained by the Dining Club of professors, who presented him with a life-long membership. He received congratulatory letters from Ker, Platt, and The University of London, with which institution University College was now affiliated.

Oxford University recognized his appointment by letter, and

also by an editorial in *The Oxford Magazine* of March, 1911, which read in part as follows:

> Nothing went wrong at Cambridge last week when the Electors to the Chair of Latin elected Mr. A. E. Housman. Mr. Housman is the greatest living critic of Latin poetry; and it is fitting that such a man should fill the chair of Munro. . . . If we bred a great man, yet it took us a long time to find it out. . . . Cambridge has invested in genius; and that, after all, is of all investments the safest.

The "plough" in Greats at Oxford over twenty years before had made a furrow deep enough to bring forth a man unique in his own age or in any age; in its wake had appeared dramatically a great scholar and a great poet in one and the same person.

Housman was fifty-two years old when he put on the regalia of Kennedy Professor of Latin at Cambridge, and became Fellow of Trinity College. He was already acquainted with a number of men at Cambridge because of his membership in the Cambridge Philological Society, having read papers to it at intervals since 1889. Mr. Gow first met him on one of these occasions in 1910, but was disappointed in his appearance: his height was unimpressive, (Gow was tall; Housman an average five foot eight); and though later study revealed the fine lines of face and skull, Gow thought Housman seemed rather commonplace on first view, and that he heightened that effect by his impassive silence. His hazel eyes, expressive and framed with heavy dark brows above, suggested the fires within that otherwise were smothered. Housman never smoked, and at dinner had to be spurred by good wine to talk at all, and almost never could be led into small talk, which he apparently knew nothing about.

He was a man of fixed habits, extremely shy, ill at ease among strangers. Previous to the Revised Statutes of 1878, Fellows of Colleges at Cambridge were not allowed to marry, on pain of losing their fellowships; the removal of this restriction meant nothing to Housman, who was a bachelor by choice. If the wild idea of marriage had entered his head, he could have taken a charming old house near the "Backs" and the Cam, with a view of winding water and arching trees and green grass—beauties he could have enjoyed all the rest of his life. As it was, he did not have much choice, and was allotted a small suite of three rooms on the third and top floor of Whewell (pronounced Yule) Court, stairway K, across the street from the gateway to Trinity. The building was a part of the College, but masked its identity by having let the ground floor front to tradesmen, who advertised their monotonous wares in the windows. It was constructed around a square of ground within, covered with grass and well-defined walks.

Forty-four stone steps led up to his small apartment, steps indented by many predecessors who from the looks of the place might have been monks climbing to their citadel. The stairway was a spiral affair. From the ground floor the door of the suite occupied by Housman was visible three flights up, a weary climb. But he complained not at all: he had always cared little for ease or beauty of environment, so far as the appointments of living were concerned; or if he did care, he was stoical about disciplining himself against comfort. His Whewell Court rooms were barren and bleak, which a bachelor's rooms do not need to be; later they were littered with books and papers, which a scholar's rooms do not necessitate. But Housman accepted the rooms because they were remote and off the beaten path; they allowed the privacy that he demanded. He was to live in this suite for the next twenty-four years.

His dormer windows looked out upon the dreary prospect of housetops, chimneys full of rooks and an occasional pigeon; smoke, and a couple of hopeless trees fighting for survival among the cobblestones below. The closest approach from town to the rooms was by the Sidney Street entrance.

He went to Cambridge at intervals during the summer of 1911, and wrote Laurence from there:

11 June 1911

... Although I had very few official duties during the Cambridge term I was much occupied with social duties, which are a deal worse, and either from the climate or the heat was generally tired when I was not occupied, so that I have not thanked you for the proofs of your play.[4]

He was being acclimatized, but the process wore him out!

He finally moved from Pinner in the early part of October with his etchings of "Melancholia" and "The Knight, Death and the Devil," his picture of Jackson's boating crew, the portrait of his Holden ancestor, his books and papers, and his silver cup.

It was hard for him to feel at home in his new suite. There was actually no sitting-room. Housman used the room that faced Sidney Street for a study, and here for many years he got along with the commonest sort of furniture: an American roll-top oak desk, ugly but useful, and several chairs and tables of a strictly utilitarian nature. The walls were soon lined with books, however; the chairs were full of them, and piles of manuscripts surrounded him, then and ever. The bedroom was narrow and dark, extremely austere, with no conveniences except the strictly Victorian wash-bowl set which he really liked to use, and which he always employed for his morning sponge bath—an "honouring of tradition" he once said. The other room was an all-purpose one, with a convertible dining table and chairs, a sideboard, an arm chair or two, and a comfortable but nondescript sofa. This room too as time passed was lined with books from floor to ceiling. Presumably Housman did most

[176]

of his meeting with callers in this commonplace cubicle, which was on the Whewell Court side of the unit. He was served his breakfast there by the bedmaker, and sometimes his luncheon, when he was working hard on research material, or was ill.

He was always plagued by throat infections, and seldom a winter passed without at least one of these visitations. Unless seriously ill, he always took his dinner in Trinity Hall, sitting at the Fellows' Table, or High Table, at the end of the room at right angles to the long side table. Through long habit impervious to the metallic clatter of voices and dishes, he did a good deal of his entertaining here, usually of men who were visiting him on some matter connected with publications, or scholarly conferences. He entertained women almost never. Food in Hall was excellent, and the wines, usually chosen by a committee of dons, later including himself, were an educational experience. If the don's committee refused to pay for as expensive wines as Housman wanted, he often made up the difference from his own pocket, especially in purchasing the Madeira and Burgundy.

About a half-mile separated the Whewell Court rooms from Hall, and the Latin classrooms were about the same distance away —both located within Trinity Court. The average man would think he had taken quite enough exercise in getting around his daily duties under such circumstances; not so with Housman. He immediately resumed his afternoon walks, usually across the Cam river, breathtakingly lovely in springtime, with its blossoms and swans and green banks, and out into open country, not so lovely, but one of the prosperous agricultural sections of England.

Casual acquaintances at Cambridge were disappointed in him at first. They had expected a person very different—a man who would thrill and fascinate them, as *A Shropshire Lad* had done— but here was a sad-eyed, grim looking don, slight and easily overlooked. Very few people realized that behind his silent mask there was a man who yearned for companionship, because he had none of the external art of making friends—no small talk, no easy give and take, no passing cigars around, no ready smiles. There is humorous truth in A. C. Benson's summary of the impression Housman made on him: "He appears to be descended from a long succession of maiden aunts."[5] His students in class were the first ones to recognize him for what he was, and although they were irked because no likeness to his poetry could be discovered in his lectures and he never made any reference to himself as a poet, the discerning ones soon recognized a mind of remarkable distinction and precision. But both faculty and students overcame their early prejudice against him as he became more at home with them.

Nothing in his outer demeanor suggested the great struggle it had been for him to enter the new world of Cambridge. If it was hard for his associates to understand him, it was much harder for him to accept them, and it took several years for him to feel relieved of nervous tension at social gatherings. Platt declared once that Housman would have been a happier man if he had never left University College, although at Cambridge he had found an "asylum" (his own word) for the most part hospitable and generous. His schedule of teaching was not very burdensome, and he was allowed time to pursue his research, and to progress with his greatest contribution to the world of Latin scholarship, his five volume *Manilius,* produced in all over a period of thirty years, as well as to continue studies in Juvenal, Catullus, Horace, Lucan, and others.

In Cambridge Housman lectured regularly twice a week, so that his courses in the Michaelmas and Lent Terms consisted of about sixteen lectures, those in the Easter Term perhaps of twelve. He usually repeated courses at intervals of about four years, and during the last ten years, he regularly repeated, in each of two academic years, a course on the special books prescribed for textual study in Part II of the Classical Tripos for those years. One of these was his valuable *Application of Thought to Textual Criticism,* especially helpful for teachers and would-be writers of criticism.

The Latin writers he lectured upon were Catullus, Horace, Cicero, Juvenal, Lucan, Lucretius, Martial, Ovid, Persius, and Plautus. Surprisingly enough, he did not lecture on his greatest research work, *Manilius,* nor upon his old love, Propertius.

The subject matter dealt with in regard to these writers was intricate and highly specialized; it covered all sorts of knowledge from the horoscope of Augustus and the time of revolution of Venus, Mercury, and Mars, to such matters as disjunctives coupling interrogatives and choriambus and ditrochaeus in dactylo-epitrite rhythm! To read the complete notes in one of his criticisms appalls the average student. Here was a scholar not only broad in knowledge but mercilessly accurate in his findings and determinations.

Very shortly after Housman went to Cambridge, in the fall of 1911, he declined to be nominated for election as a Fellow of the British Academy.[6] Why he should have taken this action, God alone knows. Perhaps to his mind such election would have been demeaning.

The students in his classes were certainly much more worthy of his mettle than those of University College, a fact which took some drudgery out of lecturing. During his later years, there was usually a row of dons present as auditors, but, attending strictly to his manuscript, he did not look at them any more than he did the regular students.

To illustrate how completely he separated textual criticism from literature in his lectures, and how sternly he kept himself to criticism alone, one amazing deviation was recounted by Mrs. T. W. Pym, a student of Housman's classical courses at Cambridge. She relates an unforgettable incident when Housman was discussing Horace, Odes iv 7:

> During my time at Cambridge, I attended his lectures for two years. At five minutes past eleven he used to walk to the desk, open his manuscript, and begin to read. At the end of the hour he folded his papers and left the room. He never looked at us or at the row of dons in the front. One morning in May, 1914, when the trees of Cambridge were covered with blossoms, he reached in his lecture Ode VII in Horace's Fourth Book, "*Diffugere Nives, redeunt iam gramina campis.*" This ode he dissected with the usual display of brilliance, wit, and sarcasm. Then for the first time in two years he looked up at us, and in quite a different voice said:
>
> "I should like to spend the last few minutes considering this ode simply as poetry."
>
> He then read the ode aloud with deep emotion, first in Latin, and then in an English translation of his own. [*MP* V]
>
> "That," he said hurriedly, almost like a man betraying a secret, "I regard as the most beautiful poem in ancient literature," and walked quickly from the room.[7]

In discussing this incident, Laurence Housman said that his brother's fear of betraying emotion extended itself to the lecture room, and that he avoided for the most part any display of feeling which could be ridiculed or misinterpreted. No doubt this fear was well-founded, for after the instance recalled by Mrs. Pym, she said a young man left the class that day with the remark: "Do you know I thought for a minute the old fellow *was going to cry!* I felt quite uncomfortable." Housman certainly would have been uncomfortable if he had known the student said it. Would they sense that he was a Pirithöus, still in chains?

As time passed, the circle of friends Housman made slowly widened. Of these, Mr. A. S. F. Gow and Mr. R. V. Lawrence, Bursar of Trinity, were closest. The Master of Trinity, Sir J. J. Thomson, he grew to know intimately later.

Housman's friendship with the Thomsons dated from his membership in the Family Club of Trinity College. The Family Club is a dining organization, Jacobite in origin, founded at Trinity during the period when the Stuart family was banished to France. The first members were Jacobites, in sympathy with the Stuarts and especially with the deposed king. The club goes back, therefore, to the days of William of Orange in the seventeenth century. At that time, it would have been a risky thing to drink to the deposed king openly; hence the Family Club was founded and given a name that sounded trite and domestic, but really referred to the Stuarts. When the members met, they drank "to the family over the water," using no names; but even that was risky on account of the presence of waiters, so they disguised the toast by merely passing their wine glasses over their fingerbowls to indicate symbolically that they were drinking to "the family over the water."

This extremely exclusive club persisted at Trinity long after the need for it was gone; it exists today, and to be one of the twelve members is a mark of great distinction. The club when Housman belonged to it had the primary aim of "good conversation, good food, and good wine." Each member entertained the group once a year, and the twelve meetings occurred during University terms, never outside of terms. The hosts went to a great deal of trouble to select the food and wines, which were chosen with the discretion of the connoisseur. Occasionally outside guests were invited, but no one from the University faculty. If the host were married, he could, for instance, invite his wife and daughter to the dinner. Perhaps the reasons for this exclusiveness were humane, and were observed in deference to possible hurt feelings if the single invitation did not lead to a membership, which it almost certainly did not.

Mrs. Joan Thomson Charnock, daughter of Sir J. J. Thomson, as a young girl attended a number of these dinners, and after the death of her mother in 1951, she was probably more qualified than any other living woman to describe the club as it was when Housman, who was a loved friend of her youth, belonged to it. She attended some of the dinners when her father was host, and went to two of them when Housman entertained the club.

The dinners she described occurred in Housman's rooms in Whewell Court; the food was choice and well served, and the wines!—according to the Housman tradition, the wines were superb. Burgundy, Madeira, and port were Housman's favorite dinner wines, and when his dinners occurred, Mrs. Charnock remembers the Madeira as especially fine. At his death, much of his Madeira he left to Sir J. J. Thomson and he bequeathed the rest of his wines to Trinity College.[8]

It was at one of these Family Club dinners, given by her father, that Mrs. Charnock, then a girl of fifteen, first met Housman. The dinner was arranged, and the appointment day came; then suddenly an unexpected and important guest descended upon the Thomsons. Thirteen would be at the table! Not particularly sympathetic with superstition, Lady Thomson still felt that it would be more comfortable to seat fourteen; thus her daughter Joan came to be present. In addition to being very young, she was also somewhat timid. Highly intellectual, an eager listener and a remarkably clear thinker, she had been used to association with the select minds of Cambridge all her life, and had developed a mature viewpoint, but at the moment she was nervous.

Seeing her apart from the group, however, and sensing she was as ill at ease as he was, Housman came up and talked to her. He did the amazing thing of making small talk, which he notably detested, in order to put her at her ease. He succeeded; they were soon conversing; and Housman, his face alight, was sending out peals of that beautiful silvery laughter that those who knew him intimately remember with delight. Places at table were not assigned that night, but as usual, the host was at the head of the board. Housman chose his seat next to Joan, and she customarily sat next to Housman at the subsequent dinners of the club which she attended.

Mr. A. S. F. Gow is a member of this club, into which no new member can be elected unless the vote be unanimous. Among other important members when A. E. H. was one of them, Mrs. Charnock recalls Mr. S. C. Roberts, now Master of Pembroke College, who is also a writer, and who knew Housman very well; Professor Newell, who has since died, and the former librarian of Cambridge, Mr. A. F. Scholfield.

Mrs. Charnock said that the Family Club dinners of Housman were long remembered. There was an unusual touch of distinction about them; the entrements and sauces were exotic. Housman was fond of serving duck and fish, and always demanded the chef to blend the flavor of the humble onion in meats and salads, for he used the onion much as the French do, from whom he procured a number of his choicest recipes. He often made the salad himself; that is, he tossed it at the table, and blended his ingredients for the dressing there, usually just before the guests were seated. Bread and butter he abominated, but served hard rolls and biscuits instead. At such dinners he invariably was a delightful host, apparently happy and full of animation.

Mrs. Charnock said that she had just returned from London when she was invited to one of his dinners. While in the city she had been taken to a one-act play of Barrie's. She told Housman at table that the play was not attractive to her, because the chief female character was hard and disagreeable. She described this character to him, and said that she was unbelievable, that no woman could have such a heart. He received her remarks in a deprecative mood, but when it came time to leave, he said goodbye to her with these earnest words: "Keep your good opinion of your own sex." This sentence ended one of the most satisfactory talks that she ever had with him.

Often over the years Housman took means of showing his fondness for this intellectual young girl whom he found congenial. At one Family Club dinner when the Master of Trinity was host, the lecturer Charles David Seligman was a guest at the last minute, because he had arrived unexpectedly for a series of talks to be delivered the next day; and Joan had to give up her place to him. When she entered the drawingroom after dinner, the face of Housman glowed with friendly interest as he came up at once and said: "Sorry you were not at the dinner." He then piloted her to a corner of the room and talked to her about poetry for an hour. Incidentally, he remarked that he had no interest in first editions of books. He said that people who collect first editions are usually so stupid they have no idea of what the contents are. He turned sharply around to her, his eyes snapping.

"Why, they even pay as much for *mine* as for a first edition of *Matthew Arnold!*" He told her then of his distaste for autographing books, and how superficial he considered the request.

This was spontaneous and worthwhile conversation, showing that Housman was perfectly at ease with Joan Thomson. She was fond of him and grateful to him for his friendship and he knew it. She could not understand why other people had a hard time talking to him, or could not talk to him at all. Once she overheard with amazement a conversation about a dinner where Housman had been one of the guests.

"Whatever did you do with Professor Housman?" asked a friend of the hostess, in honest admission of her own defeat at a similar occasion. Mrs. Charnock saw the ladies interchange helpless smiles.

Housman never showed the young Joan his darker side, as he

[184]

disclosed it to Mr. Gow; but he did give her occasional bursts of confidence. Most important of those was that he could not tolerate the idea of a man loving more than one woman in his life. There was nothing personal in this statement, although she interpreted it so at the time; it was not a declaration of a personal code. If it had been, he would not have said it; it was a general remark, made to bolster her faith in both men and women, a faith which Housman fostered in her and which he never ridiculed. She had an ingenuous outlook on life that both fascinated and amused him. He found her refreshing and lovely, and she did him good.

She recalled that when caught unaware, Housman often had a look of intense sadness on his face, an expression that she sometimes glimpsed as she saw him pass the Thomson bay window on his way back from his afternoon walk across the Cam. But this sadness he never explained to her and he assiduously cultivated her faith and happiness in living. It was as if she might have been the daughter that he never had, and that he would have directed in these channels if his life had been different.

Mrs. Charnock's general description of Housman's appearance was suprisingly similar to that given by the sexton of Ludlow church:

> He looked like a tired army officer. He was erect, so erect that he seemed to be a soldier out of uniform, and his face was marked by struggle and battle, when it was in repose. However, the expression of his mouth could be singularly sweet and kind, and that is the expression I best remember.[9]

Housman felt the same protective interest for his sister Kate, whose home he visited with great pleasure; and for his brother Basil, whom he liked to visit often at Tardebigge after Basil had lost his health. The brothers frequently went upstairs together, from whence peals of laughter tantalized Basil's wife Jeannie below. "What *are* they so amused over?" she asked herself, her slightly twisted mouth curved upward in a sympathetic attempt to enjoy whatever delighted her beloved Basil. That the jokes were apt to be risque ones she never found out. The fact that Housman felt most comfortable and happy with his least sensitive and perceptive brother and sister who were more ordinary than the others suggests that he wished for a normalcy in his own life which he could never attain.

Mrs. Charnock felt very strongly that Housman was starving for love and affection, the kind of love that only his own home and family could have given him. She spoke of remembering one Christmas season when she observed him in the house of friends where there were children, and how he gently lifted a little boy upon his lap, and picked up his wooly toy from the floor; then holding the child carefully on one knee, with the toy poised on the other, he amused the small boy into bubbling delight, and apparently took pleasure in doing so.

"Mr. Housman had a happy look on his face as he held the boy," she said, "and I could not refrain from thinking that this was the life he was really fitted for, and that he had somehow unfortunately lost." Grant Richards also recalls similar occasions when the poet took great interest in the Richards' family of four.

Housman formed by degrees many literary friendships at Cambridge, which brought him satisfaction, if not affection or happiness. Some of these arose from the appreciation felt for his poetry, for example the one with Sir William Rothenstein. Others were of a purely scholastic nature as was the one with Dr. J. W. Mackail, eminent Latin scholar of Balliol College, Oxford, who lived in Kensington and who was the father of the novelist Angela Thirkell.

A few typical letters he wrote to Mackail over a fifteen-year period give insight into this kind of scholastic friendship which Housman carried on with the very few men he considered worthy of it. The subject of the first one is *Manilius*:

> Trinity College, Cambridge,
> 4 May, 1916.
>
> Dear Mackail,
>
> Many thanks for your notes. What I say at 113 is that the political oratory (rostus) has no business in the middle of forensic matters. As to *numerosis,* in 172, although I think *pro spatio magna* can mean "of a length proportional to the distance," I do not think that *magnus* could mean "great or small" without help, nor *numerosis* "many or few"; and if it could, what a thing to think of saying!
>
> *Longa dies* in 482 is the long day of midsummer.
>
> At 325 as a parallel to *gradus,* perhaps you would prefer Sophocles Ai. 7-8.
>
> It is not for equality but for sense that I adopt the future in 361, as in 333.
>
> Yours sincerely,
> A. E. Housman

Though written with a twinkle in the eye, there was certainly nothing personal in that letter, nor in this one, sent to Mackail, 28 February, 1920:

> .... In reading Virgil I often cry: "Out, hyperbolic fiend! how vexest thou this man! . . . but if epic poets are debarred from useless epithets they will never fill their 12 or 24 or 48 books. . . . Virgil's besetting sin is the use of words too forcible for his thoughts, and the *moritura* of Aen. XII 55 makes me blush for him whenever I think of it . . .

This comment is especially interesting: "Virgil's besetting sin is the use of words too forcible for his thoughts," an error Housman avoided in his own poetry.

An interesting bit of news about *ASL* is found in a letter to Mackail written 23 March, 1926: "While the book (*ASL*) was printing, I took out five pieces, [one of these was "The Sage to the Young Man"] and put in the three now published as XXXIV, XXXVII, and XLI. . . . LX originally bore the title 'The Return of the Native.'"

A more personal letter to Mackail is typical of the length of A. E. H.'s private letters to casual friends, letters which were usually limited to the making or breaking of appointments:

> Trinity College, Cambridge
> 26 D., 1929

Dear Mackail,
It was very unlucky that I was out when you called. If you, or you and the Lord Lieutenant, happen to be in Cambridge one of these days about 1 o'clock, we could lunch off our cold Christmas sideboard: boar's head, game pie, beef, ham, tongue, plum pudding, mince pies.

> Yours sincerely,
> A. E. Housman

Shades of the good old days, before rations and budgets were bringing the Cambridge dons their share of austerity!

He wrote on the completion of *Manilius*:

> Trinity College
> Cambridge
> 18 Dec. 1930

Dear Mackail,
I am glad of your approbation and grateful for your condolence and congratulations; though the condolence is not needed, for I am always glad when a job is finished. I shall now be getting out an *editio minor,* just text and apparatus in one volume, but it will be a thin octavo, not suitable for your genteel pocket, as I want a roomy page. I do not mean to impoverish myself any more for the public weal, and I have no doubt that either of the

University presses would undertake it. The Cambridge Press has volunteered to produce a new edition of the Juvenal, which is now printing.

Yours sincerely,
A. E. Housman

Housman's dislike of publishers' high prices comes out here; again to Mackail:

17 Dec. 1931
. . . . I hope you have not been buying my second edition, [*Juvenal*] which our press sells at an absurd price: they overpay their workmen and therefore overcharge their customers . . .

And a sad personal sentence from one more letter to Mackail:

12 Dec. 1933
. . . . I am so much better than I have been in the course of this year that I do not like to boast myself "very poorly," but I am uncomfortable, and depressed by slow progress . . . .

These letters were presented to Trinity College by Mrs. Mackail in April, 1946, ten years after A. E. H.'s death.[10]

Housman's friendship with Sir William Rothenstein was based not on scholastic interests, but upon Rothenstein's faculty for making acquaintances with famous people who interested him as men rather than as geniuses, although he thought that genius went along with the individual himself and could not be dissociated from him. He had a remarkable ability to read character, and to put personality into his portraits. His sympathies were broad and liberal beyond those of most men, a fact which made him tolerant towards the intolerant and unusual. Rothenstein admits that he was flattered by the fact Housman granted him the key to his inner circle, but at the same time, he certainly tried Rothenstein's patience sorely. For all the friendship between these two men, it was one-sided; the poet always withholding himself, ungracious about sitting for portraits, and unwilling to return favor for favor unless it suited him.

As a result, Rothenstein tried over and over to capture Housman on paper unsuccessfully. Housman eluded him, disliked Rothenstein's drawings of him, and never missed a chance to say so. But he maintained friendship with Rothenstein through it all, entertained him occasionally, knew the family well enough to jot notes once in a while to Mrs. Rothenstein, and one summer once or twice walked over to visit them in the country, where they were staying not far from Woodchester, during the time that he was a house guest of his childhood friends, Minnie and Edith Wise.

Rothenstein tried in all five times to draw Housman but none of his portraits can compare with the single delineation that Francis Dodd accomplished in 1926, four years after the publication of *Last Poems*. This great portrait, seated three-fourths to left, hangs in St. John's College, Oxford.

Rothenstein in his *Men and Memories* succeeded in picturing Housman better in words than he did with the pencil:

> Housman, I believe, had a secret fund of affection, but a certain frustrated and sombre twist in his nature kept it in cold storage; he certainly discouraged any show of affection towards himself. Like McTaggart of Trinity, he was an unashamed Tory and a bitter patriot. He had scant sympathy with idealists, since every ideal has its inherent danger, being in conception one thing, in action another. The horizon, however high a man may climb, remains on a level with his eye. In the perfectibility of mankind Housman had no belief; there was the beauty of Nature, and here and there men living with courage and decency. More one could not expect.[11]

Rothenstein gave Housman his own fine celestial globe just after he had finished Book Four of *Manilius*. Housman was looking everywhere for one, prior to working on Book Five, the section most astronomical, so that the gift was a godsend. Nevertheless he curtly refused to grant Rothenstein a small favor afterwards when the artist invited him to write a five-hundred word sketch of Thomas Hardy for a book of portraits he was publishing. He also refused, after a great deal of bickering, to sit for a memorial portrait of the distinguished men chosen as Hardy's pallbearers.[12] Rothenstein finally gave up the project, worn out with the reluctance of Barrie and Housman to cooperate with him, although the other men in the group including Baldwin and Bernard Shaw, gave whole-hearted support to the plan.

There were bound to be many uncongenial acquaintances that Housman had to put up with because of his position. Some were casual, as when important guests were placed by Housman at High Table, where they could not get a word out of him, and where some of them, indeed, could not think of a word to say to him, as was the case with J. M. Barrie; or worse, when the feeling aroused by the guest's presence made Housman acrimonious, as was apt to happen when he was near Frank Harris. Housman was a man of intense likes and dislikes, and sometimes just a glance at a stranger was enough to condemn him for all time. His dislike for Frank Harris, John Galsworthy and Maurice Hewlett was based partly on a distaste for what they wrote. Galsworthy he detested, and almost refused to be a pallbearer at Hardy's funeral when he found out that Galsworthy was also to officiate in that capacity.

There was nothing half way about Housman, for if he gave his heart, he was eternally loyal about it, but if he withheld it, he could be cold to the point of rudeness. He was notably rude to people who, it seemed to him, were trying to seek him out as a curiosity, or trying in some way to ingratiate themselves for personal gain, types which he usually could ferret out with one unerring glance.

When one such offensive chap said: "I have the pleasure of knowing your brother Laurence," Housman turned on his heel and whipped out in reply: "Knowing my brother Laurence is no introduction to *me*."

The regular round of dinner parties at Cambridge was a great trial to Housman, and often they proved as great a trial to the hosts that invited him. He was asked often because of his dinner party status: the Kennedy Professor and Fellow of Trinity was important, too high up in the hierarchy of notables to overlook. After a few agonized attempts from the hostess to draw him out, he was left pretty much to his own devices, and he waded through the seven or eight courses—touching the high spots of soup, lobster, oysters, The Main Course, followed by pudding—and emerged able to cope with the final flourishes of fruit, cheese and nuts, bolstered up, of course, by the wine and brandy that accompanied them. It was a world for the epicure, that time before 1914, the end of an era when women swept grandly in to meals which they had planned but never seen until they came to the table, and where men adorned their persons, and fostered their dignity by learned conversation interspersed with gossip.

The Cambridge circle was certain of its own perfection, though it would not have said so; to be received therein was to join a group of grandees who were quick to look down their noses at those whom they deemed inferior. That Housman was received, yes even cultivated by this circle is evidence that he had passed the board of censorship with regard to dress, manners, and morals. After all, worse things could be than silence, and after a time, the men discovered that Housman was an excellent listener, which endeared him to them, as they all loved the sound of their own voices. He gradually lost his distrust of their intentions, and as time put their respect beyond question, he melted a good deal, and passed quips with the ones he knew best. But he was never a diplomat, and contradicted them with asperity if he wanted to.

When Housman appeared in top hat and tails he was an impeccable figure, turned out, as the ladies had to admit, quite suitably. For the first time in his life, he bought all the clothes he wanted. He went to the best Cambridge tailor (though some of the Fellows and Heads patronized only London tailors, and appeared with the finest Bond Street could offer on their backs). He was fitted to formal attire, and to striped pants with black coats to match for less formal occasions. He bought fine tweed suits for his lectures, and surmounted them by the most elegant quality of regalia he could find. He was notably fussy about his regalia, and was known to buy new when some very important occasion seemed to demand that he should look his best, not for his own sake, but in order not to bring shame to the Cambridge procession of professors. Yet he never gave the impression of being overdressed, and casual inspection would pronounce him to be a very modest looking man. There is something terribly tragic in the clothes of the dead, and when his brother Laurence went through his things in the summer of 1936, he was surprised at the number of clothes he had, all neatly and silently standing upright on their racks, giving testimony to the fact that the clothes had become a part of his mask, so that they looked like him, as if a strange ghostly emanation from their wearer clung to them.

In December of 1916 Housman was made a member of the Trinity Wine Committee, and on New Year's Day, 1917, he journeyed to London on the important and to him, very pleasant mission of tasting and testing wines with the other members of the Wine Committee. Later on, Housman often supplemented the supply of the finest out of his own pockets, if his tastes called for more expensive wine than the faculty budget was able to pay for.

A common interest in books and wines drew Housman and his publisher, Grant Richards, close together. Richards had a beautiful Hungarian wife and four children all of whom Housman liked, and he often visited them in their own home, or in summer cottages they took from time to time along the coast of Cornwall overlooking the Channel. The Richards family liked picnics, and they discovered that Housman was unusually cheerful on such expeditions, willing to scramble up and down to remote coves as if he were a boy again, then wandering off for a stroll by himself.

Mrs. Richards was one of the few women that Housman entertained at Cambridge. On October 31, 1916, Mrs. Richards was his guest for the first time, during a bookselling tour the Richards made through a war-scarred England and Scotland. Housman was delighted to have her, and although there was thirty-one years difference in their ages, he found himself at ease with her, perhaps because of their mutual interests in her children. She had reason to be grateful to him, the next year, when on one visit to the Richards home, Housman defended the youngsters from a sizeable viper, which coiled and hissed at their bare legs. Like a flash he was on it, and attacked it with such energy that he broke his stick. Later on he had occasion to thank Richards for a new cane: "October 23, 1917. I am grateful though ashamed to receive your present of a new stick. The old one perished nobly in the destruction of a venomous serpent, and I only hope the new one may make as good an end."[13]

His friendship with Richards lessened in later years but remained for many years on a convivial basis centered upon their mutual interest in books, wine, and French food. Richards learned early never to intrude upon Housman's privacies; the attempts he made met with such alarming rebuffs that they were not often repeated. Their companionship was most satisfactory when they met as gourmets to discover little known but delicious foods and wines in such home settings as the living room behind the shop of Monsieur and Madame Perrier at Dole, near Arbois, France, where Madame smilingly ladled out her entrancing soup and her husband attended to the rare bottles of wine that went with the feast. Richards appears amusingly to have been a Duncan Hines of French cuisines; Housman was often guided on his tours by Richards' itinerary.

Both Housman and Richards knew all about wines: The *Pouilly Fuisse* at Quingey, the *Montrachet* and *Hermitage Rochefine* at Besancon, the *Chambertin* and *Gavillon,* and the great *Chablis* wine not far from Dijon. They liked to dine on chicken and *Chablis,* or fish done with cheese and a *Meursault Goutte* or a *Chateau Le-Tour-Blanche* at Fontainebleau. *Grand Luxe* hotels they usually avoided. Housman never ate a great deal; he ate slowly and enjoyed food, and he drank with the same exquisite palate, tasting and enjoying but seldom over-indulging, although Richards recalled one night when they both were a bit high, and went singing happily around the winding streets of Montmartre under a French moon. The two men shared a liking for French novels and letters, including autobiographies, and Richards rarely lost a chance to send Housman the latest of these which he could procure. Baron Corvo's letters were among these, along with forthcoming books of Proust and Gide.

As the years went on, these jaunts became less frequent and finally lost their savour, and the correspondence between the two was desultory towards the last. That the gradual withdrawal came on Housman's part is certain; and although the poet was friendly with Richards to the end of his life, his friendship was based on the unswerving loyalty to the few he had admitted to his inner circle, a loyalty with arrogance in it, based on the impossibility of his having made a mistake.

Chapter XXIV, in Richards' book, *Housman 1927-1936,* was a denial of rumors regarding A. E. H. that had been better left unwritten. It was based on the author's desire to clear his own reputation more than to serve Housman's. Whisperings must have gone around that the relationship of these two men had an unwholesome motive for its basis. Of course nothing could have been farther from the truth. Richards had a particularly happy home life; his beautiful, talented wife and their children were his greatest pride and delight. Had that fact not been undeniably clear, Housman would never have allowed himself to be as intimate with Richards as he was; nevertheless, the gossip flared up at times, and Richards thought this chapter was a way to silence it, after the victim of these innuendoes was gone. At the time Richards' book was published, only four years after Housman died, it would have been fitting not to touch upon the secret of his life at all, a reticence which would have been both courageous and appropriate. Housman certainly had made his own place both as a man of nobility and of genius; he did not need Grant Richards to defend him. Richards knew nothing about measuring the distance between temptation and resistance; he did not always resist the temptations that beset him, trivial as they were, thus he could not envisage great renunciations; by necessity he ignored them. He had been somewhat unreliable in forwarding royalties due Housman, (which A. E. H. accepted after 1922), yet with all this, Housman did not chide or embarrass him. He knew Richards was constantly in debt, and he never demanded payment past due. Richards said after his death: "He was my friend, faithful and just to me, and generous. Would that I had learned more from his friendship, and gained more from his ever-patient wisdom."[14] Richards could not have said otherwise, for never did he have a better friend, or one whose patronage aided his reputation as a publisher more, or one that he was able to use so satisfactorily for his own advantage. But he could not deceive or manipulate Housman. There was no time that the poet did not keep his own accurate accounts, and he knew exactly what his publisher owed him.

Never in his life was Housman able to achieve that easy friendship with his associates which brightens and stabilizes the lives of most men; he remained lonely, and during the Cambridge years he allowed his loneliness to grow on him; he even made a cult of it. He was bitterly ironical at times, but filled with human sympathy at heart. The fact was that as he grew older, he was sorry for all his fellow men, born without their will into a world in which he found much less good than ill. "Yet, in the face of that sorrow, he kept his end up, and was active, mentally and physically, and had a lively sense of humor, and a beautiful ringing laugh. He never mistreated animal, child, or man," said his brother Laurence.[15]

Housman was a master of intellectual cruelty, however, which he expressed in witty and scathing terms against all sham pretentious scholarship in matters of classical exegesis, and thoroughly enjoyed doing it. He made himself the most hated and feared of all contemporary classical authorities, and he "didn't give a damn!"

As time passed, his face in repose was glum, lit by deep-set hazel eyes that were a reflection of loneliness within.

Dr. Jackson and his family visited England several times, both while he was located at Karachi, India, and after he had removed to Vancouver, British Columbia. On these visits he met Housman; and on one of them Housman stood as godfather to one of Jackson's sons, Gerald C. A. Jackson, and wrote a humorous poem to the child. But these meetings were rare, and nothing authentic is known of them. Most of them were unshared by others, and probably they caused Housman more sorrow than pleasure. Although after 1920 Jackson was aging very fast, Housman still saw in him the young man he once had been, and loved the recollection, not physically any more, but spiritually; loved with pain and sorrow the man who was now sixty-three years old—his comrade to "The West."[16]

It is possible that the final visit of Dr. Jackson to England (1921) and the hours Housman spent with him, brought about the sudden completion of *Last Poems,* 1922, Housman's final gesture to poetry during his lifetime. The first poem "The West" identifies Jackson as 'the comrade' and is a veiled dedication of the book to him.

8

Last Poems and Honors

RICHARDS HAD BEGUN teasing Housman for a new book of poetry as early as March, 1900. After he discovered that such requests met with tart refusal by a terse postal card, he kept silent, fearing Housman's reaction to further interference. Richards never attempted to telephone to Housman, who hated telephones, and would not use one. He seldom wrote Richards more than a card or brief note, but finally a laconic card that made Richards tingle with excitement arrived on September 5, 1920: "Suppose I produced a new volume of poetry, in what part of the year ought it to be published?"

Another card arrived in the editor's office April 9, 1922: "It is now practically certain that I shall have a volume of poems ready for autumn. I desire particularly that the price should be moderate."

On June 20 the manuscript arrived, and Richards locked himself up with it. The long anticipated volume appeared October 19, 1922 —a four thousand edition in dark blue cover—which was modestly titled *Last Poems*. Housman himself gave this off-hand explanation for his publication of *LP* in his preface to the book:

I publish these poems, few though they are, because it is not likely that I shall ever be impelled to write much more. I can no longer expect to be revisited by the continuous excitement with which I wrote the greater part of the book [referring of course to the period preceding 1896] nor indeed could I well sustain it if it came; and it is best that what I have written should be printed while I am here to see it through the press and control its spelling and punctuation.

By the end of the year twenty-one thousand copies had been sold. Composers vied with each other to set his verse to music; the book was done in Braille; a miniature edition was requested for the Queen's doll-house![1]

The epigraph of *LP* controls the mood of the entire volume—a wistful melancholy like that of a gray autumn day with winter coming. Although Housman had translated a French folk song by Theodore de Banville for his epigraph, the poem became his own:

> *Nous n'irons plus au bois*
> *Les lauriers son coupés . . .*
>
> *We'll to the woods no more,*
> *The laurels all are cut . . .*

The high, wild woods of the epigraph are the realm of emotional inspiration Housman was relinquishing with reluctance upon the publication of *Last Poems*. The depth of his regret is apparent in the twilight tone of the repetitive "no more, no more," and in the word "bare" which describes the aridity of the poet's life and future output.

Last Poems had been re-worked and polished with an artist's hand. It was a less rebellious offering, more uniform, and more stable in emotion than *ASL*, with thought that was sometimes more intricate and mature. But few readers would place it higher than *ASL* in its ability to reach the heart, nor does it show much development in range or method. At least half the poems were clearly written many years before.

The volume was influenced by Dr. Jackson. A strange poem called "The West" (*LP* I) is a veiled dedication to him—the "comrade" who approaches the end of life with the poet. The likelihood of the two having discussed death in their last meeting—Jackson seriously and Housman mockingly—is evident. "West" here takes on the British vernacular in which "going west" meant "death" in the wry terms of World War I:

> Beyond the moor and mountain crest
> —Comrade, look not on the west—
> The sun is down and drinks away
> From air and land the lees of day.
>
> The long cloud and the single pine
> Sentinel the ending line,
> And out beyond it, clear and wan,
> Reach the gulfs of evening on.
>
> The son of woman turns his brow
> West from forty counties now,
> And, as the edge of heaven he eyes,
> Thinks eternal thoughts, and sighs.
>
> Oh wide's the world, to rest or roam,
> With change abroad and cheer at home,
> Fights and furloughs, talk and tale,
> Company and beef and ale.
>
> But if I front the evening sky
> Silent on the west look I,
> And my comrade, stride for stride,
> Paces silent at my side.
>
> Comrade, look not on the west:
> 'Twill have the heart out of your breast;
> 'Twill take your thoughts and sink them far,
> Leagues beyond the sunset bar.

Oh lad, I fear that yon's the sea
Where they fished for you and me,
And there, from whence we both were ta'en,
You and I shall drown again.

Send not on your soul before
To dive from that beguiling shore,
And let not yet the swimmer leave
His clothes upon the sands of eve.

Too fast to yonder strand forlorn
We journey, to the sunken bourn,
To flush the fading tinges eyed
By other lads at eventide.

Wide is the world, to rest or roam,
And early 'tis for turning home:
Plant your heel on earth and stand,
And let's forget our native land.

When you and I are split on air
Long we shall be strangers there;
Friends of flesh and bone are best:
Comrade, look not on the west.[2]

—*LP* I

Another tribute to Jackson in *LP* is found in Housman's longest
and most complicated poem, "Hell Gate," an allegory symbolizing
Jackson's influence on the poet's life. Hell is conceived as a me-
diaeval city (therefore archaic today) to which Satan is returning
as a conquering hero. But mutiny of Ned, the sentinel at "Hell's
Gate" (Jackson) prevents the entrance of both Satan and one who
journeys with him (Housman). Satan and Hell finally leave "a
pair of friends alone," and the torture fires of Hell that surround
Ned and the newcomer recede before the greater power of friendship. Jackson probably read the book when his friend sent him an

early copy, but its figurative meaning would not have been very apparent to him.

Margaret L. Woods, a contemporary poet, acknowledged the gift of *Last Poems* with these words in part:

> I took it to the Tennysons [Charles Tennyson's] immediately after it came, and was pointing out to Lord Tennyson the "Hell Gate"—saying not only how fine it was but how quite in another genre from the others, when he showed me the same remark in the London Times Literary Supplement. . . . You ought to give us more like it.[3]

Dr. Gilbert Murray, famous British classicist of Oxford, in a letter to A. E. H. October 22, 1922, wrote:

> I think deliberately that "Fancy's Knell" [*LP* XLI] will stand as one of the most beautiful lyrics in the language. One can see how much you have been influenced by writing Greek and Latin verse. . . .[4]

Sir William Rothenstein wrote to Housman from his office in The Royal College of Art, upon the publication of *LP*:

> I am grateful for your poems . . . Hardy long ago prepared me. . . . But we are never fully prepared for either excellence or stupidity. Stupidity is the common commodity, and though I have never been moved by the doctrine of Christ taking the sins of men upon himself that men may be saved, it looks as though a few men do actually preserve a generation from damnation by futurity. I doubt whether you have looked on yourself in the light of a savior: I imagine you would be rather scornful of the role. . . .[5]

Housman's technique as a perfectionist is illustrated in the rough drafts of "Eight O'Clock," *LP* XV, the superlative expression of Housman's contempt and horror for hangings.[6] The poem was either written or re-worked in 1921. Notebook C, sheet 8 and sheet 9, show fascinating rough drafts with brilliant alterations in two places. A third stanza was originally present, but was finally obliterated. Housman had the unerring instinct not to detract from those dramatic last lines. The hardest word to get was "tossed," (line 4). He finally chose it from no less than eight alternatives: loosed, spilt, cast, told, dealt, pitched, passed, and the entire alternate line, "They dingled down." The search for the word "tossed" is possibly the best example in all the original rough drafts of Housman's passion for the right word. The final choice perfectly expresses the shrugging indifference of the material world to the misery of the man about to die. It crystallizes the coldness of fate, carelessly dealing out a trump that spells ruin to the player who has lost the game. The reader actually enters into the experience of the doomed man to whom the clock has assumed terrible importance.

The clock is fate; it is the hangman; it is the fury that collects its strength, and strikes. Doom has its agent in the senseless, imperturbable clock, with its sprinkling quarter hours; it snips the thread of life. The words *sprinkled, tossed, collected,* and *struck* are powerful examples of motor, or verbal imagery; and the eternity of time between the last quarter's striking and the final blow of eight is expressed in the slowing down of the movement in *collected* and *struck* as opposed to the restless speed of *one, two, three, four* in stanza one. Weight and stress concentrate in a climax of intensity upon *struck,* so that at that word, as Housman intended, one projects himself into the last agony of the sprung trap. A. E. H. was one of the great perfectionists in the history of English poetry.

Americans recognized Housman's importance sooner than Englishmen who often merely skimmed the surface of his poetry and failed to catch not only its perfection, but also its meaning, thereby falling into amusingly incorrect generalizations. An illustration of such vague comprehension was innocently recounted by Grant Richards, who was just as ignorant about the statement he quoted as was the man who said it. The anecdote was recounted to Richards by William Hickey, a member then of the staff of *The Daily Express,* who was retelling an incident in the friendship he had with S. G. Owen, then a famous classical don of Oxford, to whom he showed the late A. E. Housman's collected poems.

"We skimmed through a lot of the stuff about Ludlow and Wenlock and all that. His only comment was: 'It's a wonder he didn't mention Church Stretton. It's a noted spot.' "[7]

Owen, and Richards, too, as they "skimmed through," had completely missed the geography of *LP* XIX, "In midnights of November," (originally titled in the rough draft: "The brim of Severn freezes"). The second line of this poem refers to Dead Man's Fair, and the scene of the poem *is* Church Stretton, the only village in all England that had the traditional observance of Dead Man's Fair! Could Owen's supercilious attitude have been caused by jealousy? Or stupidity, "the greater commodity"?

There was nothing supercilious about the way America received *Last Poems.* For the first time, Housman arranged copyright with Henry Holt and Company, for not only *LP* but *ASL* also; and at last royalties of fifteen per cent began to pad his pockets. He had a similar arrangement with Grant Richards. When a new edition appeared, and how fast they followed after 1922, Housman insisted upon proof reading each one, and pounced with fury on the blunders in punctuation and the ordering of lines perpetrated by "the filthy beasts of printers"[8] whom he never failed to indict as sworn foes.

By postal card, October 12, 1922, to Grant Richards: "I knew the

[205]

printers would do something, and I only wondered what it would be. On p. 52 they have removed a comma from the end of the first line and a semi-colon from the end of the second."

When Richards offered to insert an errata slip this postal card arrived: "No, don't put one in. The blunder will enhance the value of the 1st edition in the eyes of bibliophiles, an idiotic class."

Later on the luckless printer tried to explain: "I return the printer's letter. Printers seem to regard this sort of error as the act of God. . . ."

Always it was the same story. Housman's venom was poured forth unceasingly upon the heads of the wretched printers, who never were able to suit him. When Richards happily wrote October 26, that already new editions were in the making, he received this infuriating card: "What guarantee have I that all these editions of yours are being printed correctly?"

In honor of the success of *Last Poems,* and possibly to placate their irascible author, Mr. and Mrs. Richards had Housman for dinner at the Carlton in London, November 8, 1922. Richards put the famous restaurant on its mettle that night: the dinner centered upon hors d'oeuvres, which Housman adored, a saddle of hare, a great favorite with Housman, with *blette,* a kind of Swiss chard, and truffles imported from France, and sherry from John Fothergill's cellar at the Spreadeagle at Thame. And of course, coffee. Housman was fond of coffee at night, and as much a connoisseur about it as wine. It must have been a highly successful dinner, for he was not acrimonious about printers for some time after, and Richards rushed through in all twenty-one thousand copies by the first of the year. But not without agony. Housman warned him with a letter: "You MUST NOT print editions . . . without letting me see the proofs."

Mrs. Richards rushed a box of walnuts to him, and he replied with a letter: "A heavy case has arrived and I have had it opened and have come to the top layer, but have not eaten my way further down at present. I write now to thank you before I make myself ill."

But even that didn't work. The same day he wrote by postal card to Richards: "I have found no errors YET in the second impression of *Last Poems,* but it seems to me that the stanza on page 56 ought to be leaded, or whatever you call it, in the same way as the two stanzas on page 55."[9]

Richards ground his teeth at the bitter sarcasm of the last sentence.

Housman refused an invitation to spend Christmas with the Richards family at Bigfrith, telling them that he was remaining at Cambridge for the holidays, and pleading the excuse of expecting a guest of his own. So the best they could do was to send him some of the famous John Fothergill sherry for a present, for which he thanked them very gratefully, and wished them a happy New Year.

Probably Housman had no Christmas guest at all, for the fact came out later, February 14, 1923, that either the proof-reading of *Last Poems,* or perhaps the walnuts, had really made him sick. He wrote to Richards: "I have been ill for two months, worse than I ever was in my life, with carbuncles, which I never had before and do not want to have again. At last I am better, but it has ruined my holiday."

It was not until July 24 that he crossed to Paris by the Handley-Page from Croydon at 4:30 in the afternoon, for a stay at The Continental, and then to Le Mans.

What a paradox the man was! Nothing could be more contradictory than the picture Housman presented as he waited to enter the plane for Paris: his eyes suddenly eager and youthful, his cheeks flushed with pleasure, but his dress and general appearance that of a gentleman of 1885—impeccably tailored in the best tweed money could buy, but with a high waistcoat, stiff upright collar, high shoes with the ubiquitous elastic inserts on the sides, neatly folded umbrella grasped firmly, and a small, unfashionable cap—all a complete contradiction of the rebel he really was.

He engaged a car at Le Mans and slowly followed the south coast and back by the north coast, full of beauty and delight for him. He was alone, as he liked best to be, and came home much refreshed in body and soul. He found a letter waiting from the Boosey Company, music publishers, enclosing his first royalties for gramophone rights to poems set to music by Vaughan Williams, the sum of six pounds. Also a letter with royalties was waiting from Richards. Not long after, a letter with first royalties came from Henry Holt and Company, who had sadly discovered Housman's penchant for criticizing punctuation and ordering.

"In this authorized edition by Holt there are disgraceful misprints," he wrote to Houston Martin, an American admirer.[10]

No, Holt could not suit him, or rather their printers could not, any better than the English ones, and Richards' heart must have gone out in sympathy to them.

By late 1925, Housman was hard at work doing his fifth volume of *Manilius,* his days of poetry entirely over. He foresaw publishing the fifth volume in about four years. On February 9, 1927, he acidly rejected a request from "the wireless people" as he put it, to recite his poems, though he allowed the Vaughan Williams group to go on the air, making the excuse that "with the music the words are mostly inaudible."

In August of the same year he dropped work for a month, and went to meet Richards in France in the neighborhood of Chablis and its vineyards. He had arrived at the financial freedom of reserving a room with a private bath, something he had not done before, and he ordered his meals, scorning the menu card. Crayfish, fondue, truffles, birds, with Chablis Grenouilles 1921, were high on his list of favorites, and how Housman enjoyed them! Dressed without much care, comfortably seated in a remote corner, he would taste and savor the foods and wines he liked best, never gaining an ounce after his afternoon walk of anywhere from five to ten miles. Such dinners were full of conversation about wines and books, and menus, and more books. Once in Beaune, Richards and Housman dismissed their chauffeur, and wearing cricket caps and dark, somewhat dusty suits, walked into the hotel diningroom unannounced and unknown. The waiter looked them over, and with an air of hauteur, casually threw the menu card on their table. Housman's brows drew together ominously, but he ordered the dinner of the day.

"Red or white wine?" asked the bored waiter.

"I will naturally have the wine list," replied Housman.

It was brought, and running down the list, at the foot of it actually, he spied Meursault Perrieres and a Montrachet, both 1919. They were not the most expensive wines, but Housman knew from memory that they were by far the best the list offered. The effect of his order for a bottle of each was electrifying. Out from the rear scuttled a *maitre d'hotel* with abject apologies. The waiter had make a mistake! The menu shown was not the one they should have seen. Would the gentlemen please pardon? Then he placed a much more imposing card in Housman's hands.

"I perceive Monsieur knows well his wines," he said, bowing low. The sly twinkle had come into Housman's eyes; Grant Richards was not restraining his laughter. What a meal it was! A highwater mark of the chef's cookery. On this night the two men were jolly and a little unsteady on their legs, but none the worse for it the next morning; in fact, they had never felt better in their lives.

The journey with Richards lasted for fifteen days, and Housman returned to Cambridge and the grind of *Manilius*. He stayed during the holidays, and when summer came, he spared only two weeks for France. On this trip he took out travelers' insurance on his life for the first time. When he returned safely to Cambridge, he began his round of lectures and most of his spare time went to the final volume of *Manilius*. He was now seventy years old, and found the endless research more onerous; he fought going to sleep at his desk by getting up and exercising with a pair of dumbbells. After his blood began circulating again, he worked regularly until midnight. In late January he had an attack of painful lumbago, but that did not stop him. In March his routine was broken by a trip to London where he collected a batch of material from the British Museum for his book.

On May, the 7th to be exact, he attended a memorable dinner in London, as the guest of the nimble writer and decorator turned master-restaurateur, Monsieur Boulestin, who admired his poetry. The other guests were Grant Richards and A. H. Adair. They drank a bottle of that rarest of fine wines, the white Haut Brion.

His companions did not know it, but for Housman, the dinner was a private celebration of his just having declined the Order of Merit! The O. M. is such a highly prized honor that few men refuse it. The reasons for his refusal are best told by his brother Laurence:

I had for some time felt a brotherly concern that the one honor which I thought he would be willing to accept, the Order of Merit, had not been offered him. Since others were feeling as I did, I broached the question—would he accept it? He replied that he would not, and when, disappointed, I asked why, he said that, though he had always known it would be offered to him if he lived to the age of eighty, he had decided against accepting any honour, and against this particular one because it was not always given to the right persons. He had condoled, he said, with the poet laureate, Robert Bridges, for having had to receive the honour at the same time as John Galsworthy, whose writing they both disliked, and Bridges had admitted the circumstance had not given him pleasure.

I suppose I pressed him further, for suddenly he blushed (an unexpected gift which he had retained from the days of his youth) and said: "Well, as a matter of fact, Mr. Baldwin did write to me not long ago to say that the King was ready to offer it; and I believe it was offered at the same time to Bernard Shaw.[11] But for the reason I have already stated, and because I could not have the trouble of going to be received by the King, I declined. 'But,' he added, 'I don't want it to be known; it wouldn't be fair to the king.' "[12]

A. E. H., Tory of Tories, never a pseudo-Tory, eternally loyal and reverent to the Crown, did not want anyone to find out that he had declined a favor that his monarch offered him.

Even in his explanation to his brother, Housman did not mention the subconscious reason for his refusal—that, as he had written "This is me" in the margin of T. E. Lawrence's book, when Lawrence had confessed his passion for fame and his shame at wanting it—so now he renounced the fame that he desired greatly in order to be true to himself. It certainly was not easy for him to do it; his renunciation was as painful to him as a haircloth shirt would have been. It was a noble and a strange thing to do, but the sacrifice made him more at ease with his memories.

He showed his deep trust in Joan Thomson when he told her about it. She listened in astonishment and regret, but with her rare insight she said nothing in the way of disappointment or reproach. There was silence for awhile, and then he turned to her with a smile both fond and cynical, and said: "You know, it's quite a distinction to have refused the Order of Merit!" They both laughed. "It certainly is," she agreed.[13]

Grant Richards also knew of the refusal by the method of worming it out of Housman, thereby infuriating him alarmingly. A. E. H. deeply resented Richards' intrusion into what was none of his business, and he never liked him as well afterwards.

Housman's letter to the King's secretary, declining the honor, in its quotation from Lord Cornwallis, tested the King's power of sympathy, we should think, to the last degree:

> With all gratitude for His Majesty's most kind and flattering wish to confer upon me the Order of Merit, I humbly beg permission to decline this high honour. I hope to escape the reproach of thanklessness or churlish behaviour by borrowing the words in which an equally loyal subject, Admiral Cornwallis, declined a similar mark of the Royal favour: 'I am, unhappily of a turn of mind that would make my receiving that honour the most unpleasant thing imaginable.'[14]

Apparently the King was as understanding as Housman expected him to be, for in the official reply, Royalty assured him that his reasons were appreciated.

Rejection of the Order of Merit was preceded by a number of other refusals which were probably based on the same reasons as the ones offered for declining the O. M. As far back as 1905, when Housman was still at University College, Glasgow University had offered him the honorary degree of Doctor of Laws; then followed offers of honorary degrees of various kinds from Cambridge in 1928, Liverpool in 1931, and North Wales in 1934. All were rejected with a sweeping gesture: "the honour would not be congenial or appropriate."[15] "The hell-defended fort"[16] had been gained, but the conqueror was unwilling to wave his banners from the top of it. How silent and secretive he was, how willfully he pushed aside the few legitimate joys that might have made him happier, only such facts as these are able to prove.

Yet there was nothing secretive about his poetry. It was there that his mask slipped, and only by his poetry can the depths of his personality, with all its brilliance and its tragedy, be known. He was as far as possible from the obscurantist school of poets: there was no hysteria or type-juggling in his lyrics. He wrote of anguish and aspiration equally well, without any savaging of structure, melody, or comprehension.

He never strained his brew through a sheaf of explanatory notes before he offered it; he was extraordinarily fitted to know the bitter stuff that life is made of, and he did not offer to lessen the sour taste of it; his draught is undiluted and invites the shock of recognition:

> 'Tis true, the stuff I bring for sale
> Is not so brisk a brew as ale:
> Out of a stem that scored the hand
> I wrung it in a weary land.
> But take it: if the smack is sour
> The better for the embittered hour;
> It should do good to heart and head
> When your soul is in my soul's stead;
> And I will friend you, if I may
> In the dark and cloudy day.
>
> *ASL,* LXIX

The catholicity of his poems included all men:

> They say my verse is sad: no wonder;
> Its narrow measure spans
> Tears of eternity, and sorrow
> Not mine, but man's.[17]

Housman viewed man as a generalized dilemma: a composite and an enigmatical composition which was forever asking the meaning of life and never finding out. A similar viewpoint caused Gauguin to paint his vast picture after he had attempted suicide: *D'où venons nous? Que sommes nous? Où allons nous?* Whence do we come? What are we? Whither are we going?

Preys to extreme sensibility, men like Housman and Gauguin suffered from struggles which did not trouble the calm of their prosaic associates. All life to such men is a tragedy of uncertainty staged on a background of earnest melancholy.

Creative art becomes a solace to them; in fact, such creation is a necessity. It is interesting to note that the tragedy of life painted by the French school known as "the rebels of art"—especially Gauguin, Degas, Van Gogh and Toulouse-Lautrec—are often similar to that painted in words by Housman: scorn of conventions, compassion for evil-doers, a twisted interpretation of sexual experience. They disclose man as a personal emanation from an Impersonal Nature—a Nature that can be beautiful, but pitiless.

Without using their bizarre coloring, but rather choosing the greys of traditional background, Housman agreed with the French rebels, expressed his vehement anger in their bold outlines; and wrote about the lust or love of his men and women in the same hieratic mood.

The natural melancholy of Housman was also influenced somewhat by the Age of Decadence in which he matured, a period that still influences thought today, presenting the world as a "waste land" through which man wanders—a nothingness in a meaningless universe. Startled into agnosticism, the Age of Decadence invented new philosophies which Housman rejected. No cult suited him; he accepted no pattern of philosophy; but the fact emerges that he was definitely influenced by French philosophies. Baudelaire he had read in early manhood. He read all of Proust and Gide over and over, and carried everything they wrote on his shelves.

He pondered over existentialism; he re-read René de Gourmont's *Décadence* (1922) and Willy's[18] *Le Troisième Sexe* (1927); the latter was sent to him by Grant Richards. The effect of these books on his thought was considerably greater than that of Heine, whose influence he readily admitted.

By 1930 Housman had put poetry away permanently. His academic load gradually was shifted from his shoulders as the faculty increased. According to the figures of Sir J. J. Thomson, in 1882 there were twenty-seven professors, two readers, seven demonstrators, and five teachers in Trinity. In 1934, two years before Housman's death, there were seventy-two professors, twenty-nine readers, two hundred twenty-nine lecturers, and thirty-five demonstrators. The larger part of this increase had come from 1920 onwards, and it must have arrived at the greatest impetus several years after the war.[19] Since Housman joined the faculty in 1911, he saw the University grow by leaps and bounds. The war work done within Cambridge gave the University new prestige, and its revamped objectives of adapting its curriculum to the needs of business men as well as professional ones increased its enrolment rapidly.

Housman was growing old at Cambridge in a new world in which he was more of a stranger than he had ever been. Competition among students and professors alike was more strenuous. The examination which at Oxford had been classed "The Moderates," at Cambridge was known by the less frightening term of "The Little-Go," and usually came earlier. To pass it well meant the go-ahead signal for the student to compete for higher honors, and the hope of taking a position among the four first "Senior Wranglers" at the end of the course, when "The Tripos" examinations were held. Housman's duties included the preparation of questions pertaining to Latin for these examinations and the passing upon the papers afterwards, but as the years went on, he had assistants who took on a considerable part of this load. In the early 1900's the use of the typewriter was comparatively unknown at Cambridge, and even after it became popular, Housman never used it, but did every bit of his meticulous Latin copy for his books in a clear, cramped hand of amazing precision and exactitude.

Of late years much of the final worth of a man who is graduating from Cambridge is determined by the original accomplishments in research which he may have either started or completed; and students of unusual promise may now get substantial grants of money to help them in advanced research. Of course this evaluation is more useful in the Mathematical Tripos, for instance, than in the Classical; however, the general objective of discovering the originality and creative ability of scholars in all branches of learning is emphasized, and Housman took on his share of these evaluations.

During Housman's tenure at Cambridge he saw University life alter completely from that of his own undergraduate days at Oxford. A much larger percentage of the students were married; in fact, after the war, it was as common for students to be married as single. The advent of women students from Newham and Girton Colleges into the classes at Trinity College was an accepted thing. Greater informality existed between the sexes; they sat in mixed groups in class if they wanted to, and between classes they walked together and took refreshments together as they pleased. At certain times, men students of Trinity were allowed to invite women students to their rooms! Dramatic clubs were another means of bringing students together, such as *The Marlowe* Society and *The Footlights,* and Greek plays were occasionally given. The musicians of Cambridge produced operas; dances were the rule rather than the exception; and receptions of special importance became increasingly numerous. While these social activities may have crowded in upon examinations, they certainly brought about a normal and wholesome relationship between men and women, at a critical time when such relationships were needed and highly valuable. Sports also became increasingly important; but they never have reached the furious momentum which characterizes the American universities. They were more popular in games where only two players, or at most four, are needed, such as lawn tennis, golf, or "squash racquets."

As the sports of rugby, cricket, and hockey became popular, there were fewer young people resorting to walks for their exercise, which they got in plenty from these games of give-and-take, withal a more normal and satisfying form of diversion with social significance. One wonders whether, if Housman had been submitted to such an environment in his undergraduate days, it might not have altered the order of his life.

Housman benefited at least in one way by the establishment of rugby matches with paid admission at Cambridge; the Rugby Club founded a lectureship in Classics! But there is no account of Housman ever having attended any of the sports.

Cambridge University today has much more practical objectives than characterized it at an earlier date. It has, for instance, an active Board of Appointments, which, in the year Housman died (1936) secured positions for 596 graduates and post-graduates, many of whom entered the world of business. Housman was affected in his classroom objectives by this new policy of training students for practical service outside the old established patterns of The Bar, The Church, The State, or The Professor. Now it was taken into account that schoolmasters should be trained in teaching methods, and Housman to meet this demand organized two courses which he taught with high success on the application of thought to textual criticism—actually the science of teaching the classics. These courses were popular with the advanced students in the classics, and resulted in a number of them securing valuable posts upon leaving the University.

Housman's hours of teaching the classroom were never onerous; he was never required to lecture more than nine hours a week and in his last years much less than that, but he never considered his teaching negligible in importance to his research. His work in the classroom often led him to further investigations which he might not have considered if the need for such had not been indispensable for his lectures. His classroom work further served to keep his mind from going into a rut; every year it was a new challenge, for he was never satisfied to give the same old stuff over and over.

He had to meet the fact that more women would be in his classes. However, he had expected this, for women had been admitted to Cambridge in 1897. There is some account that he was rude to them; he was certainly remote. His method of lecturing without looking at them must have been trying, and tended to make him appear more impersonal and distant than ever. But there was something about him that fascinated them; possibly his "mystery," but more possibly the fact that they instinctively felt themselves to be admitted into an opportunity to observe the workings of a superior intelligence, the brilliance and cogency of which allowed no denial.

Astounding changes had marked the pathway for the Atomic Age. Housman had been born into a world of comparatively tranquil existence, with no electricity, no telephones, no radios or cinemas, no modern plumbing, no automobiles, no aircraft, no X-rays, nor wonder drugs, nor nylon, nor radium, nor atomic bombs.

But the facilities for discovering how to make them were there. During the war years, Cambridge University teemed with scientific curiosity and invention. The Cavendish Laboratory, under the energetic leadership of Sir J. J. Thomson, was the English hub of research into electrons, isotopes, and Röntgen rays, and was paving the way for the atomic age. The pulse of science was quick and hot; as in America, men spent their lives bent over test tubes and computations. Housman was in sympathy with this research, but he wished with painful nostalgia that he could go back to the world of his boyhood, to the comfortable rural culture untouched by the machine age, to the sweet country air of the Valley House and Fockbury House, places fertile for individual living. His happier life was always lived in the world of his imagination.

The Mass of the Moving Charge, as physics knew it, he knew nothing about, but now he was well acquainted with the moving charge of his breast, where his emotions began to suffocate him. Life had worn him down, and his heart was performing its final experiment with life, beating on a fine thread which might snap under pressure.

He sat alone in his room more than ever and often dreamed of the days of his youth. On cold, blustery nights of late autumn and winter, he heard the trees hit the windows that faced Sidney Street; the windows that faced the Whewell Court side of the apartment rattled with the force of the west wind. But west winds were dear to him; they blew from the hills of home; they had gathered strength in Worcestershire. When his loneliness was greatest, he could not think of any new lines of poetry, but he repeated lines that comforted him, whispered from a great distance by the Shropshire Lad:

> Into my heart an air that kills
>   From yon far country blows:
> What are those blue remembered hills,
>   What spires, what farms are those?

That is the land of lost content,
I see it shining plain,
The happy highways where I went
And cannot come again.
                    —*ASL*, XL

The miles of years receded rapidly behind Housman now; sometimes out of their jumbled limbo he caught experiences, but these recollections were like unrelated cuttings from cinemas, played by another person; he no longer thrilled to their emotion.

He was no longer in love with anything in life. Scholarship, which he had decently married and slept with for over forty years, was now a jaded mistress whose veins were dry and shrunken. There would be no more offspring from that union.

Jackson had been dead for eight years; he had lived wisely and well, but his influence on his friend's life was to remain his only historic achievement. If he and Housman had never met, the poet might have been less a poet, but almost certainly his mental complex would have been the same. It is impossible to imagine Housman ever contemplating marriage. Aside from his mental twist, he possessed two characteristics which would probably have kept him a bachelor in any case: hypersensitivity and a passion for perfection which would have made his demands in love too high. These tensions, with their attendant stringencies, would have precluded marriage in all probability. But it is barely possible that he might have had a comfortable marriage if it could have been abnormal or irregular—if the sexual element could have been absent. If he had married someone much older (as Walter Cross married George Eliot), or, in late maturity, if he had mated with someone much younger who needed him or was afflicted in some way, the marriage might have beeen a valuable venture. Such a marriage for A. E. H. would have been a form of justification for living. His intense need to be

[220]

all in all to someone who could be all in all to him would have been satisfied. However, in the accepted meaning of marriage relationship he certainly would not have been happy or at ease.[20]

But he had known great loves: loves that had nothing to do with people. The love of Nature in trees, hills, and flowers. The love of the stars and the planets. The love of the soft, lush landscape of a Worcester springtime, May orchards snowing bloom across England, blowing beauty into the valleys and drifting banks of blossoms upon the woodlands. . . . Those he had known, but in old age his life was often as bare and deserted as a looted castle after a war. Winds of suffering beat upon him, and always the annoying impedimenta of living—shaving, dressing, lecturing, note-making, necessary correspondence, conferences—cluttered the corridors of his mind to his increasing irritation.

Loosing their grasp on the revolving globe, his nearest human loves were at last far distant; they had taken their endless way to the wind's twelve quarters (*ASL* XXXII). They were entities no more, only wraithlike recollections. His mother first, then Herbert, Robert, Lucy, and Basil; Jackson had died before Basil by seven years. Then Sophie Becker last of all. He thought of them as they had once been: his mother with her noble, serious expectancy; Sophie Becker, clever, sane, and cheering; Lucy, the majestic Roman Mater, piloting his vacillating father as best she could—they had all been a part of his inner life, and he had loved them all in widely different ways. He had loved Herbert, clean of stain, buried in the Veldt; he had loved Jackson, his "Mo"—it was bitterly sad to contemplate that all the youth and virility of Jackson lay shrunken in the shell of an uncouth disguise within the cold Canadian earth.

Walking remained the main solace of Housman, and because of exercise, he retained in old age an unusually youthful appearance regardless of his inner sadness. Sir J. J. Thomson was much surprised to find out that Housman had passed his seventieth birthday, and sorry that he had not recognized the anniversary in some way, at least by a note of congratulation. He mentioned this feeling to Housman when he next saw him, and Housman replied that Thomson was not the only one who misjudged his appearance: that a teamster on a country road had come up behind him, as he was taking his usual afternoon walk, and mistaking him for a country boy, had cried out: "Hey, there, lad! Get out of my way!"[21] This incident Housman repeated with a good deal of relish. As the unmistakable signs of age crept into his bones, he fought them silently, as he had fought everything else, would not recognize them as such, and concealed them successfully from other people.

He realized now a new misfortune: his life's work was actually done. Never could he start another project like *Manilius*; never could he succumb to the devastating passion that it would demand of him to write another poem. Mentally he was static and quiescent; only some unusual demand upon him would make him rise out of his lethargy, and that demand did not come until 1933.

Analytical of himself as always, he realized that now he had slackened his pace and was waiting to go into "The West." How long would he wait? At night he sat musing in his lounging chair, book in hand, looking at the fire and occasionally dozing.

He often heard the Cambridge clocks strike midnight. How many of those clocks there were! Fortunately they had never bothered him, for they were connected with physical time. It was only psychical time that had ever troubled him; in that he resembled Proust. What a difference there was in the two ways of measuring it! One, the insensate time of the calendar, tossing its quarters down from the steeple; the other, the time of the soul measured by whether it "trots withal," or whether it drags through eternities of grief.

He usually made himself go to bed at midnight, if not before; of late, he had not been sleepy. Only a year or two previously when he was finishing *Manilius* he had used his dumbells to keep awake; now he tried to use them to get to sleep. But all they did for him was to make him breathless, and he furiously flung them in a corner. When he finally turned out his light, he was still sharply aware, and when he slept it was but fitfully. He was propped up on two pillows, and when his nerves were too tense to sleep at all, he watched the moonlight that flooded his room, or listened to the branches sweep his window.

After bad nights he liked a cup of tea as early in the morning as he could get it, and this his bedmaker sometimes brought him, but the bedmaker was not there for much of the time, and for none of the early afternoon. About tea time into the midst of his lonely desolation he would hear her apologetic knock at his door. In she would come, with the little tray, and the hot tea, the stimulating tea, steaming in the pot, and she would bustle quietly, in order not to disturb the master, who, God bless him! looked pale and weary enough in his big arm chair, and shrunken too, so that with all his age, she felt as if he needed mothering.

She would build up the fire to a rosy glow, pull down the blinds, turn on the light, pour the tea. She would watch him, as he silently concentrated on the tea, his thin facile hands around the hot cup, his face buried in the savory steam. She would watch him take a biscuit, and a bit of jam, spreading the savory fruit daintily as a woman, breaking off little pieces and eating his small meal. Two cups of tea, always.

She would notice a faint glow in the tired face, a sense of relaxation in the set of his shoulders. He thanked her without saying a word, as she came to know him better. How much more grateful he was than the others who spoke oftener! How kindly his eyes followed her as she left the room! A very great gentleman, she liked to tell the other women.

His brother Laurence stood ready to be Alfred's companion now that old age had come, and he would have been a comfort to Alfred could he have brought himself to reach out and call to him—not a small beckoning of his brother's hand would Laurence have failed to follow, but there was no such invitation. Desperately as Alfred needed Laurence he would not ask for him. Occasionally he was willing to go for a short trip to view English countrysides and cathedrals, in Laurence's Williams car, with its open sides and brass front that Wills, the faithful friend and chauffeur, took pride in keeping polished "like the handle to the King's front door," but these trips were not fireside intimacies, and were kept on a friendly and impersonal basis.

There was no jealousy in Alfred's heart towards his brother, who occupied a good deal more space in the encyclopedia than he did at the time. His reaction had been only delight and pride when *Victoria Regina* with Helen Hayes in the leading role of the Queen had made Laurence Housman famous and wealthy, and able to buy his Somerset estate, to build his beautiful home and gardens, and to have the Persian rugs he wanted. Over and over Laurence and Clemence had invited Alfred to visit them at "Longmeadow," but he went only once, and that to see his brother's Nativity play, put on two miles from the estate, at Glastonbury, during the Glastonbury festival. When Laurence asked him how he liked it, his reply was typically disconcerting. With a kind smile he said: "Not so bad as I expected."

It was not the play but the subject of it, the profoundly religious feeling in it, that Alfred could not accept. The religious beliefs and social attitudes of the two men were so different that there was no hope of even discussing them together, and Laurence had learned long ago to veer off any such danger. Laurence had grown more and more liberal in his social opinions; he had given his sympathies to the Labor party, and had subscribed to some of their publications. During the period of "Votes for Women" controversy, years before, Alfred had been provoked and embarrassed when his brother supported Clemence in her fight for women's rights. Clemence had even gone to jail in London for her beliefs, and Laurence had gone down and bailed her out, with accompanying publicity. The two of them had spoken for suffrage in both London and Cambridge, and their pictures appeared in London papers as leaders in the movement. As far back as 1911, Housman wrote to Grant Richards: "There is a lovely portrait of my disreputable relatives in yesterday's *Standard*."[22] The "lovely portrait" was of Laurence and Clemence Housman in connection with their feminist activities, for which Alfred had genuine repugnance. The only women he ever loved in his life, and the only women that later he liked (Mrs. Percy Withers and Mrs. Richards, for example) were women who were of the hearth and home, wrapped in domestic affairs and looking well to the ways of their households. Model menu makers, perfect hostesses, serene helmsmen of their private vessels, such women commanded Housman's respect and once in a blue moon, his liking. Clemence would have lived up to his severe qualifications perfectly, if she had not identified herself heart and soul with the suffrage movement, and supported her brother in his nefarious schemes for the social salvation of the world with the same vigor with which he supported hers. She was a wonderful housekeeper, trained by Lucy in the hard school of necessity, and even when she was in her late eighties it was hard for her to turn over the important cooking at "Longmeadow" to her house helper, Elizabeth; worse, if Laurence came into her spotless kitchen, tiled so attractively, with mud on his boots, she was down on her hands and knees to get rid of it before he had crossed the floor. Of these virtues, her exacting brother would have highly approved. That Laurence did not is another story.

After the years when Housman was completely withdrawn from his family, he developed a literary correspondence with Laurence, beginning during his healing years at Byron Cottage. This exchange of letters was a comfort to both of them, though one fails to see how Laurence could have got much satisfaction from them, since they were almost always a series of rather bantering and sometimes scathing criticisms of poems or other writings of Laurence, criticisms he had asked for, to be sure, but which were often cruel and discouraging, although fair. Under their veil of humor were hammer blows at Laurence's manuscript which must have been hard to bear. But Laurence, always a cross between a saint and an elfish Mephistopheles, took them all meekly and asked for more. The correspondence of this period was often amusing, but it certainly arouses one's sympathy for the younger brother. Excerpts from a few letters will serve to show their flavor.[23]

Byron Cottage, North Road
Highgate
14 Dec. 1894

I have got your poems into what seems to me a rough order of merit. *Love-bound Time* I think is the most original, and it is very well written and quite as lucid as one can expect; though I rather doubt if the English language will allow the stanza beginning 'Beauty may to beauty err' to mean anything in particular: however, it sounds nice. *Prisoner of Carisbrooke* ought certainly to be included, as it has more root in earth than most of its author's lays, and occupies the proud position of distinctly meaning something from beginning to end: also I think it good in itself, though 'well-water' is rather *neiges d'antan*. *The Three Kings* is a very good verse, except the end of the 12th stanza and the

2nd line of the 13th; in the 14th too I don't like 'this tells,' though I am fraid that cannot be altered without sacrificing 'Earth, Earth, Earth,' on which you have probably set your young affections. . . . *Blind Fortune* and *The King's Gifts* I should decidedly leave out, and, for my own part, the remaining pieces; these show a certain proficiency, in a certain style, which shall wax old as doth a garment: still, I daresay some will admire them: your Scotch friend very likely, who draws large cats. I would die many deaths rather than use such words as 'a-croon' and 'a-saw'; but that holy man St. Jerome very truly observes *'nemo tam imperitus scriptor est qui lectorem non inveniat similem sui"* (the worst hand at writing in the world is sure to find some reader of his own kidney).

What makes many of your poems more obscure than they need be is that you do not put yourself in the reader's place and consider how, and at what stage, that man of sorrows is to find out what it is all about. You are behind the scenes and know all the data; but he knows only what you tell him. It appears from the alternative titles *Heart's bane* and *Little Death* that in writing that precious croon you had in your head some meaning of which you did not suffer a single drop to escape into what you wrote; you treat us as Nebuchadnezzar did the Chaldeans, and expect us to find out the dream as well as the interpretation. That is the worst instance; but there are others where throughout the first half of a poem the hapless reader is clawing the air for a clue and has not enough breath in his body to admire anything you show him. . . .

The Fire Worshipers is surely a very bad title and rather helps to confuse. "Man, Truth, and Beauty' would be, not good I daresay, but better. 'Bowels": if terrific sublimity is what you are after, say 'guts'; which has the further advantage of being one syllable, and not two, like 'bowels,' though I am aware that Aytoun rhymes the latter with 'howls.' But nobody rent Prometheus' bowels that I know of, so I should say 'side' like an ordinary creature. . . .

The Keepsake. 'She waits by the windowsill and whistles.' Do you think so, Jim? The accomplishment is rare among women. . . .

[227]

The Bleeding Arras. This fails to impress, all the more because of the evident intention to impress. By the way, arras, embarrass and harass are brazen effrontery. . . .

The House of Birth. This is less indecent than Rosetti and less comical than W. E. Henley, but that is all I can say for it.

The Two Debtors. I do not understand this, and perhaps that is why I think it perfectly odious.

King B's Daughter. Nor this; but that may be the fault of my ignorance in not knowing who this monarch was.

Alfred's severe comments no doubt aided his brother to succeed in publishing his volume of poems called *Green Arras* in the same year that *ASL* appeared; and the English public, who knew Laurence better than Alfred, received the book with much greater praise than they gave *ASL*.

By the spring of 1930, a reversal had occurred in the opinion of the critics about the relative value of the two poets. They had learned to take Alfred seriously as a poet, and after *Last Poems* there was no longer any question about his being known for himself, and not for being "Laurence Housman's brother."

In 1929, Housman's passport expired, and he hastily sat for a new picture to enable his getting a new passport. This picture turned out to be the best photograph of his late years. His necktie wasn't straight, for he had been in a hurry, and he was wearing a common tweed suit, but his pique at having to sit for the picture at all kept him from being self-conscious. The carelessly posed photograph, taken three quarters to the left shows Housman exactly as he was at the age of seventy. Sensitivity, earnestness and brooding sadness are its striking characteristics, combined with a mellowness that came to him through suffering and renunciation. His head was silvering now, his brows were furrowed with living. But there was great dignity in his face; his eyes were true and clear. Such have looked from monk's cowls, and from under soldiers' helmets; eyes

that have reflected tragedy and have known great fear and loneliness and bravery. It is, too, the face of a man who had followed
the advice of Solomon: *And with all thy getting, get understanding.* But it is an imperious face, with pride written upon it, stony
determination too, such as scientists have known when they were
willing to reject many experiments to find truth at last. There is no
triviality in that face, no dalliance.

In the spring of 1930, the living children of Edward and Sarah
Jane Housman gathered together for the last time at the home of
their invalid brother, Basil, in the village of Tardebigge. Alfred,
Clemence, Kate, and Laurence arrived to spend some days with
Basil and his devoted wife, Jeannie, and although the sojourn was
darkened by the rapidly declining health of Basil, they were quietly
happy together, and came closer spiritually than they had been
since childhood. The following year Basil died, December 1, 1931.
Jeannie continued to keep her home and survived her husband a
number of years, and Alfred occasionally visited her, always at ease
in her company, and he wrote to her frequently.

Jeannie Housman wrote her impressions of the poet to Laurence
after his death in 1936:

> There is one thing I don't understand in all that is written
> about Alfred—they all speak as if he never had any happiness in
> his life; surely that cannot be true. I never knew that side of his
> life, he always seemed to enjoy things and to be happy, and enjoy
> amusing others with his clever nonsense. I have known him and
> Basil laugh until they cried. It hurts to think of him not getting
> some real happiness out of life, he deserved it, apart from his
> success and fame that must have given him satisfaction; but his
> kindness to others must have meant pleasure to him also.

Housman suffered a long period of depression after the publication of the last volume of *Manilius* in 1930. It was based on psycho-

logical reasons as well as physical ones; when Housman was work-ing on his book, he was not thinking of himself. When he had completed the thirty-year project, he suddenly took time to discover that he was old and very tired. But he sternly refused to admit his weakening even to himself, and he continued to take his walks, insisting on his legs maintaining the brisk pace they had always practiced, and consciously holding the same erect posture that had always reminded people of an old soldier. But he often boarded a Cambridge public bus that ran along Sidney Street to take him out to the country instead of walking, and from the end of the bus line he pursued his walk of several miles with spartan courage though his step had begun to slow down. Then he would board the bus again from the outskirts of the city to get back to Whewell Court, and he commended these buses to his friends—a form of transportation he had despised in his younger days.

He lived less comfortably in Whewell Court than he had lived, and he told his brother that he climbed his forty-four steps, two flights up, hoping he would drop dead at the top.[24] No wonder: the rooms were always bleak and drear when he arrived. A gas fire that consumed the oxygen had to be hastily lighted; he had a particularly cold and damp study and bedroom. Over and over he had been offered more convenient and commodious quarters, but he went on with his austerity and his hot water bottle and his tepid bath from a wash bowl in the morning. He had fallen into a weary state of body and mind in which his "go was gone"—to use Gerard Manley Hopkins' description of himself.[25]

He seemed to take grim satisfaction in his dark, plain, useful furniture which contradicted his love of beauty. For many years he had used a small straight-backed chair for his writing, but in late years procured an uncushioned Windsor chair for his handsome new mahogany desk. It was in this chair that he completed the final volume of *Manilius* and wrote *The Name and Nature of Poetry.*[26] He had very little sense of possessiveness in his mellow years; his one bitter lesson in possessiveness had taught him well. He definitely did not want to become too fond of anybody or of anything; the serenity of complete detachment grew on him, and was his main armor against "cheat and charmer."[27]

He continued consistently to renounce honors as they were rapidly offered him in his last years. He also refused a flattering request to lecture in America, which he never had the slightest desire to visit.

He liked American writers much better than he liked Americans (or America) and claimed to have introduced *Gentlemen Prefer Blondes* to the English public by first popularizing it among the dons of Cambridge. Mark Twain, Artemus Ward, Edith Wharton (whom he called upon in Paris), Sinclair Lewis, and Theodore Dreiser were other American authors whom he admired, and among poets, Edna St. Vincent Millay.[28]

When Housman was importuned to deliver the annual Leslie Stephen Lecture at Cambridge in 1933, he somewhat reluctantly accepted this honor, probably because there were some things he wanted to say that had never been said by anyone before him. He chose for his subject *The Name and Nature of Poetry,* and incorporated with his opinions about these some of his doctrines about literary criticism.

This lecture, his swan song, was given May 9, 1933, in the Cambridge Senate-House before a large gathering of some of the most brilliant minds of his University and elsewhere. Housman spoke honestly and simply, with such lucidity and assurance and downright sincerity based on experience, that he gripped his audience, though many chose to disagree with him; for as one might expect, he threw away all previous conceptions both of poetry and criticism and offered his own ideas in the place of them.

Aside from the extracts already quoted to show his method of writing, there were several autobiographical sentences in the lecture that deserve notice:

"All my life long the best literature of several languages has been my favorite recreation. . . ."[29]

"It is twenty-two years today since I last, and first, spoke in this Senate-House."[30] He had declined the position of College Orator during the interim. The fact that this position of honor had been offered him suggests how highly his ability to write in Latin was evaluated, as the Orator according to precedent often delivered his addresses in the Latin language.

"My ears are not contentedly attuned to the choir of captives singing hymns in the prison chapel, but can listen to the wild music that burdens every bough in the free world outside the wall. . . ."[31]

"When I am drinking Parolo stravecchio in Turin, I am not disturbed, nor even visited, by the reflexion that there is better wine in Dijon. . . ."[32]

"Whosoever will save his life shall lose it, and whosoever will lose his life shall find it." That is the *most important truth which has ever been uttered*,[33] and the greatest discovery ever made in the moral world; but I do not find in it anything which I should call poetical. On the other hand, when Wisdom says in the Proverbs "He that sinneth against me wrongeth his own soul; all they that hate me, love death," that is to me poetry, because of the words in which the idea is clothed; and as for the seventh verse of the forty-ninth Psalm in the Book of Common Prayer, "But no man may deliver his brother, nor make agreement unto

God for him," that is to me poetry so moving that I can hardly keep my voice steady in reading it. And that this is the effect of language I can ascertain by experiment: the same thought in the bible version, "None of them can by any means redeem his brother, nor give to God a ransom for him," I can read without emotion.[34]

This passage is a strange one to have been written by an avowed atheist. Its real significance is disclosed between the lines. Unconsciously Housman disclosed the fact that he chose to call himself an atheist for lack of a better term. He certainly did not believe in the God of the Church of England, nor in the philosophy of a life hereafter; that is true. Yet religion as it bears upon morals in human action affected him profoundly. He was a reader of the Bible from early life, though he chose to spell it with a small "b," but he discriminated between the creeds it gave birth to and its social teachings. Of God he had no conception that he was willing to admit, but here again is his merciless demand for truth and accuracy asserting itself in a positivism which excludes everything but knowable things. He believed without doubt that most people who affirm God are either misguided or hypocritical, because he knew that the finite mind cannot pierce infinity, no matter how hard it tries. All he could believe, if he had chosen to believe at all, would have been actually not belief, but merely adherence to a prescribed pattern, and with such imposed creeds Housman would have nothing to do. So the easiest way out was to avow himself an atheist, and an atheist he was, by the accepted pattern society likes to term atheism.

In the Leslie Stephen Lecture Housman had succeeded in stimulating his listeners again. He had experienced one of those regenerative comebacks that always has distinguished the English nation and its men at times of crisis. He was a sturdy son of England to the backbone, able to revive from hardship, over-effort, and austerity, and flower forth into new achievement. His auditors received his message as if they had felt the impact of a blow. Some agreed with him; others disagreed completely.

What? No poetic ideas? Poetry is a method of expression, not the thing expressed?[35] It may be inadvisable to draw out the meaning of poetry?[36] Shakespeare poured out his loveliest poetry in saying nothing?[37] Poetry is more physical than intellectual?[38] These were iconoclastic opinions and to accept them would be to cast a blow at the new school of scientific criticism of poetry, a craft well liked by dull men—preposterous possibility!

Housman took sardonic pleasure in throwing his monkey-wrench at the vanguard of "new" poets and critics, hoping to unseat them from their pedestals. A lesser man could not have said what he said; but Housman spoke with authority and had to be reckoned with. As time goes on, *The Name and Nature of Poetry* has taken its place with Wordsworth's and Coleridge's dissertations on the same subject; it is a classic, and anyone who wants to understand the difference between poetry and pseudo-poetry would do well to read it. James Southall Wilson says:

> *The Name and Nature of Poetry* has the ease and inevitability of expression that implies the utterance of thoughts that are not new to the mind from which they come.
> Written by any poet, the book would have been a valuable record of poetic experience and a beautiful statement of a poetic creed. But as the mature speech of the author of *A Shropshire Lad, The Name and Nature of Poetry* will be garnered up with the essays by great poets on poetry: with Sidney's, with Coleridge's, with Arnold's.[39]

Housman suggests the tests of physical response to find out what is pure poetry.

"Meaning," says Housman, "is of the intellect; poetry is not."[40]

He holds, as Herbert Read does, that in the eighteenth century "the place of poetry" was usurped by wit. In that century, the true poetic accent was possessed by four men—and they were all four mad—Collins, Christopher Smart, Cowper, and Blake.

Chauncey B. Tinker comments:

Some of Housman's critical assertions in *The Name and Nature of Poetry* are so old-fashioned as to seem today almost novel.

It was extremely disquieting to have Housman withdraw poetry from its intellectual and moral relations as not of the *esse,* or even the *bene esse*, of poetry at all.

"Meaning is of the intellect; poetry is not," he said.

Of course what Housman was thinking of was "poetry is not the thing said, but the way of saying it." Arnold too believed in the doctrine of "poetic touchstones," by which a poet's value may be tested by his power at times to produce passages of splendor which fill the heart or overwhelm us. It is this indescribable perfection of utterance that is for Housman the mark of true poetry.[41]

Housman lived up to his standard in his own short fervent lyrics. He could not sustain for long the excitement which he felt when writing poetry. In *The Name and Nature of Poetry* Housman dealt with poetry in its purity—the purple passages. He quoted only short illustrations in his lecture, lovely bits of song. He jeered at those poets and critics alike, professors of literature included, who were not able to discriminate between the great and the near-great in poetry. His essay was like a shot in the arm. He completely ignored that phenomenon known as "modern poetry." This exclusion was of course deliberate, and Mr. Tinker says: "In all the eloquence of this stimulating book there is nothing more eloquent than this silence."[42] Actually Housman's essay was the earliest attack made by the rear guard critics, who a few years later were openly to come to blows with the vanguard poets and their sympathetic reviewers.

Housman would have cried, "Capital! Capital!" had he lived to read the open attack on the "obscurantists" summed up neatly by Mr. Ben Lucien Burman:

> Only the dullest reactionary can fail to recognize that we live in a changing world, and that we and our methods of expression change with our new conditions. But it is one thing to welcome change and growth, and quite another to enthrone incomprehensibility and make it the cult of greatness.
>
> Because we cannot understand the poor creatures in a madhouse is no sign that they speak with the wisdom of Solomon. Words must communicate or they are worthless . . . Literature is life in all its variety, its beauty, its ugliness, its sorrow, its laughter. The disciples of the obscure accept no such definition. They permit no grace . . . they abhor what is known as "regionalism" . . . and thus bar out most of the great books of the world. Thomas Hardy was regional, so were De Maupassant, Victor Hugo, and Cervantes.[43]

Mr. Burman bases the reason for "the cult of unintelligibility" upon a feeling of insecurity in the world today, the fact that "culturally and politically we are still in our swaddling clothes."[44] He says "we are prone to accept frauds at their own valuation"[45] that valuation being boosted by much publicity. In other words too often professors and students alike vie at airing their pseudo-culture by glibly trying to discuss the unintelligible intelligently.

Housman would have cried amen to what a foremost American poet, Miss Louise Bogan, said recently about trends away from obscurantism. She startled many readers by declaring that our present mannerist art and literature is in the process of becoming obsolete in a "natural renewal of romantic idealism." She stated that "it is only in periods of idealism that order and integrity come back to thought; that a time of abundance is at hand." Two years had brought great changes in our way of thinking, she recognized, and added: "Americans must work away from the abstract toward the real, the organic, and the humane. Virtuosity in thought is particularly useless at present."[46]

The "cult of unintelligibility" that Mr. Burman talks about was what Mr. Gilbert Murray likened to a "stream of mud," in a letter to Housman after publication of *Last Poems*, in which Murray summed up his opinion with the prophetic words: "It will make a dreadful difference."[47]

The Name and Nature of Poetry backed Mr. Murray's opinion and was intended to do so. Housman wasted no time in telling what the obscurantists are; he spent his time extolling what they are not. He emphasized the virtues they do not possess: spontaneity, tonal purity, lucidity, beauty, emotional honesty, simplicity—all resulting in immediate understanding and response from the reader. And where he frankly says poetry may mean nothing, and cites some of Shakespeare's lovely little songs to illustrate his point, he says it still goes straight to the heart because of its ability to produce an immediate response in mood and emotion on the part of the reader.

Housman was old and wise when he wrote that final message to the world of poetry. He abstained from pique and petulance. He upheld an ancient standard by which to distinguish good poetry from bad, assuming his audience was willing to practice discrimination.

The group of English critics who were boosting obscurantists wasted no time in retaliating against Housman's lecture. Mr. Gorley Putt wrote:

Many who enjoyed the charm of Professor Housman when he delivered his Leslie Stephen Lecture will be sorry to see its appearance in cold print. . . . It would have been over-sanguine to expect much lively criticism of English poetry from a professor of Latin, but Mr. Housman's qualifications were such that his most jocular utterances have been echoed with solemnity.[48]

Conversely, among *The London Times* leaders, where solemnity is wont to be found, there appeared on the morrow of the lecture a whole column of skittish triumph: "When the whole lecture is published . . . and the world learns the full sacrilege of Mr. Housman's remarks . . . there will be some pretty outcries—or perhaps a dignified and discreet silence."

The champions of "modern poetry" were caught and they didn't like it. They chose, with Mr. Putt, to assume an attitude of amused sarcasm:

> Cultured people who feel that *A Shropshire Lad* is . . . the last appearance of the real thing in modern poetry have welcomed this pamphlet [*The Name and Nature of Poetry*] as making it safe for them to be quite explicit about the state of their taste. There has been a good deal of amusing explicitness.[49]

The same weak irony appeared in another piece by Mr. D. W. Harding and Mr. L. C. Knights:

> There is, of course, room for a good deal of difference of opinion about the merits of contemporary writers and their relative importance in the future. All the same, one could hardly be anything but amused by the trumpetings with which the *London Mercury*, in its June editorial, turned out the Old Guard against the Reactionaries—those who have reacted, that is, against the traditions of nineteenth century poetry. Professor Housman's lectures on the Name and Nature of Poetry provided the occasion.[50]

The article which was mentioned from the June number of the *London Mercury* said in part:

> It [*The Name and Nature of Poetry*] was like a buglecall, or the All Clear signal after an air-raid: the population stirred

again, saying "Thank Heaven that's over!" For during at least
ten years, the field of poetry and poetical criticism has been invaded by swarms of people who haven't the least conception as
to what poetry is, and who have affixed the name to things which
have no relation at all to what has been called poetry through all
the long past.

Mr. Harding and Mr. Knights continue:

It seems that the invaders are in flight and the editor of the
Mercury ... can now, beer-mug of stout fellowship in one hand,
knightly sword in the other, flourish defiance behind their backs.

Aside from the attitude of tolerant amusement, there is not a
single barb Mr. Harding and Mr. Knights were able to hurl against
the "Old Guard," which had reinforcements coming up from the
rear as far back as Homer.

When Housman read with venom these spirited reactions to his
lecture, and many more like them, he must have laughed with
sardonic glee at the hornets' nest he had stirred up. Indeed the Old
Guard had sprung suddenly to life in his defense. Mr. Herbert
Palmer dared to muster his missiles against the new poetry with
deadly aim: "The Eliotites are poets of obscurity, prosiness, experiment, and despair."[51]

The Saturday Review (London) said with delicate sarcasm
December 10, 1933: "Mr. Powys [who had written on Eliot in *The
Week End Review*, May 20, 1933] is naturally incensed that Mr.
Eliot's emotions do not find "immediate and careless expression,"
like Shakespeare's, in his verse."

Housman was gratified that he had struck a telling blow against
obscurantism without actually in words attacking it at all. His remark "that poetry was not the thing said, but the way of saying

it," had gone a long way. He would have agreed with Gerard Manley Hopkins when the Jesuit scholar wrote in his diary in 1864:

> It is a happy thing that there is no royal road to poetry. The
> world should know by this time that one cannot reach Parnassus
> except by flying thither. Yet from time to time more men go up
> and either perish in its gullies, fluttering *Excelsior* flags or else
> come down again with full folios and blank countenances. Yet
> the old fallacy keeps its ground. Every age has its false alarms.[52]

Regardless of Housman's devotion to his literary gods, and his
success in defending them, he never was able to win his personal
war or to achieve his peace. Peace was not for him, and all he could
do in old age was to declare a truce with his hidden struggles. But
in old age he was able to crystallize his opinions with a surety and
independence that he could not have approached in his younger
days, and his importance when he expressed those opinions must
have been gratifying to him.

But he still nursed loneliness and made it a fetish. He still sat in
his stiff chair three flights up in Whewell Court and growled and
snarled at shoddy scholarship, and pounced relentlessly upon un-
wary newcomers into the classical world when he detected sham
notes in their output. It was only when he relaxed at last before his
fire at night that the mist came to his eyes. Then he took up his
time-worn volumes of poetry, or a book he wanted to read, perhaps
the latest detective fiction, that made his face less grim.

It was impossible by this time for a stranger to pierce the hard
shell of his reserve. He distrusted admirers, and treated only his
most distinguished visitors with any consideration. But he still felt
compassion, especially for youth, or for people in trouble. An interesting example of his compassion for people in trouble was one
which occurred not long before he left his Whewell Court apart-

ment. He noticed that his bedmaker who had served him for many years seemed sorely depressed. He finally inquired what was the cause of her trouble, and she told him that her husband was ill, the family in poverty, and that she had exhausted her resources.

Housman immediately gave her a generous supply of bank notes, but said in a tone of exasperation, "Why didn't you tell me before? I would gladly have helped you." He then visited the husband, and assisted him in various ways to lighten the family burden.[53]

Another much earlier example of his generosity, not so easily accounted for, was lavished upon his favorite gondolier in Venice, a man he calls "Andrea" in *MP* XLIV (page 206, Penguin edition). His first reference to this man occurred in early letters to his stepmother, and they seem innocent enough.

15 Oct. 1900

I suppose I had better take the contents of Venice in the order of date. The first is the best: the Byzantine architecture as represented by the cathedral of St. Mark, which I should think is the most beautiful, though not the grandest, building in the world. It might be possible to erect in the Gothic style a more beautiful building, but I doubt if such a one exists. . . . I used to go there nearly every day; but it would take years to exhaust it.

The few remaining palaces of the same architecture I did not think much of, though Ruskin cries them up a great deal. Of Gothic they had two sorts in Venice: one for the churches, very thin and poor, with naked red brick on the outside; another for their palaces, exceedingly rich and elegant, but rather timid and monotonous. Of this the Doge's palace is the great example: you know its stupid general design, like a clothes-horse with a blanket on it; I am bound to say the reality is better than the pictures, because one can see that the flat and tame upper half of it is composed of red and white marble, although the pattern is no better than you see on the cottages in the Stourbridge Road at Bromsgrove.

The painter best represented in Venice is that lurid and theatrical Tintoret, whom I avoid, and Paul Veronese, whom one soon sees enough of. There are surprisingly few Titians, though two of them are very fine and famous. The best paintings to my thinking are those of Giovanni Bellini, who belongs to the previous generation, and his pupil Cima de Conegliano, mostly Madonnas and groups of saints; also two painters both called Bonifacio Veronese. . . .

My gondolier expressed a wish that he were your son. He wanted me to come to Venice next Christmas, and I explained that at Christmas I went to see you; and then he made this remark. The reason is, that if he were your son he would be well off and have no family to provide for: so at least he says. At present he has to earn a living for one wife, two sisters, one mother, one mother-in-law and half an uncle (who was once a champion oarsman and is now paralysed); which is pretty good for a young man of twenty-three who has had one eye kicked out by a horse.[54]

Housman's peculiar friendship with this gondolier lasted apparently until 1926, when he wrote a letter to his sister Kate, a letter that showed extraordinary solicitude for this man.

2 June 1926
. . . I should write to tell you that I am going abroad on Saturday for a fortnight or three weeks: first on a short visit to Venice, where my poor gondolier says he is dying and wants to see me again, and then to Paris. . .

23 June 1926
I got back safe yesterday, after three days' beautiful weather in Venice and a very dull time in Paris till just the last. My gondolier was looking pretty well, as warmth suits him, but he is quite unable to row and gets out of breath if he goes up many stairs. He is being sent by the municipal authorities for another three months' treatment in hospital, as they still find bacilli in his blood, and I suppose he will go steadily down hill. I was surprised to find what pleasure it gave me to be in Venice again. It was like coming home, when sounds and smells which one had forgoten stole upon one's senses; and certainly there is no place like it in the world: everything there is better in reality than in

memory. I first saw it on a romantic evening after sunset in 1900, and I left it on a sunshiny morning, and I shall not go there again. . . .[55]

The gondolier died, but his family, who seem to have adopted Housman, continued to pester him for funds after "Andrea's" death. He finally broke from them in disgust, and he never did see Venice again. One wonders what bond held "Andrea" and Housman together for so many years. One also wonders what urge caused the fastidious Housman to break down the class barriers which he was noted for observing. The fact that the gondolier wrote letters to Housman, and that his family also presumed to do so—letters which Housman answered—shows an intimacy that baffles explanation. The world of romance, the Grand Canal under the spell of moonlight, the slow steering of the gondola, and then no steering . . . how far will one's fancy carry him?

When a young student named Houston Martin read *A Shropshire Lad* while he was an undergraduate at the University of Pennsylvania about 1930, he was deeply stirred, and bought a copy for himself. He then wrote to Housman, telling him ingenuously of his admiration and devotion, and asking him to autograph his copy. Housman was quick to discover the honesty and freedom from ulterior motives that the letter displayed, and he wrote to young Mr. Martin, answering a question or two about the poems, but he refused to autograph the book. "Don't send it to me," he warned. Martin never did, but the correspondence did not stop there, and in all eleven letters were written to the young American, almost entirely about the Shropshire Lad. Very few Americans, with the exception of Mr. Witter Bynner, received as many letters from Housman as did Houston Martin. They were sent at intervals, not consecutively, and the poet got to know his distant admirer rather well. Housman told his brother Laurence about him, and some time after, Laurence asked about his brother's opinion of Mr. Martin.

In reply, Housman wrote dryly to his brother (1934) : "Mr. Houston Martin is a lunatic, but not unintelligent. I have expressed so much contempt of his aims and activities that he has now let me alone for some time."

Yet a few weeks before his death, he wrote a letter in the hospital to this same ingenuous and delightful young American friend who had done him good and brought a little brightness into his life by his honest praise and appreciation. The wine of true affection was sweet and heady even to the last. But the tone of this final letter was like all the others—witty, almost bantering, and quite impersonal.

Housman's sensuous intensity all his life made everything he enjoyed more pleasurable to him than to the average man: the color of skies, reflections in water, the sound of bells, the odor of flowers, the taste of fastidious foods and wines, the feel of good woolens and linens. Opposed to these delights, his intellectuality made him individualistic to the degree that he substituted his own ego in place of "the laws of God" as given through the established Church, and so had to bear his own guilts and temptations without spiritual intervention. Herein lay his soul struggle, typical of the revolt against tradition (of which obscurantism was but one expression with which he did not agree).

Housman had enough faith in his intellectualism to believe it would strengthen him with sufficient spiritual endurance to render him relatively impervious to suffering, but he was disappointed, for he had too much of the nature of a potential Christian to be satisfied by intellectuality alone. He believed that to relinquish his own errors to religious forgiveness—to cast the burden—was a deplorable kind of spiritual inertia that could result only in stagnation. He had to carry his own load of sin, and make, so far as he could, his own atonement.

This fact again identifies Housman with the unrest of the twentieth century, with its fluxion of confused opinions about the significance of both man and God: the flesh and the spirit. The groping of man to understand himself and God, without God, had become a malady. Man's preoccupation with his own soul and body had resulted in a sense of worthlessness so far as their value or significance was concerned, and had caused him to beat more furiously than ever against his limitations and restrictions, both in actual living, and in expression through philosophy and the arts. Housman lived to see this rebellion express itself in mass slaughter; if he had lived another decade he would have seen the drama unfolded on a bloodier stage ten times as wide and far reaching. And nobody would have been quicker than Housman to say that "the world runs ruinward."[56]

Housman constantly held up with almost exalted fanaticism the value of Virtue and Knowledge as the only satisfactory goal of mankind in his unsatisfactory existence. Paradoxically, he never recommended it more strongly than when he depreciated it as a means of securing happiness. "I covet truth" is a fine doctrine, but one that is susceptible to the amusement of the true cynic, who can easily tear away the veil of delusion about its curative value. Housman never deviated from the opinion he voiced about the failure of knowledge to bring about a state of happiness; an opinion which he first expressed in his Introductory Lecture at the University of London in 1892:

Entire happiness is not attainable either by this [truth] or by any other method. Nay it may be urged on the contrary that the pursuit of truth in some directions is even injurious to happiness, because it compels us to take leave of delusions which were pleasant while they lasted. It may be urged that the light shed on the origin and destiny of man by the pursuit of truth in some directions is not altogether a cheerful light.

The lecture on *The Name and Nature of Poetry* was given at five o'clock in the afternoon, May 9, 1933, and after the congratulatory fanfare was over, Housman was entertained at dinner by the Vice-Chancellor of the university, where a select group was present to continue their praises. Housman longed to get away. He was sick of "the infernal lecture"[57] and at ten o'clock he climbed wearily to his rooms, where he found Grant Richards waiting for him. He asked Housman for the right to print his lecture in book form, and Housman snapped out that he had already promised it to the Cambridge University Press. The evident fatigue of Housman was depressingly apparent, and Richards left very soon. When the volume appeared less than a month afterwards, Housman sent Richards a copy, with the words: "You'd like this, perhaps." The reply came, "Of course—but please inscribe it to me." The terse reply was not very agreeable: "I'm damned if I will. I don't like the lecture. I was over-persuaded into writing it. I wrote every line against my will. I shall inscribe no copy to any one."[58] Housman sent only ten copies of the book as gifts, and two of them went to his own family.

Snow came early that autumn, and with it winds and fog. Housman missed a Family Club dinner, and was suffering with an attack of lumbago when Richards called on him October 27 at his rooms in the midst of a heavy snow-fall. The men lunched and dined together. Richards was depressed by the starkness of Whewell Court, and urged him to seek more comfortable and convenient rooms, which were available at the time. But Housman brushed off the suggestion and changed the subject. He hated any alteration in his routine, and the bother of moving loomed before him like an insurmountable obstacle. Richards was not the only one concerned about Housman's poor accommodations, and out of the solicitous devotion of Mr. Gow, a change for the better was soon to be effected.

Housman's true feeling about his quarters he revealed in a remark to Laurence, when his brother thought he climbed the forty-four stone treads too fast for his age and condition: "I go up them with reckless speed," he explained with a hint of malice, "because I am overcome with joy at the prospect of getting there!"

Four

The Mask Cast Away

Happy he on the weary sea
Who hath fled the tempest
and won the haven.
Euripides

9

Oh whence, I asked, and whither?

THE LESLIE STEPHEN LECTURE was the beginning of the end for Housman. Only by great effort had he written and delivered the address, and a severe depression followed, when Housman's faithful Doctor Wood told him definitely that his heart was failing. The poet wrote to Grant Richards in July, 1935:

> The continuation of my life beyond May 1933 [when he delivered his lecture] was a regrettable mistake. The bright side of the weakening of my health since the end of February is that it encourages me to hope for an earlier termination of the affair. The heart is regarded by the doctor as the chief culprit, but partly it is just old age. . . . I have been passing a quiet three weeks in the country.[1]

Tardebigge, near Bromsgrove, was the place of his holiday, under the hospitable roof of his brother's widow, Jeannie. Here was a spot where Housman was surrounded with unselfish love, which he desperately needed. Jeannie lavished her services in his behalf, but unostentatiously, so that he was not made ill at ease. They were able to talk and even laugh, as they recalled old times—for instance the day when Alfred had been best man at Basil's and Jeannie's wedding, and how he had made a speech at the wedding supper commending a religious observance of a certain African tribe, which, he said, made a practice of eating the mother-in-law at the wedding feast. It had been a typical instance of his dry humor, and had been received with shouts, particularly because he was on very friendly terms with both the newly-made mothers-in-law.[2] During this visit in 1935, Alfred was pleased to find Jeannie much restored in health, and overcoming the shock of Basil's death at last.

Housman was invited to go to the Percy Withers estate at Souldern Court, near Bletchley, as often as he cared to come. He had visited the Witherses first in May, 1922, after Mr. Withers had recovered from his war injuries. Mrs. Withers, a typical twentieth-century woman, was not only trained in the ways of domesticity, but also she was a science First, and during her husband's convalescence at Cambridge, she had worked in the Cavendish Laboratory. She was adept at handling Housman; he had learned that there was nothing to fear from her, she never ruffled him. So with her he was amiability itself. She never fussed, never bothered him, never openly admired him. Perhaps she had heard the story of the woman who had invited Housman to her home and then tried to make a social lion out of him. When her determination became apparent, her charm and hospitality went for nothing. "This must cease!" Housman cried in agony; "She has seen the last of me!"[3]

No doubt his freedom from embarrassment with Mrs. Withers caused him to go to Souldern Court oftener than to any other place in England during his last years. The affection Dr. Withers felt for him was completely disinterested—of this Housman was certain, just as certain as he was that Richards' interest was not unselfish. Percy Withers venerated him, loved him for himself, and Housman was quick to note the difference. Mr. Withers treated him as if he were a precious musical instrument, he kept him in the right atmosphere; he tuned him to a nicety with fastidiously chosen guests for his pleasure; he touched his heartstrings gently and lovingly, alert to sense the slightest strain upon him, and immediately to protect him from it.

After Housman was released from the nursing home in November, 1933, he had gone to Jeannie, but on the way there he stopped to take lunch with the Witherses en route. How worn and frail he looked, and how subtly altered in appearance! The change greatly grieved his friends, but they felt better when he quickly broke into a hearty chortle upon seeing the array of fine wines awaiting his choice, which omen made them hope their fears were groundless.

After lunch, he stayed long enough to stroll about the flower garden, refused to sit down, and finally proceeded on his way refreshed and rested.

He did not plan to visit them again until the following May, when in anticipation of his coming, he wrote: "I fear I shall not be a worthy walking companion for you." Only a year before, they had taken their usual five mile walks. Mr. Withers was perturbed, but he comforted himself with the thought, "Well, after all, it's what you can expect from a man seventy-five years old." But the visit did not come off as intended, and Housman wrote to him later in pencil from sickbed:

> You probably know all about Cheyne-Stokes breathing described in Arnold Bennett's *Clayhanger*: sleepless nights spent in recurrent paroxysms of failure of breath, which can be combated if one is broad awake, but which overwhelms one if one dozes . . . if I were in proper health I should at this moment be representing Cambridge at the tercentenary of the French Academy.

Withers was unreservedly grieved and worried, to the extent that he wrote at once, asking the privilege of motoring to Cambridge for Housman and bringing him home as soon as he was able to travel. A pathetic letter came in reply, a letter so overcome by the affection lavished on him that he could not express his gratitude; he wrote that he would have liked to have suggested it, but had been afraid the Witherses could not conveniently keep an uncertain date open for him. They could indeed! Ten days later, Mr. Withers motored to Cambridge, and took Housman to Mr. Withers' new home, where he had very recently moved, halting at Buckingham for tea, which refreshed Housman; but at no time on the trip was he able to talk. Mr. Withers with daring sagacity about how to make Housman happy and comfortable, had invited the President of Magdalen College, Mr. Gordon, and his wife for the night. He left Housman free not to meet them unless he wished, but he agreed heartily to the idea, and the evening turned out to be one to remember with joy. Nothing about it was so memorable as Housman's high spirits, vitality, and good companionship. Mr. Gordon was a main reason for the success of the evening; "the best in everyone is, I should suppose, the customary attendant on the presence of the President of Magdalen,"[4] Mr. Withers remarked later.

It was not until the next day that the severe illness of Housman was painfully evident. The new home of the Witherses was an old watermill converted into a house by additions; it was near a lovely stream, and had spacious lawns and gardens. It was artistic, charming, and wholly comfortable. The private sitting room of the family, which faced the gardens and hills, Mrs. Withers turned over to Housman for his own use, and here he remained during his stay, often not disturbed for hours at a time. He sat in an armchair near the windows, with newspapers and books, and a book he had brought with him; but frequently when Mr. Withers came in to see how he was, he was found to be in heavy slumber, the slumber of exhaustion after terrible nights. His host longed to fuss over him, but he was kept from it by his wife, who assured her husband that their guest wished to be left alone, free from intrusion. She was right, for when Housman returned to Cambridge he wrote to her:

> I was glad to hear that you said I seemed happy while with you, for indeed the fact was so, and everything conspired to give me peace and enjoyment, and I make warm return of thanks to you and your husband for your care and kindness.

Another friend at Cambridge felt the same disinterested affection for Housman that Percy Withers displayed, and that man was Mr. Gow, his former student and now a co-Fellow of Trinity, who had felt increasing dissatisfaction over Housman's living quarters. He realized that Housman would never change them himself, so he took the job in hand, and by his own initiative, moved Housman from Whewell Court to the first floor of Old Court, Stairway B, while Housman was taking his customary motor trip in France that summer, this time in Dauphiné and Savoy. Knowing Housman as he did, it must have taken a good deal of courage to invade his sanctum. However, there had been numerous opportunities for escape from the dreariness and discomfort of Whewell Court, and one such chance had almost been taken three years before, when Mr. Gow had persuaded him to move to a suite of rooms in the gatehouse. It was repainted, ready for occupancy, even to an elevator, which Housman had paid for himself. At the eleventh hour he recanted. He was not as anxious for the immense gain in location and charm, and freedom from undergraduate clamor, as he was for staying where he was put, without the pain of upheaval, and the loss of all that had been home to him for twenty-four years. It had been a wrench long ago when in middle life he left Mrs. Trim at Pinner; it seemed an impossible thing for him to move now.

Mr. Gow said little more, but he felt justifieed in taking the responsibility for the change when the time came, and relieved his old friend of all the inconvenience of moving, for he even had his books shelved to his liking, and his papers in place, when Housman returned. Mr. Gow must have been well rewarded when he saw that Housman was contented with the move, now it had taken place, and actually enthusiastic about its benefits.[5] The suite was delightfully situated on the ground floor, with the spacious charm of the Great Court at his doorstep, and everything inside for his comfort. His windows were framed in ivy, which reminded him of the latticed ones of his childhood at Perry Hall and Fockbury; the sunshine flooded the apartment nearly all day.

This move occurred in late September, 1935. Housman had cut his visit in France short because of a slight accident which would have been less of a shock to a younger and stronger man. As he was getting into a taxicab in Savoy, he hit his head severely, cutting a disagreeable gash above his temple. Although he went on with his trip, the unexpected misfortune annoyed and exhausted him to such an extent that in two weeks he returned to England by plane through a storm—a dangerous crossing—so that he arrived in his new apartment in a much weakened condition.

"I doubt if I shall ever go to France again," he wrote his brother. This was his last journey, either there or anywhere else.

Mr. Gow had barely enough time to get the Old Court apartment ready before Housman came home.

His health improved for awhile under the stimulus of complete comfort, and his old inner fire flared up enough for him to do something he had contemplated with relish for years. Without a word, one day he tore down the portrait of himself by Rothenstein which had hung in the faculty Combination Room at Trinity, and bearing the wretched thing away, he flung it savagely into the fire. The portrait had been more than an annoyance to him; he had abominated it, the more because many people thought it was a good likeness. But he had to come to terms with Trinity, and finally substituted a portrait in his possession that he liked better, yet had bitterly condemned, one which he said with some venom that he had intended to throw in the fire before he died. The portrait which he did not wish to survive him hangs on the wall of Trinity to this day.[6] Although it was by Rothenstein also, he detested it only mildly. He never fussed at photographers, who showed him as God had made him; but he loathed portraits that showed him as Rothenstein had made him.

In the new suite, the closets were amply large for the suits, greatcoats, canes, umbrellas, ulsters, haberdashery, regalia, dressinggowns, and all sorts of shoes, overshoes, and slippers that Housman had accumulated with a finicky old-maidishness for correct attire; and now, for the first time in his life, he had the services of a valet, who must have been kept busy caring for his extensive wardrobe. When Mr. Withers visited the new suite, Housman flung open the closet to display the neat array, and spent some time showing him the wonderful bathroom, turning on the hot water time and again to prove how deliciously steaming it really was.

Housman had remained active during the entire summer of 1935. Both in 1934 and 1935, Laurence Housman and he took holidays together, visiting the homelands of Worcester, Gloucester, Herefordshire, and over into Shropshire, driving in Laurence's car, with his chauffeur Wills at the wheel, in 1934; but because of Alfred's failing health in 1935, they elected to make Cambridge their headquarters, and to visit churches, abbeys, and cathedrals in the country close enough to return to Cambridge at night.

Wills was again at the wheel, and on this trip he was somewhat scornful of A. E. H.'s tip—a half crown! "Quiet he was—said almost nothing on those trips," Wills told me. However, when the two brothers were alone, A. E. H. talked more than he had for many years, dwelling largely upon the past, Laurence Housman told me, and especially he spoke with intense love of his mother, and of her intimate talks with him. But the nature of these he chose not to disclose. In fact, he suddenly became cross, as if Laurence were guilty of trying to draw him out, and turned to him snappishly with these words: "More I will not tell you!" Again he showed one of his most unfortunate characteristics—unwillingness to share his deepest loves with others.

The last motor trip the brothers had together, in early October, 1935, they returned to Cambridge every evening, and Laurence remained over night with Alfred at Trinity. They were tired by nightfall, for they were making the most of the exhilarating autumn days, and sometimes did not reach Old Court until time for late tea. On this series of drives they visited more places, churches, abbeys and cathedrals than Laurence could count. Alfred knew them nearly all, and had a marvelous memory for their main points of interest and their style of architecture—even for those which he had not seen for a score of years. There was hardly a cathedral in England that he did not remember better than Laurence did; architecture was an interest which they shared deeply. Their only difference was that Laurence preferred Norman, and he Early English (Wells Cathedral was his favorite). "Of course," he said dryly, as if to discount the genuineness of his brother's preference, "to extol Norman is now the fashion." Alfred believed that one of the duties of windows was to let in light, and he expected architects to plan them for that purpose. Strange to say, monastic gloom in cathedrals did not please him as it pleased Laurence.

This final trip together made another deep impression on Laurence—his brother's remarkable memory of poetry. One day as they rode along they were discussing Keble, and Laurence happened to mention "Sun of My Soul," saying that he could not remember the poem to quote the lines he wished. Immediately Alfred quoted it all with unhesitating accuracy.[7] Many of the hymns with which he was brought up in the Church of England, and which his mother had him learn by heart before he was eight years old, had remained a part of his subconscious life, and surely had been unrecognized guardians over him at moments of his greatest temptations. But his memory was not limited to hymns, and when on the same occasion his brother discussed Landor with him, and started a quotation he could not finish, Alfred placed it at once in *Imaginary Conversations* and supplied the missing portion, though he said he had read Landor but little.[8]

On the last evening of the visit, Wills escorted the two men into the new suite, carrying a small satchel which the brothers had taken with them. Since the air was a trifle chill, the bedmaker had built a cheerful fire to greet them, and she had placed in the window a small blooming geranium because she had learned to love the silent old man whom she served.

"I was afraid of him at first," she told Laurence, "but after I knew him, how kind and grateful he was, everything was all right, and I loved your brother."

The apartment looked very handsome. The imposing modern library covered one entire wall, and much of the opposite one was devoted to the classical texts and reference books, all neatly arranged. The warm bedroom could be seen, with door half open. The same pictures and photographs he had cherished for so long were on the walls. He called from the bathroom, "Come see! It's hot at once!" as if the miracle were still to be wondered at. Laurence exclaimed about it over and over, to please him, but he thought, "Why, oh why, hadn't he procured these comforts years before?

Why had he punished himself by keeping to the stark Whewell Court citadel for twenty-four years?" His view of his brother had not been close enough, perhaps, in the withdrawn period to realize that A. E. H. had written a truce with himself, first through the means of poetry, and last, through self-punishment, through self-denial of many things he would like to have enjoyed, but could never accept; the inevitable result of his remorse for his deflection from the normal. Now, at seventy-six, with all the struggle of youth long past, he had forgiven himself; his atonement was finished. He could laugh when his water ran hot from the silver tap, and he could lie down in a warm, comfortable room without stabs of conscience.

Soon the bedmaker knocked. She knew the master was coming home, she had been watching for him, and now she came in and brought to his table, drawn before the fire, the steaming tea, and special scones she had made, with bilberry jam. She drew the shades, and carried Wills off for his share of the refreshments, which were better than ordinary. The tea was the finest Twining blend, smoky and rich, the scones had been made from a family recipe brought from Cumberland. The brothers were alone an hour, and while they had tea, probably A. E. H. discussed the will he was about to draw up with his solicitor, and in all likelihood told Laurence that he was to be his executor.

Finally a wave of exhaustion came over him, and Laurence rose to go. His brother did not get up. "Can't you remain over night?" he asked surprisingly. But Laurence said no, Clemence would be expecting him, he had promised her to return that night. Wills came in to help his master put on his ulster while Alfred still sat in his chair, a look of tragic sadness on his face as he said good-bye. He continued to stare fixedly at Laurence as he stood in the doorway, so that Laurence received the strange impression that he had become just so much space to his brother, and that he was gazing through him at something behind him. Laurence raised his hand in a mute gesture of farewell without any return wave given; then he gently closed the door and left him.[9] He had no way of knowing that Alfred's mind had projected his sight into the past, and that, as he looked unknowingly at Laurence, he was seeing the land of long ago, and the face of his mother; and the dearly loved children were looking up to him, calling him "Wa-wa," while they were all walking together down Worms Ash Lane, on the way to "Mount Pisgah." Long after Laurence had departed he sat there, looking at the closed door, his long thin fingers straight out on the arms of his chair, and such a broken look about him, such a shrunken, disconsolate appearance, that when the bedmaker came in to carry the tea things away, she longed to comfort him.

"Mr. Housman, sir, could I bring in your dinner tonight? I'd be glad to do it, sir." He roused and came back to the land of the living. "No, I thank you," he replied kindly. "I'll go to the Hall as usual." He looked at her gratefully, and after she had gone, the glow of her kind intentions warmed him to the extent that he felt comforted by the small incident which had broken into memories buried deep enough in his background of thought for him to believe them forever gone.

All his life he had turned to books for his main solace; now he reached for the nearest at hand—Max Beerbohm's *Caricatures*, as it happened, and before many minutes passed he began to smile sardonically. This was the kind of art he understood best, consequently he never failed to find enjoyment in caricatures of himself and others.[10] Some of the other books he turned to again and again in his old age were Selden's *Table-Talk*, which he always kept near at hand, finding it "serviceable and cleansing," Lecky's *History of England* in the eighteenth century, and Arnold Bennett's *Old Wives' Tale*.[11]

After their October holiday, Laurence Housman had his brother much upon his mind. He found a good pretext to visit him again in November, 1935, as he was to be the speaker at a Peace conference in Cambridge. When he called at Old Court, he was greatly concerned to discover that Alfred was in the Evelyn Nursing Home. He took a taxi to the Home on Trumpington Road, and the nurses allowed him to see his brother, but admonished him to make the visit brief. Alfred was glad to see him, but not inclined to sympathize with his reason for being in Cambridge.

"He knew what I was there for: the evening before there had been a torch-light procession to advertise the meeting. 'Last night,' he said, 'your people were making a great deal of noise outside, disturbing everyone. If that is what you call a peace movement, I would prefer that it should remain sedentary.' "[12]

In reference to their former meeting in the summer, Laurence asked his brother whether he had left any prose autobiographical notes which he might wish to pass on to the world after he was gone. The poet hesitated. "Nothing but my poetry, which I shall authorize you to use as you see fit," he finally replied.

Then the old impish expression that he put on when he wanted to tease his brother appeared and he said: "I've often thought of doing something like that. But if I did, I'll put it in the British Museum, to be kept under lock and key for fifty years!"[13] He wrote the same thing to Mr. Houston Martin in America, in a letter published in *The Yale Review*, (Winter, 1937, p. 299). He possibly said this also to others. Laurence Housman believed that his brother intended to burn his diary about his intimate relations with Moses Jackson, but at last decided to leave the remarkable story of those

years in the care of his brother, his last sacrificial gesture to truth.
During the final months of Housman's life, the Evelyn Nursing
Home became his haven of refuge. It was a pleasant residence that
did not look like a hospital, which in 1918 had been bequeathed to
Cambridge University by Joseph Prior, a tutor of Cambridge, a be-
quest that proved very useful, as it enabled the university to support
a much needed and worthy project otherwise impossible at this
time of national crisis, when the regular revenues of the university
were at low ebb.

It was a quiet, friendly spot, and after Housman was put to bed
there, and given morphia to relieve his suffering, it was not only a
place of rest, but the means of keeping him from self-destruction,
a desire that came back full force during the last two years of his
life. This was a desire that he despised as cowardly from the depths
of his heart, and fought away with no opiates until he reached the
Home. The nurses and Dr. Wood were astonished that after two
or three days with them, he was able, or so he said, to go back to
his rooms and his lectures. The injections gave him uninterrupted
sleep at night, and afterwards he lived on the strength of them
until he was forced to return to the Home for another rest. He continued to give his lectures even after his health broke down completely, sometimes coming from the nursing-home to the lecture
room, and going back there as soon as the lecture was over.[14]

When Christmas 1935 came, Percy Withers had sent Housman
his usual letter of greeting, with his customary invitation to be his
guest when he was able. There was no reply. However much he
disliked letter-writing, A. E. H. was always scrupulously prompt
in answering letters, and when a week passed, and a second, and a
third, Mr. Withers knew there must be something seriously wrong.
Waiting became increasingly difficult but knowing how his old
friend hated to be pestered with questions, especially about his

health, he chose to go empty of information rather than bother him, nor could he think of any Cambridge friend who might have the information he wanted.

At last the message came, a brief postcard. He had been for three weeks in the Nursing Home, unable to answer letters. He was home now, and lecturing again, but "with barely sufficient strength for necessary work," so Mr. Withers was asked to forgive this poor acknowledgment.[15]

Two days later, a letter came from Mr. Withers. The valet brought the mail in to him; he sorted it out from a miscellaneous pile of newspapers, journals, and strange post marks on letters that usually turned out to be requests for things he would not give, like autographs or permissions to quote his poems in anthologies. He sighed. What did Percy want now? Didn't he know he was old and sick and desired to be left alone?

The letter began: "My dear old friend." A quick mist came to his eyes, as his lips silently formed the words. Only two others had ever addressed him so, and both of them were dead, gone from this unsatisfactory world, their essence drifting to the twelve quarters of the wind. He read on. The letter told him of a love beyond compassion, an affection neither casual nor uncertain. Mr. Withers offered to go to Cambridge at a day's notice, to serve Housman in any way he wished, to be his nurse, and to remain with him as long as his services were useful. The letter dropped from his hand. He sat very still in the chair, and presently the tears came against his will. How could a man be so kind, and yet show the impulsiveness of an imbecile? He was touched at the solicitude, moved beyond his control, as he thought of his nightmare hours before dawn, his dread of sleeplessness, his struggle with suffocation, and nobody at hand to administer the antidote. What a wonderful aid Percy

[264]

could be to him, soothing him, relieving him, most of all, giving him the human sympathy he needed.

But his long years of self-denial would not allow acceptance of such a mercy. The longer he thought of it, the more provoked he was that the letter had come to stir him up, to harp on his predicament, to tempt him to take the easier way. He pulled note-paper out, and wrote four full pages by way of reply, an unusually long letter for him. It could not be called by any stretch of the imagination a gracious letter. It was mainly directed at Mr. Withers' "wrong-headedness," his "far-fetched irrelevance," a letter of frayed nerves and shaky lettering. When he got it, Mr. Withers was stung and grieved. Against the judgment of his wife, he wrote an abrupt note to Housman accusing him of tartness. The swiftly following letter made atonement, made it simply, casting off all disguises, and revealing his hidden self. He wrote: "I am sorry I have written tartly: my intention was not so; and indeed the extreme and undeserved kindness and generosity of your letters moved me to tears."[16]

After this episode, Mr. Withers felt Housman must not be troubled with proposals for a visit, as any disturbance of the customary routine might bother him. Not until March did he dare to write to him again, and then made his letter short, fearing to tax the strength of his friend with a reply. But Housman did reply—a letter written in pencil, quite unrecognizable, many of the words could be only deciphered with difficulty. The half-completed signature bore little resemblance to his name, and was vigorously scored out. Then, as if with a supreme effort, his own name, correctly spelled, was written firmly underneath. The news the note contained was typical: "My term was conducted to a triumphant end, but finally I had such bad nights that I was obliged to resort to the Nursing

Home. After two very wretched nights, I was wondrously relieved by morphia, which I submitted to at last, and now things are going on well."

His determination did not falter. Wryly he thought how painful was the travail to produce a skeleton. His flesh was dying, and he realized as never before the truth of a poem that he had written long ago:

'Tis long till eve and morn are gone:
Slow the endless night comes on,
And late to fulness grows the birth
That shall last as long as earth.

'Wanderers eastward, wanderers west,
Know you why you cannot rest?
'Tis that every mother's son
Travails with a skeleton. . . .

Empty vessel, garment cast,
We that wore you long shall last.
—Another night, another day.'
So my bones within me say.

'Therefore they shall do my will
Today while I am master still,' . . . .
—*ASL* XLIII

Laurence and Clemence Housman knew well that A. E. H. would not allow sympathy as he neared death, probably because he could not endure without emotion the expression of love behind it. They knew that their brother dreaded having his stoicism break down, that to subject him to compassion would have been an indignity. They knew he wanted to maintain his detachment until his thoughts blew clean away from him. It was for this reason, and

[266]

not because of lack of affection, that neither they nor his sister Kate were with him during his last days. His final note to Laurence, a barely discernable scrawl in pencil, with the date wrong by ten years, was confined to literary matters, to which was added one terse sentence about the state of his health. This note was written in April. About the same time, he wrote a short note to Mr. Houston Martin in America, with much the same thought. There were no more letters to anyone.

For now the Merry Guide[17] was shed of delight and laughter, and was close by his side. The "thymy wold" was past; "the blowing realms of woodland" were far behind. The road they had trudged on had been long and steep and rough, so that now the effort to follow was very great. Because of Housman's courage to meet his lectures at Trinity, his fellow-workers did not realize how ill he was and only Mr. Gow and Sir J. J. Thomson knew the truth. Mr. Thomson saw him on the day that he gave his last lecture. He was terribly ill, and the thought came to the Master of Trinity that his old friend must have invincible determination to lecture in such a state.[18] Mr. Gow took him to the Evelyn Home the next day, and neither of them saw him again, although they inquired for him constantly. Books which were sent to him by solicitous friends were returned unopened. The only flowers that went into his room were a little basketful of Lent lilies[19] that Joan Thomson knew he liked. Spring was early, and the lilies had not died on Easter Day.

Dr. Wood, the specialist who had been his doctor for several years, had grown very fond of him. Housman had been a courageous if intractable patient. At times of great pain he had maintained rarefied dignity—Dr. Wood had never seen greater self-control. The nurses discovered the same thing, and their interest in Housman soon became personal and beyond the call of duty. They prayed for him, told him so, and he thanked them kindly, and said with all honesty that their prayers did him good.

The mask he had assumed in early manhood was gone. His intellectual arrogance was cast aside as well; precision and accuracy failed him. Sometimes he asked, "What day is it?" not really caring or remembering. Like a wanderer in the desert who dreams of rest if he can reach the mirage in the distance, and so lets fall his burden a piece at a time—useless, cumbersome impediments in the battle against death—so A. E. H. cast from him, one by one, the accoutrements of his mind, until even courage was gone. His mind that had perversely compelled him to think, to reason, to criticize, "to lay his hand upon his heart"[20]—was winding up its affairs.

About two days before the thirtieth of April, he was able to talk when his doctor visited him. To Dr. Wood's surprise, he reached out his hand, and having lost the burden of reserve, he clasped the doctor's fingers closely for about half an hour. His sunken eyes expressed an affection that was deeper than gratitude.

"You have been very good to me," were the words that Dr. Wood quoted to Laurence Housman later. "I know that you have brought me here over and over to keep me from destroying myself."[21] He gazed at the physician with a look of fixed, intense pleading. He then asked him if it would be possible for him not to suffer any more pain. Dr. Wood knew what he was asking for—complete release. He bent over him and said with compassion: "I promise you, you shall not suffer any more," and after that, he did not.[22]

In order to cheer him, just before he left, Dr. Wood told Housman a thoroughly naughty story. The hypodermic was already taking effect, and Housman was able to throw back his head and laugh heartily. "I'll tell that tomorrow on the Golden Floor," he said, with his final spark of cynical humor.[23]

[268]

Dr. Wood was gone. Housman held out his hand again with a light feeling of loss of the body. Someone took it; could it be the Guide who was leading him? he wondered at a great distance. The nurse continued to clasp the slender fingers until oblivion came.

Night had enfolded him. Outside there was a wind, with a last-of-April shower, blowing the latch insistently with ghost-like fingers. Suddenly the door blew open in an urgent gust, and as quickly closed again. The hours went on, the rain diminished, tapped gently, and was silent. Dawn had come, with a faint pipe of birds in the hedge and muffled silence in the room. The watchful nurse bent over him. His pulse was as slow as time and eternity; she could perceive no action. For at last Housman was a part of time gone and eternity to come. His fingers relaxed. His seventy-seven years of travail were over, and the "immortal part"[24] had started on its endless way.

The news of Housman's death was flashed around the world, an event of more than mere literary or academic interest. Literature and scholarship would feel his loss, and in many hearts the loss was deeply personal. *The London Times,* May 1, 1936, had a leading article of nearly a column and an obituary of two columns, which was written by three men.[25] A few days later—May 5— *The Times* had a further column under the heading: "Professor Housman: Appreciations," written by Canon B. J. Kidd, (The Warden of Keble), Mrs. T. W. Pym, (a former student), Sir Percy Nunn, and Grant Richards.

Laurence Housman and N. V. H. Symons, N. C., I. C. S., son of Mrs. Kate Housman Symons, completed the plans for the poet's funeral. They went to the Nursing Home on the afternoon of May 1, and saw A. E. H. lying in the little chapel which was a part of the Home, a still and peaceful form at last. He was covered with a fine linen sheet over which had been placed a silk pall of gold and purple, and he lay beneath the altar of the chapel. Laurence said his expression was "imperious Roman" to the last. It was a fine face, from which suffering and struggle had been erased by the magical hand of death. Yet the face, said his nephew, was not serene. It was rather the face of a fighter that has laid down his armor, but retained his challenge. "It was," he said in conclusion in a letter to his mother written the same day, "the face of an autocrat and an aristocrat facing a silly mob and defying it." Noel laid his warm hand on his uncle's cool forehead, and said farewell.[26]

On May 4, the impressive final service was held in Trinity College Chapel, where all that was left of Housman was placed before the high altar midst the mellow radiance of candles and the subdued light of stained glass windows.

Three hundred people came to do Housman homage, among them the notable men of Cambridge and elsewhere, some of whom were deeply moved at the loss of Housman as a friend, quite aside from his loss to the world of scholarship and poetry. The service, planned by his family, was very simple, as he would have wished it to be. The twelfth chapter of Ecclesiastes was read, its haunting beauty and pagan poetry never more impressive. It was followed by a hymn, the tune being one by Melchior Vulpius, harmonized by John Sebastian Bach; the words were written by Housman in 1925 and entitled "For My Funeral." This poem was never seen until Housman sent it just about a year before his death to the Dean of Trinity Chapel. In the letter that accompanied it, Housman asked that the hymn might be sung at his funeral.[27]

O thou that from thy mansion
Through time and place to roam,
Dost send abroad thy children
And then dost call them home

That man and tribes and nations
And all thy hand hath made
May shelter them from sunshine
In thine eternal shade:

We now to peace and darkness
And earth and thee restore
Thy creature that thou madest
And wilt cast forth no more.
—*MP* XLVII

As the congregation sat there that brief hour, they all felt the loss of an individual force, but some discerned not loss—rather a presence. Those who loved A. E. H. were surrounded by him, he was everywhere—an invisible resurrection of memory and influence. To the right of the door as they left the chapel a bronze tablet was later placed in the wall by Trinity College as a memorial to A. E. Housman.

The next day the body was taken up to London for cremation. The ashes were placed in a bronze box, with an engraved inscription thereon which gave the name and dates of birth and death.

The final burial was private, and occurred on July 25, 1936, at Ludlow, the ancient town in South Shropshire that the poet had made famous. At the graveside, along the north wall outside the fine old parish church of St. Lawrence, were gathered Laurence Housman, his sisters, Clemence and Kate, and Kate's son with his wife, Dr. and Mrs. Gerald Symons. It was about noon when A. E. H.'s sister Kate, having seen to it that the engraving upon the bronze was placed in the direction to her liking, sorrowfully scattered over the urn a little boxful of earth that she had brought with her from the old home grounds at Bromsgrove, some from Fockbury, and some from Perry Hall.[28] The little group stood silently, each one thinking his own thoughts, remembering their brother of the old days when he was close to each of them, and their accepted leader. Then they turned away. The urn was buried in the ground, and over it to mark the exact spot there lies a smooth square of stone with the letters: A. E. H.

Later a bronze tablet was placed in the outside wall of the church directly above the grave, which bears these words:

IN MEMORY OF ALFRED EDWARD HOUSMAN
M. A. OXON.
KENNEDY PROFESSOR OF LATIN AND FELLOW OF
TRINITY COLLEGE IN THE UNIVERSITY OF CAMBRIDGE
AUTHOR OF "A SHROPSHIRE LAD"
BORN 26 MARCH, 1859. DIED 30 APRIL, 1936.
GOOD NIGHT, ENSURED RELEASE
IMPERISHABLE PEACE
HAVE THESE FOR YOURS.

This tablet, the square of stone in the ground bearing its initials A. E. H., and the living cherry tree that Laurence Housman caused to be planted near the grave, but on the opposite side of the walk, are all the visible testimony at Ludlow that A. E. H. once lived.

Those, and the hills of Clee in the distant West, and the orchards in the spring, the soldiers on the streets of Ludlow, the lovers lying two by two in the meadows or in their graves, the great constellations at nights in the heavens, and the eternal foolscap on the face of the moon.[29]

Stars, I have seen them fall.
—*MP* VII

Notes

Notes

Notes

CHAPTER ONE

1. Symons, *Alfred Edward Housman: Recollections,* (A. E. Housman Memorial Number of *The Bromsgrovian,* November, 1936, published at the Bromsgrove Preparatory School, Bromsgrove, England, for the Housman Memorial Fund, with various contributors.). (Hereafter cited as *A. E. Housman: Recollections*), p. 8.

2. Laurence Housman, *The Unexpected Years* (Indianapolis, Indiana: Bobbs-Merrill, 1937), p. 19.

3. *Ibid.,* p. 49.

4. Symons, *A. E. Housman: Recollections,* p. 10.

5. Laurence Housman, *My Brother A. E. Housman* (New York: Scribner's, 1938), p. 20.

6. *ASL,* no. L, ll. 1-4.

7. Housman, *The Unexpected Years,* p. v.

CHAPTER TWO

1. Housman, *The Unexpected Years,* pp. 19-20.

2. Conversation with Laurence Housman.

3. *Ibid.*

4. Letter from Laurence Housman to author, 1952.

5. Housman, *The Unexpected Years,* p. 84.

6. A story Laurence Housman recounted to the author.

7. A. C. Benson's thumbnail sketch of A. E. H. in Grant Richards, *Housman, 1897-1936,* (Oxford University Press, 1942), p. 300.

8. Symons, *A. E. Housman: Recollections,* p. 8.

9. Conversation with Laurence Housman.

10. Housman, *The Unexpected Years,* p. 51.

11. Symons, *A. E. Housman: Recollections,* p. 10.
12. A recollection told to the author by Laurence Housman.

CHAPTER THREE

1. Conversations with Laurence and Clemence Housman.
2. Symons, *A. E. Housman: Recollections,* p. 8.
3. Conversation with Clemence Housman.
4. Richards, p. 270.
5. Conversation with Laurence Housman.
6. Laurence Housman showed the placard to the author and explained in detail its influence on their later lives.
7. Symons, *A. E. Housman: Recollections,* p. 23.
8. *Ibid.,* p. 16. "I was small, and a dunce through my inveterate hate of lessons . . . Basil, with prosaic and mechanical tastes, went a different way." (He became a doctor.)
9. It was a delight to hear Clemence read a few lines, or to hear Laurence read from his *Little Plays of St. Francis,* as he paced back and forth in "Elbow Room," and sometimes broke into tears when emotion in the lines overcame him. He was then eighty-six years old, and Clemence eighty-eight. Both of them were keenly alert, physically and mentally.
10. Personal letter from Clemence Housman to the author, December, 1951.
11. It was interesting indeed to see this book in the A. E. Housman library at "Elbow Room"—a book he had kept all his life, unused.
12. A. E. Housman, *The Name and Nature of Poetry* (Cambridge: Cambridge University Press, 1933), p. 46. (Rudyard Kipling remarked about this passage: "Housman is so right.")
13. Conversation with Laurence Housman, at which time he showed the author the first and only short story A. E. H. ever wrote, and granted permission to quote the small part given.
14. Scribner's, 1938.
15. Quoted from a letter from Laurence Housman, 1952.
16. Clemence Housman died at ninety-four in 1956. Laurence Housman is ninety-two.

CHAPTER FOUR

1. Pollard, *A. E. Housman: Recollections,* p. 30.
2. Laurence Housman, *My Brother,* pp. 40-41.

3. Symons, *A. E. Housman: Recollections*, p. 16.
4. Pollard, *A. E. Housman: Recollections*, pp. 30-31.
5. Richards, p. 322.
6. Pollard, *A. E. Housman: Recollections*, p. 31.
7. Housman, *My Brother*, pp. 41, 52.
8. Richards, p. 270.
9. *Collected Poems.*
10. *Ibid.* This poem was first published in *Waifs and Strays* at Oxford.
11. Pollard, *A. E. Housman: Recollections*, p. 33.
12. When Housman attended Oxford, the college required four years of residence for a degree.
13. Symons, *A. E. Housman: Recollections*, p. 24.
14. Italics added.
15. Italics added.
16. By letter, in 1952, from Laurence Housman.
17. Symons, *A. E. Housman: Recollections*, p. 24.
18. *Collected Poems.*
19. Note A. E. H.'s *Diffugere Nives, MP,* no. V.
20. André Gide, *Corydon,* Fourth Dialogue, notes p. 213 (New York: Farrar, Straus and Company, 1950).
21. Quoted from a letter to the author from Laurence Housman, 1951.
22. Laurence Housman, *A. E. Housman: Recollections,* p. 36.
23. Richards, p. 322.

CHAPTER FIVE

1. Housman, *My Brother,* p. 60.
2. Ker, *A. E. Housman: Recollections,* p. 46.
3. An expression Laurence Housman used in a letter to the author to describe his brother's attitude after "the heavy change," (1952).
4. Their intimate relations at these times, which Housman fully describes in his diary of this period, lie locked in the British Museum, not to be published until the centenary of his birth—disclosed in a letter from Laurence Housman to the author, October 7, 1957.
5. *MP,* no. XLIV.
6. Italics added.
7. Housman, *My Brother,* pp. 128-31.
8. His birthday.

9. The Patent Office.

10. As recounted to the author by Laurence Housman.

11. Quoted from a letter to the author from Laurence Housman, 1952.

12. Percy Withers, *A Buried Life* (London: Jonathan Cape, 1940), p. 67. "The first of the lyrics came as early as 1886." This fact was told to Withers by Housman when the poet was past seventy.

13. Perhaps Housman did tell a Frenchman this fact, but Laurence Housman probably referred to a passage he had inserted in an earlier book of his own. Houston Martin's letter from Housman, December 14, 1933, gave this information and was published by Laurence Housman in *My Brother*, p. 194.

14. The name of Byron Cottage has nothing to do with Lord Byron.

15. A. S. F. Gow, *A. E. Housman, A Sketch* (Cambridge: Cambridge University Press, 1936), discusses the list more fully, pp. 60-137.

16. *Ibid.*, p. 9.

17. *LP*, p. 125.

18. As told to the author by Laurence Housman.

19. Richards, p. 270.

20. A. E. Housman, Introductory Lecture, University College, 1892. (Mimeographed pamphlet, University of London.)

21. This amusing cartoon was included in R. W. Chambers, *Man's Unconquerable Mind* (London: Jonathan Cape, 1939), p. 376. Mr. Chambers was a student under Housman at University College and later a famous contemporary.

22. A. E. Housman, Inaugural Lecture, Cambridge University, 1911.

23. Chambers, pp. 381-82.

24. Quoted from a letter to the author from Sir Mortimer Wheeler, 1951.

25. Italics added.

26. Richards, p. 271.

27. Chambers, p. 383.

28. Withers, p. 67.

29. A. E. Housman to Maurice Pollet, from *My Brother*, Laurence Housman, p. 72.

30. Richards, p. 270.

31. John Sparrow, Introduction to *Collected Poems of A. E. Housman* (The Penguin Poets, London: Jonathan Cape, 1956), p. 12.

32. Housman, *My Brother*, p. 99.

33. A. E. Housman, *The Name and Nature of Poetry*, pp. 45-46. Housman said in this book that one stanza in the last poem in *ASL* had stumped him; that the other three had come spontaneously. The elusive stanza took a year in the making. Many people asked him which stanza the difficult one was, but he never told them. Among these was Houston Martin. In a letter of October, 1956, Laurence told the author that it was the third stanza. The poem was written in this order: 1, 2, 4, 3.

CHAPTER SIX

1. As recounted by Pollard to Laurence Housman, with whom he was on terms of life-long friendship.

2. Conversation with Laurence Housman.

3. Sir William Rothenstein, *Men and Memories,* (London, 1920), Vol. II, p. 141.

4. Chambers, p. 375.

5. Housman, *My Brother*, p. 81. Laurence Housman later sold one of these copies for £80.

6. Conversation with Clemence Housman.

7. Letter to the author from Laurence Housman, 1952.

8. Letter to the author from Laurence Housman, 1952. This interpretation is different from the one the author published in *The Explicator* in June, 1950. The change is the result of Laurence Housman's explanation which A. E. H. had given him.

9. Symons, *A. E. Housman: Recollections,* p. 26.

10. The tumultuous drama of the Wenlock Edge lines appealed to Dr. Vaughan Williams, dean of English composers, who used them as his key song in his famous "Wenlock Edge Suite," published by Boosey in London, and now available in excellent record album form in America.

It is generally conceded that Dr. Vaughan Williams accomplished a good interpretation in his Wenlock Edge Suite. Throughout the poem, the tempo set for the struggle of man is like a tiny centrifugal force inside the patient, slow, almost motionless action of eternity. This tempo Dr. Williams interprets well.

Mr. Percy Withers, in his long friendship with Housman, once essayed to play the records for him, while the poet was making Mr. Withers a house visit, but his reaction was very unfavorable. Withers decided that Housman had no liking for music nor understanding of it, though actually A. E. H. was stirred violently but negatively—more probably because he had a natural sensitivity to the high-pitched tenor of the Wenlock Edge Suite, set as high as A in register. Also, he was repelled by the considerable amount of dissonance and minor notes which best expressed Williams' somewhat radical style. Housman recoiled at what seemed to him to be the wrong setting for his Shropshire Lad, who, according to his creator, would probably have been best interpreted in a simple ballad setting. But Housman was opposed to poetry being set to music at all, or to musical recitative, and only in his late years did he grudgingly comply with such requests.

11. *The Culprit, LP,* no. XXIV, ll. 1-2.

12. Italics added.

13. Quoted from a letter from A. E. Housman to Arnold Stein, Rare Manuscript Division, Housman Collection, The Library of Congress.

14. Richards, p. 449.

15. Laurence Housman made it plain to the author, as did his sister Clemence, that Sophie Becker had a "comfortable friendship" with A. E. H., that it was never disturbing to either of them, and that Housman's regard for her was a solace to him throughout his life. She was almost sixteen years older than Housman, and in a way took the place of the mother he had lost.

16. Withers, *A Buried Life.*

17. From the A. E. Housman Collection, Library of Congress:

> *ASL,* no. XXXIII, was written at least three times with great passion and difficulty, before it reached its final form. Verse 1, line 2, "powers" read "heavens"; line 6 read "if truth" (almost obliterated); also "if strong resolve could save"; line 7 for "end" read "fall"; line 9 did not suit Housman; in the left margin appear these words all rejected:
>
> Long care and . . . .
> contriving
> devising

On the right hand margin appear:

> Fear and not hopes
> Long fear. . . .

Line 10, "will" chosen after "hope" and "pains" were rejected. Line 13, "but now" very significantly read "There is none": The line read as a whole at first:

> there is none: that all is over. . .

Line 15, "Town" read "an end."

18. André Gide, *Corydon,* (New York: Farrar, Straus and Company, 1950).

19. Mr. Gow told me this in a conversation I had with him on July 26, 1951. I asked him if he thought such unhappiness to be unavoidable in the invert personality.

"No, certainly not," he replied emphatically. Mr. Gow obviously did not wish to be drawn out further, but his frank reply to that one question took for granted the central tragedy of Housman's life.

20. A letter from Alfred Housman to Laurence Housman, which he permitted the author to copy in part.

21. Quoted from *The Yale Review,* Eugene Davidson, (Winter, 1937).

22. H. W. Garrod, *The Profession of Poetry and Other Lectures,* (Oxford: Clarendon Press, 1929). This was a collection of essays and lectures which Professor Garrod delivered over a period of years.

23. A remark attributed to "a Scotch legal gentleman" who threw *ASL* in the fire. Richards, p. 219.

24. Cyril Connolly, "A London Diary," *The New Statesman,* May 23, 1936.

25. Laurence Housman quoting George Meredith, *A. E. Housman: Recollections,* p. 36.

26. Comment of Witter Bynner (who, when editor of McClure's Magazine, was the first to publish in an American magazine single poems from *ASL*). Quoted here from *A Shropshire Lad,* with notes by Carl J. Weber, Colby College: Waterville, Maine, pp. 124-25.

27. Comment of Evan Pughe who said, "I first read *ASL* on the Messines Ridge (World War I). A new officer said to me one evening, 'Have you read this?' and drew from his pocket a long, narrow red edition of *ASL*. From that time I was a devotee of Housman." *Ibid.*, p. 125.

28. Comment of J. B. Priestly, *ibid.*, p. 125.

29. Comment of Louis Untermeyer, *ibid.*, p. 123.

30. F. L. Lucas of King's College, Cambridge, under the title of "Few, but Roses," *The New Statesman,* October 20, 1923.

31. Christopher Morley, *Plum Pudding,* (New York: Doubleday, 1921) p. 192.

32. André Maurois, *The Quest for Proust,* (London: Jonathan Cape, 1950) p. 229.

CHAPTER SEVEN

1. Gow, p. 55.

2. Housman, *My Brother,* p. 147.

3. *ASL,* no. LXII, ll. 21-22.

4. Housman, *My Brother,* p. 102.

5. Richards, p. 300.

6. Housman, *My Brother,* p. 112.

7. Richards, p. 289.

8. The history of The Family Club, and the facts which follow were told to the author by the Charnocks, 1951.

9. From personal conferences with Mrs. Joan Thomson Charnock.

10. From the A. E. Housman Collection in Trinity Library; used by permission of Trinity College.

11. Rothenstein, p. 149.

12. In addition to Housman, other pallbearers at Thomas Hardy's funeral in Westminster Abbey were Stanley Baldwin, Ramsay McDonald, Bernard Shaw, John Galsworthy, Edmund Gosse, Rudyard Kipling, Rev. E. M. Walker (Provost of Queen's College, Oxford), and A. B. Ramsay (Master of Magdalene College, Cambridge).

13. Richards, p. 154.

14. *Ibid.,* p. 283.

15. Letter to the author from Laurence Housman, February, 1953.
16. "The West," *LP*, no. I.

CHAPTER EIGHT

1. Richards, p. 207-8.
2. Permission of Henry Holt and Company.
3. A letter to A. E. H. from Margaret Woods, in the A. E. Housman Collection, Rare Manuscript Division, Library of Congress.
4. A letter to A. E. H. from Dr. Gilbert Murray, *ibid.*, Library of Congress.
5. A letter to A. E. H. from Sir William Rothenstein, *ibid.*, Library of Congress.
6. Clarence Darrow, the famous criminal lawyer, used this poem and one or two others by Housman, in his defense of criminals—notably in the Loeb and Leopold trial.
7. Richards, p. 373.
8. *Ibid.*, p. 201.
9. *Ibid.*, pp. 203-4.
10. *The Yale Review*, Winter, 1936.
11. Shaw declined the honor.
12. Housman, *My Brother*, pp. 112-13.
13. Conversation with Mrs. Joan Thomson Charnock.
14. Housman, *My Brother*, p. 113.
15. *Ibid.*, p. 112.
16. This quotation is taken from the first stanza of "The Sage to the Young Man," *MP*, no. IV.
17. Appropriately placed by Laurence Housman at the beginning of *More Poems*. These quotations are used with permission of Henry Holt and Company.
18. "Willy" was Henry Villars, the collaborator of Colette. Housman considered Willy to be spurious and second-hand.
19. Sir J. J. Thomson, *Recollections and Reflections,* (London: George Bell & Sons, Ltd., 1936).
20. See the natal horoscope of A. E. Housman. Housman, *My Brother*, p. 279.
21. Thomson, *Recollections and Reflections.*
22. Richards, p. 104.

23. Housman, *My Brother,* pp. 156-60.
24. *Ibid.,* p. 118.
25. Letter from Hopkins to Alexander Baillie, January 14, 1883.
26. Laurence Housman uses this chair and desk in "Elbow Room."
27. *MP,* no. VI.
28. Housman, *My Brother,* p. 85.
29. A. E. Housman, *The Name and Nature of Poetry,* pp. 2-3.
30. *Ibid.,* p. 1.
31. *Ibid.,* p. 26.
32. *Ibid.*
33. Italics added.
34. A. E. Housman, *The Name and Nature of Poetry,* pp. 34-35.
35. *Ibid.,* p. 35.
36. *Ibid.,* pp. 35-36.
37. *Ibid.,* pp. 39-40. "Even Shakespeare, who had so much to say, would sometimes pour out his loveliest poetry in saying nothing."
38. *Ibid.,* p. 40.
39. J. S. Wilson, "The Name and Nature of Poetry," *The Virginia Quarterly Review,* July, 1934.
40. A. E. Housman, *The Name and Nature of Poetry,* p. 37.
41. C. B. Tinker, "On the Name and Nature of Poetry," *The Yale Review,* September, 1933.
42. *Ibid.*
43. Ben Lucien Burman, "The Cult of Unintelligibility," *The Saturday Review,* November 1, 1953. Quoted by permission of Mr. Burman.
44. *Ibid.*
45. *Ibid.*
46. *The Partisan Review,* September-October Number, 1952. The three midsummer numbers of *The Partisan Review,* 1952, contain sober discussions by a dozen critics on the general subject "Our Country and Our Culture." Miss Bogan's article is a part of this series.
47. From a letter from Gilbert Murray to A. E. H. in the A. E. Housman Collection, Rare Manuscript Division, Library of Congress. The letter was written after publication of *Last Poems.*
48. Mr. Gorley Putt, *Scrutiny,* (published quarterly at that time by the Cambridge University Press) September, 1933.

49. *Ibid.*
50. D. W. Harding and L. C. Knights, "Flank-rubbing and Criticism," *Scrutiny,* September, 1933.
51. Mr. Herbert Palmer, *Everyman,* May 27, 1933.
52. *A Hopkins Reader,* Edited by John Pick, (New York: Oxford University Press, 1953).
53. As recounted to the author by Laurence Housman.
54. Housman, *My Brother,* pp. 141-42.
55. *Ibid.,* pp. 150-51.
56. *MP,* no. XLIII.
57. Richards, p. 275.
58. *Ibid.,* p. 276.

CHAPTER NINE

1. Richards, p. 280.
2. Housman, *The Unexpected Years,* p. 304.
3. Withers, p. 97.
4. *Ibid.,* pp. 108-9.
5. *Ibid.,* pp. 121-22.
6. *Ibid.,* p. 123.
7. Housman, *The Unexpected Years,* pp. 321-22.
8. *Ibid.*
9. As recounted to the author by Laurence Housman.
10. Withers, pp. 83-84. Mr. Withers had loaned him these volumes.
11. *Ibid.,* pp. 98-99.
12. Housman, *My Brother,* p. 120.
13. Richards, p. 287, footnotes.
14. Thomson, p. 314.
15. Withers, pp. 123-24.
16. *Ibid.,* p. 126.
17. "The Merry Guide," *ASL,* no. XLII.
18. Richards, p. 283.
19. *ASL,* no. XXIX.
20. *LP,* no. X. These lines were in rough draft in Notebook C, page 1, but in a revised form with few corrections.
21. Housman, *My Brother,* p. 120.
22. *Ibid.*

[285]

23. *Ibid.*, p. 121.
24. *ASL*, no. XLIII (title).
25. Richards, p. 285.
26. An excerpt from a letter by Katharine Symons' son, whom Housman called "Jerry." Quoted here from *A. E. Housman: Recollections*, p. 60.
27. Three hundred copies of Housman's funeral service were first printed with an error; Ecclesiastes was spelled Ecclesiasticus. Later one hundred more copies were published with the error corrected. The evening newspapers of May 4, 1936, in London, Cambridge, Oxford and Birmingham carried the item of Housman's funeral service.
29. Symons, *A. E. Housman: Recollections*, p. 29.
30. "Revolution," *LP*, no. XXXVI, l. 8.

List of Sources

List of Sources

BOOKS

Brenner, Rica. *Ten Modern Poets*. New York: Harcourt Brace, 1936.

Chambers, R. W. *Man's Unconquerable Mind*. London: Jonathan Cape, 1939.

Dodds, John W. *The Age of Paradox*. New York: Rinehart, 1952.

Garrod, H. W. *The Profession of Poetry and Other Lectures*. Oxford: Clarendon Press, 1929.

Gide, André. *Corydon,* (Four Dialogues). New York: Farrar, Straus and Company, 1950.

Gow, Andrew S. F. *A. E. Housman: A Sketch*. Cambridge University Press, 1936.

Haber, Tom Burns. *The Manuscript Poems of A. E. Housman*. University of Minnesota Press, 1955.

Hopkins, Gerard Manley. *A Hopkins Reader,* edited by John Pick. New York: Oxford University Press, 1953.

Housman, A. E. *Collected Poems,* (Tenth Impression), with notes by John Carter. London: Jonathan Cape, 1939.

Housman, A. E. *Collected Poems,* with notes by John Sparrow. The Penguin Poets, London: Jonathan Cape, 1956.

Housman, A. E. *Manilius,* Vol. I. Grant Richards Press, 1903. Discussed and explained by Clemence Housman, Somerset, 1951.

Housman, A. E. *The Name and Nature of Poetry*. Cambridge University Press, 1933.

Housman, Laurence. *My Brother, A. E. Housman*. New York: Scribner's, 1938.

Housman, Laurence. *The Unexpected Years*. Indianapolis, Indiana: Bobbs-Merrill, 1937.

Maurois, André. *The Quest for Proust*. London: Jonathan Cape, 1950.

Richards, Grant. *Housman, 1897-1936*. Oxford University Press, 1942.

Rothenstein, Sir William. *Men and Memories*. London: 1920.

Stevenson, Lionel. *The Ordeal of George Meredith*. New York: Scribner's, 1953.

Thomson, Sir Joseph John. *Recollections and Reflections*. London: George Bell & Sons, Ltd., 1936.

Weber, Carl J. *Housman, With Notes*. Waterville, Maine: Colby College, 1946 (Jubilee Edition).

Wilde, Oscar. *De Profundis*. New York: The Philosophical Library, 1950.

Williams, Charles. *Poetry At Present*. Oxford: Clarendon Press, 1930.

Wilson, Edmund. *The Triple Thinkers*. New York: Oxford University Press, 1949.

Withers, Percy. *A Buried Life*. London: Jonathan Cape, 1937.

ARTICLES AND PERIODICALS

Bibliographical Notes and Queries: Vol. 2, Number 9: 5, 6, January 1938; the order of service for Housman's funeral; and "Check List of Housman's Writings," Vol. 2, November, 1938, by John Sparrow.

Bromsgrovian, A. E. Housman: Recollections, November, 1936. A. E. Housman Memorial Number, published at Bromsgrove Preparatory School, Bromsgrove, England, for the Housman Memorial Fund, with various contributors.

Cambridge Review, "Obituary of A. E. Housman," May 8, 1936.

Explicator, published under the auspices of the University of South Carolina, Dr. Edwin J. Whitesell, Director. Darrell Abel, December, 1949; William Bache, October, 1951; Robert J. Kane, June, 1950; Brewster Ghiselin, March, 1946; Maude Hawkins, June, 1950; A. E. Housman Number, March, 1944; Elizabeth Nitchie, June, 1952.

London Mercury, an editorial, June Number, 1933.

London Times Literary Supplement, Notes on A. E. Housman, April 24, 1937; October 19, 1922; October 24, 1936; November 5, 1908; April 22, 1926; November 7, and 14, 1936; April Memorial Number, 1946, with a drawing of Housman on the cover.

Mark Twain Review, Housman Memorial Notes, Vol. I, 1937, (secured from Duke University and long out of print).

Oxford Magazine, "A. E. Housman at Oxford," November 11, 1937.

Punch, 163. October 25, 1922, A caricature of A. E. Housman with a copy of *Last Poems* in his pocket. (Library of Congress.)

Partisan Review, Louise Bogan, September-October Number, 1952.

Saturday Review, Ben Lucien Burman, "The Cult of Unintelligibility," November 1, 1953; Melville Cane, "Is Poetry Returning to Lyricism?" January 16, 1954; Basil Davenport, Vol. 9: 673-74, July 1, 1933; A. E. Housman Memorial Number, April, 1946.

Scrutiny. (A local periodical of Cambridge University, no longer published.) Vol. II, Cambridge Press, 1933-34 (secured from Duke University).

Virginia Quarterly Review, J. S. Wilson, "On the Name and Nature of Poetry," July, 1934.

Yale Review, Eugene Davidson and Houston Martin (with letters from Housman to Martin), "Notes on A. E. Housman," Winter Number, 1936; C. B. Tinker, "On the Name and Nature of Poetry," Vol. 23, September, 1933.

UNPUBLISHED WORKS

Allen, T. J. *The Life and Poetry of A. E. Housman,* a Master's thesis, Queen's University, Kingston, Ontario, Canada, 1937.

Housman, A. E. Introductory Lecture, University College, 1892. Mimeographed pamphlet, University of London.

Housman, A. E. *Original Fair Copy of A Shropshire Lad,* Trinity College Library, Cambridge University, England, 1951.

Housman, A. E. *Original Fair Copy of Last Poems,* Fitzwilliam Museum, Cambridge, England, 1951.

Housman, A. E. Original Manuscripts, Letters from A. E. Housman, photographs from the collection of Laurence Housman, displayed at his home in Somerset, 1951.

Housman, A. E. *Original Rough Drafts* of his poems, The Rare Manuscript Division, Library of Congress, Washington, D. C., 1949.

Hyder, C. K. *Concordance to the Poems of A. E. Housman,* University of Kansas, 1941.

Wright, Dr. Louis Booker. *Modern Trends in Poetry,* a paper delivered before students, professors and editors at Coker College, Hartsville, South Carolina, October, 1953.

LETTERS

Letters from Mrs. Joan Thomson Charnock, Cambridge, England.
Letters from A. S. F. Gow, Tutor of Trinity College, 1952.
Letters from Clemence Housman, 1952-1954.
Letters from Laurence Housman, 1949-1956.
Letter from Mr. E. Slade, Oxford University, Oxford, England, with permission to use the Francis Dodd portrait of A. E. Housman, 1953. (Other letters of permission have not been included.)
Letters from Sir R. E. M. Wheeler, C. I. E., D. Literature, Institute of Archaeology, Regent's Park, London, N. W. 1, 1951-1952.

CONVERSATIONS

Conversation with Mrs. Joan Thomson Charnock, daughter of Sir J. J. Thomson, who was Master of Trinity College, Cambridge, 1951.
Conversation with A. S. F. Gow, Trinity College, Cambridge, 1951.
Conversations with Laurence and Clemence Housman, Somerset, England, June-July, 1951.
Conversation with Col. R. K. Morcum and his niece, Miss Darrant, Fockbury, Worcestershire, England, 1951.
Conversation with Col. C. L. Wood, Perry Hall, Bromsgrove, England, 1951.